T0305143

# Innovation Networks in Industries

# Innovation Networks in Industries

*Edited by*

Franco Malerba

*Professor of Industrial Economics and Director,
KITeS-Cespri, Bocconi University, Italy*

Nicholas S. Vonortas

*Professor of Economics and International Affairs and
Director, Center for International Science and Technology
Policy, The George Washington University, USA*

**Edward Elgar**

Cheltenham, UK • Northampton, MA, USA

Published by
Edward Elgar Publishing Limited
The Lypiatts
15 Lansdown Road
Cheltenham
Glos GL50 2JA
UK

Edward Elgar Publishing, Inc.
William Pratt House
9 Dewey Court
Northampton
Massachusetts 01060
USA

A catalogue record for this book
is available from the British Library

Library of Congress Control Number: 2009928596

Mixed Sources
Product group from well-managed
forests and other controlled sources
www.fsc.org  Cert no. SA-COC-1565
© 1996 Forest Stewardship Council
FSC

ISBN 978 1 84720 376 2 (cased)

Printed and bound by MPG Books Group, UK

# Contents

*List of contributors*                                                          vii
*Preface*                                                                       viii

1   Innovation networks in industries and sectoral systems: an
    introduction                                                                1
    *Franco Malerba and Nicholas S. Vonortas*

PART I   THE CURRENT STATE OF KNOWLEDGE

2   Innovation networks in industry                                            27
    *Nicholas S. Vonortas*
3   The dynamics of networks and the evolution of industries:
    a survey of the empirical literature                                       45
    *Lorenzo Zirulia*

PART II   VARIETY OF NETWORKS IN INDUSTRIES
          AND SECTORAL SYSTEMS

4   Measuring the corporate web of science: research and
    partnership networks within the European pharmaceutical
    industry                                                                   81
    *Robert J.W. Tijssen*
5   Knowledge search and strategic alliance: evidence from the
    electronics industry                                                       105
    *Stefano Breschi, Lorenzo Cassi and Franco Malerba*
6   Partnership networks and knowledge networks in five sectors   125
    *Koichiro Okamura and Nicholas S. Vonortas*
7   What do you mean by "mobile"? Multi-applicant inventors
    in the European biotechnology industry                                     157
    *Francesco Laforgia and Francesco Lissoni*
8   Science as a communications network: an illustration of
    nanoscale science research                                                 177
    *Caroline S. Wagner and Susan A. Mohrman*

PART III   PUBLIC POLICIES FOR NETWORKING IN ICT

9   European policy favouring networks in ICT                195
     *Stefano Breschi, Lorenzo Cassi, Franco Malerba and*
     *Nicholas S. Vonortas*
10   Evaluating the links between research and deployment
     networks of innovation in information society in Europe   226
     *Lorenzo Cassi, Nicoletta Corrocher, Franco Malerba and*
     *Nicholas S. Vonortas*

*Index*                                                        253

# Contributors

**Stefano Breschi**, Professor of Industrial Economics, KITeS-Cespri, Bocconi University, Italy

**Lorenzo Cassi**, Assistant Professor of Economics, CES – MATISSE, Université Paris 1 Panthéon-Sorbonne, France and KITeS-Cespri, Bocconi University, Italy

**Nicoletta Corrocher**, Lecturer, KITeS-Cespri, Bocconi University, Italy

**Francesco Laforgia**, Università di Brescia, Italy

**Francesco Lissoni**, Associate Professor of Industrial Economics, Università di Brescia and KITeS-Cespri, Bocconi University, Italy

**Franco Malerba**, Professor of Industrial Economics and Director, KITeS-Cespri, Bocconi University, Italy

**Susan A. Mohrman**, Marshall Scholl of Business, University of Southern California, USA

**Koichiro Okamura**, Japan Science and Technology Agency, Japan

**Robert J.W. Tijssen**, Center for Science and Technology Studies (CWTS), Leiden University, The Netherlands

**Nicholas S. Vonortas**, Professor of Economics and International Affairs and Director, Center for International Science and Technology Policy, The George Washington University, US

**Caroline S. Wagner**, Senior Research Scientist, Center for International Science and Technology Policy, The George Washington University; and SRI International, USA

**Lorenzo Zirulia**, Department of Economics, University of Bologna; KITeS-Cespri, Bocconi University; and Rimini Centre for Economic Analysis, Italy

# Preface

At the turn of the millennium, the European Commission released the communication, "Towards a European Research Area".[1] This statement of goals has come to underline European strategic thinking regarding the role of the Commission, as well as that of national and regional governments of member states, in science and technology policy. The prospect of a European Research Area has provided the basic foundation for the sixth Framework Programme for Research and Technological Development and is expected to continue doing so for the seventh Framework Programme.

Networks linking scientists, research institutes, universities and firms are a pillar of the envisioned European Research Area. The communication from the Commission emphasizes the need for better coordination between national and European research centres. It also calls for more consistency in foresight exercises, science and technology watch, socio-economic intelligence, science and technology options at the national and European levels, and benchmarking exercises. It makes a plea for improved statistics and indicators at a European level, particularly the kind of indicators that address important features of the knowledge-based society.

This book traces its origins to a research project, "Network Indicators: Science, Technology and Innovation"[2] (STI-NET) funded by the European Commission to start tackling the issue of network indicators. The main objective of STI-NET was to identify, construct and analyse network indicators for European science, technology and innovation. The consortium partners studied network formation and structure and derived relevant indicators from three large longitudinal databases of European patent citations, scientific co-publications and inter-firm cooperative agreements. By creating "connectivity indicators" (i.e. combinations of indicators showing relationships among agents in various knowledge-creating functions) the study made a significant contribution in terms of constructing datasets and deriving the network tools that can be used to study both the achievements of past European RTD policy and the prospective foci of the next Framework Programme. In addition, various research papers also explored the feasibility of using such indicators to address analytical questions with clear policy implications.

This book, however, contains much more than work originating in

STI-NET. In the course of the years, researchers at KITeS-Cespri, Bocconi University, as well as at other centres in Europe and the United States, have been involved in other research regarding networks, such as: "Evaluation of Progress Towards a European Research Area for Information Society Technologies";[3] Networks of Innovation in Information Society: Development and Deployment in Europe[4] concerning ICT; and KEINS – Knowledge-Based Entrepreneurship: Innovation, Networks and Systems[5] – concerning knowledge intensive entrepreneurship. This book reflects these efforts. In particular, Chapters 3 and 7–10 are contributions from researchers and studies beyond STI-NET.

We have had two main objectives in putting this material together. One has been to open up to the reader the tremendous opportunities for significant work on policy and strategy using network concepts and indicators as well as to highlight the complexities and challenges involved. The other objective has been to tackle the network issue from a perspective that has been relatively disregarded in the extant literature but which, we feel, deserves a lot of attention: namely, the perspective of industry and of sectoral systems. This contrasts with the typical perspective of the individual organization on which the literature has tended to focus. We believe that some of the most important policy questions of our times lie at the sectoral system level (including the delineation of industry boundaries that are getting increasingly blurry). Correct as this argument about systems and boundary ambiguity might be, it also reflects the frustration of analysts in fitting a radically new global environment into the confines of old definitions and concepts. Could industries be defined more accurately in terms of sectoral systems, and therefore of both the nature of the output as well as the inter-organizational relationships rather than just the former?

A lot of people in addition to the authors have worked to make this book happen. While we cannot thank all of them here, we certainly extend our warmest thanks to Fabienne Corvers, Frank Cunningham, Vincent Duchene, Peter Johnston, Pia Laurila and Ugur Muldur, who – as officials of the European Commission – have provided guidance, feedback and support in various stages and through several research projects that built the underlying material for this book. We are also obliged to Jeff Williams at the George Washington University who worked diligently with us in editing and preparing the manuscript.[6]

## NOTES

1. Commission of the European Communities, "Communication from the Commission to the Council, the European Parliament, the Economic and Social Committee and the

Committee of the Regions: Towards a European Research Area", Brussels, 18 January 2000, COM (2000) 6.
2. STI-NET Network Indicators: Science, Technology and Innovation (1 February 2001–31 January 2005) Contract n°HPV2-CT-2001-00014 – DG Research Directorate M Unit M2. Partners: CWTS and MERIT.
3. Evaluation of Progress towards a European Research Area for Information Society Technologies (1 January–31 December 2005). Contract n. 30302 – DG Information Society and Media.
4. Networks of Innovation in Information Society: Development and Deployment in Europe (23 December 2005–22 December 2006). Contract n. 30-CE-0039054/00-44 DG Information Society and Media.
5. KEINS – Knowledge-Based Entrepreneurship Innovation, Networks and Systems (1 September 2004–28 February 2008). Project n. CT2-CT-2004-506022.
6. In the final preparation of their chapters, Franco Malerba, Stefano Breschi, Nicoletta Corrocher and Lorenzo Cassi acknowledge the financial support of the Italian Ministry for Education, Universities and Research (FIRB, Project RISC – RBNE039XKA: "Research and entrepreneurship in the knowledge-based economy: the effects on the competitiveness of Italy in the European Union").

# 1. Innovation networks in industries and sectoral systems: an introduction

**Franco Malerba and Nicholas S. Vonortas**

## 1. NETWORKS AS MAJOR PARTS OF INDUSTRIES AND SECTORAL SYSTEMS

The contributions in this book concentrate primarily on networks in industries and sectoral systems, reflecting a belief that some of the most important analytical and policy questions related to networks must fully consider the industry level (including the very structure of industries), the role of networks in different sectoral systems of production and innovation, and the delineation of real industry boundaries. Indeed, an extensive literature has developed around networks at various levels of analysis, but the bulk of these studies focus on single organizations and single networks, or are done at the macro, aggregate level. There has been little analysis at the industry and sectoral levels. We are convinced that a relevant and useful way to examine networks is one that takes industry and sectoral systems into consideration and, therefore, allows us to examine diversity in network emergence, structure and evolution, and to evaluate the differential effects of networks on firms and industry growth and performance.

In addition to the previous objective, a second goal of this book is to open up to the reader the tremendous opportunities for significant study in the areas of industry structure, firm strategy and public policy through the use of network concepts and indicators as well as to highlight the complexities and challenges involved. We strongly believe that, although extensive, the literature on networks has just scratched the surface in terms of concepts, models and indicators that can be used to address challenging strategy and policy questions.

Why focus on the industry and sectoral levels in the analysis of networks? The evidence on inter-organizational technological agreements is already very rich, pointing at their importance for fast-changing environments where flexibility is highly prized. We would argue that the existing empirical literature can constitute the basis for an "appreciative theory" that links the self-organization of research and development (R&D) networks to the rate and the direction of technological progress, to the actors involved in the innovative process and, more generally, to the evolution of industries. The formation of R&D networks is a self-organizing process because such networks are the result of uncoordinated choices of organizations over time in response to technological factors and socio-economic conditions. In turn, such factors and conditions are affected, over time, by that same network, so that the dynamics of the system are characterized by several feedbacks, mostly positive (self-reinforcing) in nature.

A useful starting point for framing the contributions in this book is to consider that networks of various types are in sectoral systems of innovation that differ to a great extent in terms of knowledge, actors and institutions. These differences greatly affect the extent, structure and dynamics of networks of agents active in a sector. This discussion can be tied into the significant efforts that have been undertaken in recent years to provide a multidimensional, integrated and dynamic view of sectors, related to the concept of sectoral systems of innovation and production (Malerba, 2002 and 2004). The basic analytical foundations underlying the notion of sectoral systems of innovation follow the traditions of evolutionary theory (Dosi, 1988; Nelson, 1995) and systems of innovation theory (Edquist, 1997). The sectoral systems approach concerns all the stages of industry evolution, from inception to maturity. This approach has both quantitative and formal (with the development of history-friendly models of industry evolution) elements, as well as qualitative and "appreciative" elements, highlighted by aspects such as learning, the knowledge base, competencies, and relationships among agents. In general, the basic elements of a sectoral system can be identified in the knowledge base and the basic technologies, products, agents (including both firms and other organizations such as universities, financial institutions, etc.), demand and institutions.

Within sectoral systems, heterogeneous agents are connected through networks that include both market and non-market relationships. On this issue, it is possible to identify different types of relationships, linked to different analytical approaches. These relationships, however, are not limited to just agents involved in the processes of exchange, competition and command. They concern also formal cooperation or informal interaction among firms or among firms and non-firm organizations, ranging from tacit or explicit collusion, to hybrid governance forms, to formal R&D cooperation. The evolutionary approach and the innovation systems literature have paid much attention to the wide range of formal and informal avenues of cooperation and interaction among firms. According to this perspective, in uncertain and changing environments networks emerge not because agents are similar, but because they are different. In this way networks may integrate complementarities in knowledge, capabilities and specialization (see Lundvall, 1992; Edquist 1997; Nelson, 1995; Teubal et al., 1991). In addition, the literature has examined the role of the relationships between firms and non-firm organizations (such as universities and public research centres) as a source of innovation and change in several specific sectors, such as pharmaceuticals and biotechnology, information technology, and telecommunications (Nelson and Rosenberg, 1993).

In this framework, network structures emerge in a self-organizing process from the initial conditions of a specific industry, the characteristics of the relevant technologies, and the norms and institutional factors that help generate rules that guide firm behaviour. Behavioural rules and network structure are linked in an interactive relationship: as rules generate the structure of the network, network structure influences subsequent behaviour. The emergent structure dissuades rule-breaking behaviour. "The dynamic between internal capabilities, ensconced in specific identities and organizational structures, and the external knowledge in the market (network) drives a co-evolution between the emergent properties in the firm and the network" (Kogut, 2000; p. 412).

Using this conceptual framework as background, the book is divided into three parts. The first part, Chapters 2–3, is methodological in nature and discusses concepts and measurements of networks. The second part, Chapters 4–8, examines empirically the structure and features of various types of networks across different sectoral and scientific domains. Finally, the third part, Chapters 9–10, introduces the public policy aspect and uses ICT as a case-study sector in which to examine policies favouring networks of research and of diffusion.

## 2. NETWORKS IN INDUSTRIES AND SECTORAL SYSTEMS: AN INITIAL DISCUSSION

As stated earlier, the first part of this book discusses the main methodological problems associated with concepts and measurements, and places the empirical discussion into an industrial framework that takes into account the fact that industries and sectoral systems evolve over time.

In Chapter 2, "Innovation networks in industry", Nicholas Vonortas provides a methodological discussion of evaluating networks in industry, and attempts to link the terminology in the networks field proper to core concepts in the field of industrial economics. The chapter draws on recent developments regarding the concepts of social capital/network resources, information/learning, network governance, network emergence, and network structure to discuss their influence on firm strategy in industrial sectors characterized by rapidly changing technologies. Distinct from human capital – or, equivalently, organization-specific attributes/ capabilities – social capital (or network resources for organizations), is understood as a set of social resources embedded in relationships and associated norms and values. The build-up of human capital and organization-specific capabilities requires investment, as does the build-up of social capital and network resources. However, the type of required investment is different. Network resources translate into informational and control benefits generated through network ties and positioning. These network resources are influenced very much by the conditions of the specific industry, the characteristics of the relevant technologies, and associated norms and institutional factors. A network balance emerges that allows both for stability, when it proves advantageous, and for a recombination of information and network renewal. This is not very different from the traditional market analysis in economics: (network) entry and barriers to such entry become key factors for network structure and its rejuvenation, exactly as they do in markets where entrants dilute the strongholds of incumbents. Similarly to achieving optimality in markets, achieving balance in networks is complex and varies across activity areas (e.g. sectors). Vonortas concludes that in order to determine the incentives (net benefits) of a firm to participate in a network one needs to address network structure optimality and the firm's positioning in the network, which, in turn, requires addressing the relationship between industry (activity) characteristics and firm strategy. Vonortas argues that this reflects the fact that networking is only a part of the more general strategy orientation of the firm, which itself is influenced by the characteristics of the economic activity in which the firm is engaged. By implication, the utility of network analysis increases if it is combined with more traditional investigations of market structure, technological advance, competitive behaviour, and company performance in different industrial environments.

In Chapter 3, "The dynamics of networks and the evolution of industries: a survey of the empirical literature", Lorenzo Zirulia reviews the empirical literature on inter-firm technological agreements. Several databases exist that track the developments in such agreements, using public announcements as the unit of analysis. While these kinds of data are subject to several biases – related to language, characteristics of announced agreements, and so forth – they all point to a number of stylized facts indicating that: alliances have increased greatly in the past two to three decades; they tend to be of a contractual nature and not involve significant investment by the parties involved; and they are overwhelmingly concentrated in high-tech activities. The incentives for forming them vary widely – even among members of the same alliance – but tend to include some form of access to market and/or resources, risk mitigation, and technology intelligence. Following a discussion of the main analytical findings in the relevant literature regarding the influence of alliances on performance and capabilities, the author turns to the relationship between technological agreements and industry evolution. He suggests that inter-firm technological agreements and related networks can be viewed as structural elements in the evolution and dynamics of industries. He proposes three interrelated themes that define the relationship between technological collaborations, R&D networks and industry evolution. The first is path dependency in collaboration and the first mover advantages it might offer to early entrants in a nascent industry environment. The second theme centres on the role of networks as both a mechanism of technological knowledge diffusion for firms within the network and an exclusionary mechanism for firms outside the network. If no firm possesses all the relevant technological capabilities to innovate, the network will act as the "locus of innovation", increasing competition within it but excluding those outside it. The network may be composed of different cohesive sub-groups, so that competition occurs among groups, rather than at the firm level, and might explain differences in exit rates, growth, economic performance and innovativeness. Finally, a third theme describes the role of networks in affecting the "collective" direction of technological change in industries.

## 3. THE FEATURES AND STRUCTURES OF NETWORKS IN DIFFERENT INDUSTRIES AND SECTORAL SYSTEMS

A central conclusion of this book is that the features and structures of networks differ from industry to industry and, consequently, from sectoral system to sectoral system. This is the result of the specificity of the knowledge base, the relevant learning processes, the basic technologies, the characteristics of demand, the key links, and the dynamic complementarities that characterize an industry and a sectoral system. For example, in pharmaceuticals, think of the change in the underlying knowledge base in the switch from old drug discovery to modern biotechnology. This change has created new types of networks and relationships among firms (large pharmaceutical companies and new biotech firms), and among firms, non-firm organizations (such as universities and venture capitalists) and institutions (such as regulations). Now compare pharmaceuticals with the knowledge base of the machinery production sector, which reflects completely different types of networks and relationships between firms (users and suppliers), non-firm organizations (such as local banks and industry associations and government) and institutions (local trust). Or consider the type of knowledge and networks in an industry such as software. Within this perspective, one common aspect affecting the evolution of different networks is the learning environment in terms of technological regimes defined in terms of various degrees of technological opportunity, appropriability of innovation, cumulativeness of technical advance, and the properties of key knowledge bases and learning processes (Malerba and Orsenigo, 1996; Breschi et al. 2000).

This background brings to mind questions regarding what kind of networks are present in different industries. We explore this issue by examining different types of networks for innovation in industries such as pharmaceuticals, electronics, instrumentation and chemicals. Networks are examined in terms of content and in terms of actors and organizations. In the first case we distinguish three broad classes of networks: scientific networks, knowledge networks and alliance networks. In the second case, we discuss universities and research organizations, companies and individuals. Of course, the categories of content and actor-based networks are strictly related in various ways.

Networks are multidimensional concepts that cut across different types of actors, different types of scientific, technology and knowledge realms, and may touch on R&D, production and marketing. In this vein, this book is one of the first to analyse networks by applying different measures to disparate industries: scientific publications to assess scientific networks; patent citations to identify knowledge networks; technological partnerships (joint ventures, formal alliances, licences) to identify partnership networks; and the movement of researchers across organizations to identify researcher mobility networks.

Often, the focus of the analysis is not the organizations within, or the physical structure of, the network, but the collaborative exchange in pre-defined industrial sectors; that is, the activity of the organization. That is to say, the examined scientific, knowledge, partnership or mobility networks are not the complete networks of the organizations that can be classified in the predefined sectors on the basis of their production. Rather, they are the inter-organizational networks constructed on the basis of the knowledge and collaborative activities of these organizations.

On the basis of this discussion, the chapters (4–8) in Part II of the book address questions such as:

- What are the main features of scientific, knowledge and partnership networks across industries?
- Are there broad differences between these networks?

• Do such networks establish effective channels of knowledge communication of different intensity across sectors?
• How do companies position strategically in these networks and how do they differ across sectors?
• What is the search process of companies in these networks?
• What are the main features of networks of mobile inventors?

In Chapter 4, "Measuring the corporate web of science: research and partnership networks within the European pharmaceutical industry", Robert Tijssen uses research cooperation data within the pharmaceutical sector to examine the scientific networks in pharmaceuticals in which at least one partner is an industrial company. The results that emerge from this study of ten European pharmaceutical companies enable a certain degree of aggregate-level benchmarking. The indicators produce a one-year snapshot of the combined firm-level research partnership profiles, in which several interesting features are observed. Most striking is the degree of similarity between the research partnership profiles of these ten companies. This shows that the distributive characteristics of the ten firms are again remarkably similar, suggesting that these research cooperation patterns within the large companies are predominantly sector-specific, rather than company-specific, and are dependent on the type of knowledge base that characterizes the sector.

However, the international orientation of the two Swiss companies in the sample, Novartis and Roche, both of which have many labs outside their home countries, highlights the impact of corporate strategies for locating R&D centres in many other countries. This outcome raises questions on how or why these firm-level research partnership profile features come about. Are they mainly determined by global, sector-specific R&D processes, by competitive pressures impacting on corporate R&D strategies, or are they still very much rooted in the traditional practice of proximity-driven preferences for partners? Can these internally driven partnering mechanisms be redirected and made more effective by introducing additional incentive systems and imposing new collaborative frameworks from the outside? Even though these partnership indicators and statistics produce a novel and unique window of research cooperation within the European pharmaceutical industry and help unravel the web of research networks involving pharmaceutical companies, a convincing interpretation of these findings requires a global perspective and sector-wide frame of reference, which cannot be provided here. Future research must be designed to answer questions such as: what does it mean for a specific European company to be near the bottom of a ranking, or to have an average score, in terms of participation in co-authored research articles?

Providing answers to such questions not only requires technical expertise on the ins and outs of the information sources and an in-depth understanding of the underlying metrics and statistical properties of the data,
but, above all, accurate comprehension requires a thorough grasp of the
relevant economic environments and geo-political contexts in which these
European multinational companies operate. We still know little about the
detailed and hard-to-observe mechanisms and organizational conditions
that are driving these research partnerships. It stands to reason that the
various types of linkages are driven by differing environmental conditions, which are strongly affected by the prevailing R&D objectives and
constraints, intellectual property rights (IPR) and knowledge appropriation regimes. Moreover, each type of research partnership and network is
likely to operate according to its own managerial models and organizational structures, including different milestones and deliverables that affect
incentives at the firm and network level.

In Chapter 5, "Knowledge search and strategic alliance: evidence from
the electronics industry", Stefano Breschi, Lorenzo Cassi and Franco
Malerba go in depth within the knowledge and partnership networks
of electronics firms and inquire empirically about the existing trade-off
between strategies of "local" search, which builds cumulatively on a firm's
established knowledge base, and strategies aimed at recombining ideas
and knowledge, drawing on areas relatively distant from a firm's current
technological base and competencies. The analysis is related to firms'
R&D collaborations. The chapter combines patent citations and strategic
alliances data for a sample of 272 publicly traded companies operating in
the electronics industry in the 1990s. In particular, patent co-citation data
are used to investigate the extent to which the pattern of search for new
knowledge overlaps across companies.

The authors argue that processes of competition and collaboration
have to be taken into account when exploring the impact on innovative
performance of different search strategies. On the one hand, competition
from other firms building on a firm's knowledge base may hamper innovation by that firm, thereby reducing the effectiveness of a local and cumulative search strategy and increasing the attractiveness of a recombination
strategy. On the other hand, forming alliances with competitors is a means
of internalizing the potential negative effects arising from competitors
exploiting a firm's knowledge base. In this case, R&D alliances are formed
among partners that perform searches in the same knowledge base and
along similar lines, rather than among companies searching in different
directions. The chapter shows that search strategies based on the cumulative exploitation of a firm's own stock of knowledge are positively related
to the firm's rate of innovation. But results show also that this positive

effect is moderated by the negative effect arising from competition from other organizations trying to exploit the same knowledge base of the focal firm. Finally, the results show a possible solution to this problem: joining an R&D collaboration by a firm that has its knowledge set crowded by too many competitors searching in its technological space reduces the intensity of competition and, in this way, increases its rate of technological innovation.

In Chapter 6, "Partnership networks and knowledge networks in five sectors", Koichiro Okamura and Nicholas Vonortas examine two different types of networks – knowledge and technology partnership – in five industrial sectors: pharmaceuticals, plastics, computers, electronics, and instruments. Their findings point to three sets of results that require further attention. First, there is an apparent difference in the networking behaviour in pharmaceuticals vis-à-vis networking behaviour in computers, electronics and instruments. Second, there is an apparent difference between knowledge and partnership networks across all sectors in terms of their effectiveness as channels for knowledge communication. Third, there is an apparent difference in the competitive positioning of European firms and firms from the United States and Japan in the knowledge networks across the examined industrial sectors. In general, all five knowledge networks are found to be highly connected. That is to say, there are paths connecting the identified companies to each other in a given sector in the form of inter-linking patent citations. These paths tend to be short: on average, a company can find any other in less than three steps. There are, however, differences between sectors in terms of the nature of this connectivity. For instance, the knowledge network in pharmaceuticals appears to be the most broadly connected, whereas the knowledge network in instruments seems to depend more on gatekeepers and information hubs for its connectivity.

The sectoral partnership networks investigated here are much smaller than the knowledge networks. They are also more fragmented than knowledge networks in all five sectors. Among partnership networks, the pharmaceuticals network seems to be the least closely connected and depends more than the other sectoral partnership networks on a few hubs for its connectivity. The knowledge network is robust to the random removal of nodes across all industrial sectors but quite vulnerable to the removal of the most connected nodes. The same is true for the partnership networks in pharmaceuticals and electronics. In fact, the partnership network in pharmaceuticals disintegrates more quickly than its knowledge network, indicating that it is more dependent on a few highly connected firms. The apparent difference in networking behaviour between pharmaceuticals and other sectors is an important finding that requires further attention in future investigations. Drug company networking behaviour seems to be different in patenting and in strategic partnering. Note that pharmaceuticals as an industry has different technology domain characteristics from computers, electronics and instruments.

The authors did find a major contrast between knowledge and technological partnerships. All five knowledge networks appear to be effective channels for knowledge flow between the participating organizations: they can all be characterized as "small worlds". The examined technological partnership networks cannot be characterized as such, even though their largest components come much closer to the small world phenomenon. This difference between knowledge and partnership networks is the second potentially important result of this study, and requires further investigation as the partnership data used in this exercise were relatively thin.

A third important result of the chapter points out differences between European firms and their American and Japanese counterparts. European firms tend to position in less crowded partitions of the examined sectoral knowledge networks. They dominate the "technology broker" partitions of the sectoral graphs, where less crowded positions are combined with high status. They also appear in large numbers in the "technology isolate" partitions, where less crowded positions are combined with low status. In contrast, Japanese firms tend to reside mostly in the partitions of "technology leaders" and "technology followers", where more crowded positions are combined with high status and low status, respectively. US firms tend to lie somewhere in between, their distribution among the four partitions resembling somewhat more that of the Japanese firms.

The dominating presence of European firms in the "technology brokers" partition across all examined industries can have two explanations. It could imply a bright future for European firms in that they are getting equipped with new, desirable technologies. Though this benefit might be tempered by the possibility that their early-stage research may not be followed with equal success in commercializing the resulting technological advancements as Japanese and US firms dominate the technology leaders' partition and capture the associated rents. Alternatively, it could be argued that EU firms tend to stick to unsuccessful technologies that die out sooner rather than later. In contrast, Japanese firms seem to follow a "fast-second" approach, keeping close to the forefront of technology but not as brokers or isolates/entrepreneurs. When they find promising technologies, Japanese firms will concentrate their R&D efforts on pushing the technology forward and reaping the benefits from commercialization. As for the American firms, their relatively more even spread in the graph indicates capabilities to follow diversified strategies. They maintain solid capabilities as technology leaders in all examined industries, including the occupation of significant positions as isolates in drugs, plastics and instruments. Unexpectedly, however, they appear relatively weak as technology brokers. Significant numbers of US firms were also found in the followers' partition across all industrial sectors. To conclude, we should add that, while characterizing the nature of the examined inter-organizational networks and the strategic positioning of companies in them has proven quite rewarding, for a fuller picture, network analysis should be complemented with the more traditional approaches in the economics and management/ strategy fields dealing with the competitive behaviour of individual companies and their market success.

In Chapter 7, "What do you mean by 'mobile'? Multi-applicant inventors in the European biotechnology industry", Francesco Laforgia and Francesco Lissoni focus on networks among companies through the mobility of inventors that move from one company to another. Laforgia and Lissoni propose a taxonomy of the phenomena of multi-applicant inventorship, defined as inventors that patent in multiple organizations, thus creating de facto links among these organizations. By making use of information on the identity and history of those applicants, they propose a taxonomy of the phenomena behind multi-applicant inventorship, which could be distinguished between true job mobility, mobility as a result of mergers and acquisitions (M&As) and residuals cases. They rely on the EP-Cespri database of patenting activity at the European Patent Office (EPO), covering the time period of 1978–2003, from which they have extracted data on all the inventors with more than one patent application signed in biotechnology-related fields and associated with a European address. Within that sample, they focus on all inventors associated with two or more patent applications, and no less than two different applicants. Job mobility turns out not to stand as the dominant source of multi-applicant inventorship. However, not all the phenomena behind "multi-applicant" inventorship may be equated to genuine job mobility creating mobility networks among different organizations. By applying their taxonomy to EPO patent data in biotechnology, the authors found that both the existence of markets for inventions and M&A activity contribute to multi-applicant inventorship, even though the existing literature has lumped all of these explanatory phenomena under the single label of mobility. Laforgia and Lissoni emphasize that it is important to identify all the various phenomena behind multi-applicant inventorship because these phenomena bear different consequences in terms of knowledge diffusion. The authors show that firm networks generated by truly mobile inventors are very different from those created by M&A-induced, multi-applicant inventorship. It is likely that the findings signal the capacity of mobile inventors to connect more firms and institutions than can other categories of inventors, therefore providing a powerful mechanism of net-worked knowledge diffusion.

Finally, in Chapter 8 "Science as a communications network: an illustration of nanoscale science research", Caroline Wagner and Susan Mohrman present the results of a network analysis of the American Department of Energy (DOE) national laboratories in their role of pro-moting research and development in nanoscale science. Network analysis was used to uncover the structure of social relationships within the specific research community on the basis of the assumption that these relation-ships transmit and diffuse information. This chapter analyses the roles and positions of the nodes within and around the DOE laboratories with sig-nificant investment in nanoscale science and technology capabilities. Six of the DOE labs established centres dedicated to nanoscale science, called the Nanoscale Science Research Centres (NSRCs), in a highly interdiscipli-nary and unstructured research design. Wagner and Mohrman analyse the network in which the labs and the centres operate (locally and globally), and the centres of excellence to which they connect around the globe. The analysis is presented over time to correlate with the time that the forma-tion of the NSRCs was announced through the National Nanotechnology Initiative (NNI) in the United States and their charters were being negoti-ated. In the earlier years, the parent laboratory is the point of reference for the network analysis, either because the NSRCs were not yet created or because the smaller centres cannot be seen in the network at a particular level of aggregation. Whenever possible, emphasis is given to the NSRCs as they emerge from within the operations of the parent laboratories.

The analysis suggests that at least two of the DOE labs are in an excellent position within the global network to trade knowledge. The DOE contract research laboratories are shown to have been key players in the nanoscale sciences even before the announcement of the creation of new interdis-ciplinary research centres under the NNI. An interesting observation is that during the years of investigation (2002–06), the NSRCs emerged from within their parent laboratories, drawing strength from the robust networks built by these DOE laboratories over more than 15 years of nanoscale research and collaborations with other institutions from around the world. As the NSRCs formed their own networks, in some cases they appear to draw off collaborators from the parent labs' networks, actually reducing the strength of the parent network in the global system while not building up the small centres into highly attractive nodes – at least not in a visible way in 2007. In other words, the creation of a spin-off research centre may actually have a short-term negative effect on the positions of both the parent and the spin-off institution while social networks catch up with the prior positions held by the parent labs. This may mean that, during the time when the spin-offs are being created and the parent labs are regaining their position, the research centres actually lose power and influence in the network as a result of the reorganization. While this may be a short-term loss, it may also mean a loss of ability to contribute to regional or national innovation for some period of time, perhaps as much as two years, as new connections are made.

All of these chapters in the second part of the book point to some general conclusions about networks in different industries and, consequently, in different sectoral systems:

- Major differences are observed in networks of R&D and knowledge flows across industries, reflecting differences in the knowledge base and sectoral systems.
- However, scientific networks pertaining to a single industry show broad similarities.
- In an industry, search strategies by companies within networks can be quite different and may involve either local search or innovative recombination of quite different types of knowledge.
- Also, in the same industry, the extent of competition within and across networks could be relevant.
- Networks among companies and other organizations involve linkages that include also the mobility of researchers that takes various forms and has various effects on innovative performance.
- The emergence of new important units within central nodes of a scientific network may disrupt the global connectivity of the parent organizations for some time and reflect a tendency for more local activity by the new units for some time at least.

## 4.  NETWORKS AND PUBLIC POLICY IN THE ICT SECTORAL SYSTEM

The final part of the book reviews policies supporting networks in a key, broad sectoral system: information and communication technology (ICT). Here, social network analysis and direct field research examine the effectiveness of public policies addressing the development of networks for the creation and diffusion of new technology.

In Chapter 9, "European policy favouring networks in ICT", Stefano Breschi, Lorenzo Cassi, Franco Malerba and Nicholas Vonortas advocate the use of social network analysis to evaluate aspects of public programmes supporting research and development, especially as these aspects relate to the "behavioural additionality" of the programmes under investigation.

Appraisals of R&D expenditures have tended to concentrate either on the resources added by public funding into the system (input additionality) and/or on the extra private and social returns resulting from public funding (output/outcome additionality). The methodology employed in this chapter concentrates on the sustainable effects beyond the infusion of resources and/or the extraction of outputs that such investments create. Sustainable effects include improving the competencies, capabilities, organizational structures and strategies of firms (behavioural additionality). The authors draw on a recent study that appraised the partnership and knowledge networks created around the R&D activities of the Information Society and Media Priority of the Sixth Research Framework Programme (FP6) of the European Community. In an effort to address questions of knowledge network effectiveness, the authors apply a novel, quantitative methodological framework for assessment of inter-organizational networks established by IST-RTD programmes in comparison with global networks developing independently of Community funding. The results of the quantitative analysis are enriched with more qualitative information obtained through a series of expert/practitioner interviews. The analysis demonstrates the applicability of social network concepts and analytical tools in appraising the relative global positioning of public funding networks and the effectiveness of the specific networks in creating leading knowledge hubs in selected technological domains. The examined programmes are found to have played an important role in generating and diffusing knowledge by attracting key industry actors and by creating and increasing network connectivity. Hubs are effective in producing and diffusing knowledge. Gatekeeper organizations – simultaneously global hubs and IST-RTD hubs – are the most effective in terms of both enriching the network with new knowledge and facilitating the dissemination of knowledge among network members. It is argued that public policy should try to facilitate the development of more European organizations that can be characterized as global network hubs and to draw larger numbers of the most technologically dynamic small and medium-sized enterprises (SMEs) into these programmes.

Chapter 10, "Evaluating the links between research and deployment networks of innovation in information society in Europe", Lorenzo Cassi, Nicoletta Corrocher, Franco Malerba and Nicholas Vonortas use network analysis to examine the structure of collaborative networks and of knowledge transfer between research, innovation and deployment activities in the field of information and communication technology (ICT) for the European Union as a whole and for several European regions. In particular, this chapter analyses the linkages between the research networks built through the sixth Framework Programme funding in the thematic area, "Applied IST Research Addressing Major Societal and Economic Challenges", and the diffusion networks built through EU programmes (eTen, eContent) and regional programmes. Research networks are found to complement diffusion networks by providing additional links and by increasing the number of organizations involved in sharing and exchanging knowledge. Two types of actors are key players in these networks: hubs and gatekeepers. Hubs maintain the bulk of ties in the networks and help the smaller and more isolated members remain connected. Gatekeepers bridge research and diffusion networks. Such organizations naturally offer greater policy leverage in establishing a European knowledge infrastructure. Moreover, strengthened inter-network connectivity among research and diffusion activities (deployment) is projected to raise the effectiveness of European research in terms of accelerating innovation. Hubs and gatekeepers partially overlap and include both research organizations (universities, research institutes) and business firms. Multinational corporations and some small and medium-sized firms play key roles in these networks. Thus, multinationals participating in research networks and in large-scale projects that link research and diffusion allow smaller organizations to access critical knowledge, technical and/or market resources, while smaller firms are effective in the deployment of specific applications. A clear policy implication follows from this analysis: if a European knowledge infrastructure is considered important and the connectivity among organizations focusing on research and innovation is a way to strengthen this infrastructure, then the connections between research networks and diffusion networks must be strengthened and the role of gatekeepers nurtured.

## 5. THE ROAD AHEAD

Clearly, more work is needed to develop a comprehensive analytical framework and an associated typology of partnerships and the networks that link them to the main features of industries and sectoral systems. For example, we need further in-depth analysis of research publication data, conclusive information from other sources on inter-organizational research networks, and illustrative case studies to R&D objectives and business strategies that drive and shape these partnerships. Further statistical analysis of the underlying relational patterns within the joint research publications of these firms might also disclose more details about how they organize.

Building on the premises that networks (a) differ across industries and sectoral systems, and thus across knowledge, technology and production space; (b) reflect social norms and institutional factors; and (c) evolve through time and as a result of changing technology, firm, and industry characteristics, the chapters in this book present a range of exploratory methodological and analytical work based on extensive network data. Methodological results have implications regarding the use and correct interpretation of network data based on scientific publications, patents and patent citations, and inter-organizational partnerships. Analytical results have direct implications for policy and were summarized in the previous section of this chapter.

Network data also can prove very useful for helping to address a much wider variety of analytical questions than can be tackled in a single book. Below, we provide a menu that, although by no means exhaustive, illustrates the possibilities of further research in this area. In the spirit of this book, all of these issues and dimensions of investigation should be examined both in a general way as well as in their relationship with the specificity of the technology, industry and sectoral system. In fact, it is highly likely that networks *differ from one industry to another and, consequently, from one sectoral system to another in several respects*:

- *Frequency of network formation.* Inter-organizational networks are increasingly regarded as a core governance mode in the knowledge-based economy. Economic success in knowledge-intensive industries depends on the commercialization of technologies that require constant organizational learning and the integration of a wide variety of know-how, skills and capabilities. These technologies have become so complex they can often only be innovated by complex organizational networks, rather than by individual firms. Can it be hypothesized that networks will be formed much more frequently around complex technologies than around simple technologies?[1]
- *Types of networks.* Technological/organizational complexity might suggest that networks formed around complex technologies will be of a different nature than the networks formed around simple technologies. For instance, if we assume that the knowledge base of a technology (for example, information and communication technologies) is more complex and more dynamic than the knowledge base of another technology (for example, bulk chemicals), this argument would imply that an information technology network may have more members and different types of ties among those members than does a chemical network. Such a hypothesis would lead to an examination of the linkage between the type of network and the type of technology.

- *Lock-ins in networks.* A firm's network(s) is a source of both opportunities and constraints. Strategic networks potentially provide a firm with: access to information, resources, markets and technologies; advantages from learning, scale and scope economies; and opportunity to achieve objectives such as sharing risks and outsourcing. Networks may also lock firms into unproductive relationships and preclude partnerships with more viable partners. Thus, the firm's network might assume greater importance as the economic environment becomes more competitive. To what extent is that true across broad technology areas? What factors account for prospective differences?

- *Cross-network differences in performance.* Network scholars propose that the concept of similarity in relational space – which differs from the concept of similarity in attributes (e.g. scale, scope, technology) – is an important way to think about competition patterns and profitability differences between firms in an industry. Therefore, do groups defined in terms of attributes overlap with groups defined in terms of relational similarities? Is firm conduct and performance contingent on these different ways of grouping?

- *Competition, positioning and networking.* Recent research has indicated that the location of a firm in a network is an important element of competition. Competition is seemingly more intense for actors that occupy similar locations relative to others but is mitigated if actors are tied to each other. Assuming an overall objective of achieving a sustained, rapid rate of technological advance in a highly risky environment, is it advisable to allow similarly positioned organizations in a network to create cooperative relationships with each other? What factors should influence the decision?

- *The value of networks as a key resource.* The resource-based view of the firm has underlined the potential for enduring benefits from a collection of resources that is inimitable and not readily substitutable. Network scholars now argue that a firm's network of relationships can create inimitable and non-substitutable value themselves and allow access to unique resources and capabilities, including network resources and social capital. To what extent does this phenomenon differ across sectoral systems? Is it more important for large, diversified firms or for smaller firms? If so, why?

- *Repeated collaborations.* It is easy to imagine that a company would confront prohibitive transaction costs should it be obliged to engage in multiple alliances with partners that it does not somehow know well, control, or trust. To mitigate the problem, firms depend on networks built on repeated interactions between members and on verifiable member reputations. It has been a researchable proposition in the business literature that membership in tight and persistent networks provides deep knowledge and a strong lever of combined trust and control over other members, thus lowering the transaction costs of collaboration in situations of incomplete contracts. Contract incompleteness is prevalent when firms experiment with new technologies and when high market and technological uncertainties are present. Does this factor alone provide a sufficiently strong argument for repeated collaboration in these circumstances? Could it be that tests between controlled populations of firms similar in all other respects except networking activity would show systematic performance differences one way or the other?

- *Networks, idiosyncratic capabilities and the appropriability of innovations.* Networks have a paradox: on one hand, firms often join to access the know-how and capabilities of their partners; on the other, they want to protect their own proprietary assets. It is now argued that building relational capital helps achieve both objectives simultaneously by facilitating learning and curbing opportunistic behaviour. To what extent is the building of relational capital responsible for differing strategies within the same industry, where some firms find it beneficial to collaborate and some don't?

- *Learning to collaborate.* Alliance networks involve costs in terms of managerial resources. It is now being established that firms learn to manage alliances as experience accumulates, and learn how to learn from their partners. It seems that these learning effects depend on firm-specific alliance capabilities. Can such learning effects be clearly quantified in terms of value? Does it mean that firms with more experience and higher social capital have permanent advantages over others? What does that mean for new companies in rapidly changing environments? Are there differences between broad technological areas?

- *Routines for absorbing knowledge in networks.* Scholarship suggests that organizations effective in learning establish routines that allow them to effectively develop, store and apply new knowledge systematically. Establishing such routines may also seem an appropriate thing to do in networks concentrating on the creation and dissemination of knowledge. Yet, we still lack a clear understanding of this issue. While recent research has pointed out the use of such effective routines in some of the most venerable industry networks, it leaves open the question of network structure. In particular, can effective learning routines be established in networks? How do these learning routines relate to the objectives of the network and its members? Do learning routines co-evolve with network structure?

- *Networks for exploration and networks for exploitation.* One of the most interesting hypotheses in network research as it applies to technological advance and innovation is whether highly connected, strong-tie networks are better suited for the diffusion and exploitation of existing knowledge while weak-tie networks are better suited for the exploration of new knowledge. In particular, it is suggested that the degree of uncertainty and the rapidity of rate of innovation influence the appropriate network configurations, promoting strong ties and dense networks in more stable environments. Such arguments are rooted in earlier research on social networks regarding the roles and advantages of strong and weak ties and strong and weak structural embeddedness. Is this hypothesis supported in European high-tech industries? How is it affected by different technological characteristics and selection environments across sectors? To what extent can one provide empirical support through European data to recent theoretical assertions that network structure is emergent in the initial conditions of the specific industry, reflecting the inherent characteristics of the technologies as well as social norms and institutional factors?

- *Networks and firm evolution.* It has been argued that the effect of alliance network composition may vary at different stages of evolution for a firm. For example, it has been shown that start-ups can enhance their early performance by establishing an alliance network and configuring it to provide efficient access to diverse information and capabilities with minimum costs of redundancy, conflict and complexity. A core hypothesis here is that, by forming alliances, start-ups can potentially access social, technical and commercially competitive resources that typically require years to acquire. How generalizable are those results across various technological fields and industries? What enables new firms to be accepted into networks given their lack of resources, prior results, and lack of social capital?

- *The dynamics of network resources for a firm.* A firm's stocks of (a) technical capital (capabilities to create new technologies, products, processes), (b) commercial capital (complementary assets required to commercialize new technologies and obtain rents), and (c) social capital (network resources emanating from prior relationships with other organizations) qualify as resources. Each of these assets adds value, is accumulated over time, and is difficult to trade across markets. However, the relationship of these asset-stocks to the alliance formation of a company may be non-linear. How are these resources defined empirically in high-technology sectors? How do companies perceive them? Does speed in the rate of evolution of an industry affect their relative importance? What factors may enable a firm to participate in a desired network even though it lacks one or more of these resources?

- *Network features in sectoral systems.* Various network features, such as network density, structural holes, structural equivalence, and core-versus-peripheral firms, have been identified as influencing the profitability of industries and firms. What role do they play in environments of fast technological advance? For example, is a network riddled with structural holes more suitable to situations of high risk and fast technological change than a very dense network where everybody is linked with everyone else?

- *Network structures and the actors of a sectoral system.* It has been argued that in exploring technological change in some industries the focus ought to be on the network of actors – the suppliers, customers, and complementors on whose capabilities and successes a firm often depends. Tightly knit networks can confer advantages when actors succeed and disadvantages when they don't, as for instance, in the case of technological change that renders actors' capabilities obsolete. What may be the repercussions of this for network structure in the face of rapidly changing, high-risk industrial environments?

- *Types of networks and types of knowledge bases of a sectoral system.* Recent scholarship has argued that when the knowledge base of an industry is both complex and expanding and the sources of expertise are diffuse, the locus of innovation will be found in networks of learning, rather than in individual firms. These inter-organizational networks sustain fluid and evolving communities of different kinds of agents (e.g. firms, universities, research institutes) and different kinds of organizational practices to access the knowledge base of the community. Path-dependent cycles of learning may be supported in such networks. How have the characteristics of the knowledge base and the distribution of capabilities among actors influenced the emergence and density of networks across industries populated by complex or simple technologies in Europe? How far can one go in identifying path dependency and its effects in these networks?

- *The co-evolution of networks and sectoral systems.* Both exogenous and endogenous forces shape network evolution over time. A key research issue is to put networks in industry in a dynamic framework: that is, to examine industry evolution and network dynamics. This means that one must fully examine co-evolutionary processes.

In fact, changes in network structure, content and function are the result of co-evolutionary processes involving actors, knowledge, technology and institutions. These processes are sector-specific and often path-dependent. Here, local learning, interactions among agents, and networks may generate increasing returns and irreversibilities that in some cases may lock sectoral systems into inferior technologies. In general, one could say that changes in the knowledge base and in the relevant learning processes of firms induce deep transformations in the behaviour and structure of the agents and in their relationships among one another. These transformations may also be seen in the structure, content and function of networks. The convergence of industry boundaries in the information technology area, for example, has shaped the strategic networks that impact that sector. Partner decisions also affect how networks evolve. It is then conceivable to think of lock-in and lock-out situations that can be the result of network evolution. If it is not costless to shift instantaneously across groups, such evolution can be the source of differential returns. Choices made by actors early in the life of the network will affect future returns. By definition, evolution is faster in environments of rapid technological advance. How do technologies, industry boundaries and networks co-evolve? To what extent is this co-evolution in rapidly changing environments the result of firms using networks to reposition in new, higher profitability activities?

## 6. POLICY IMPLICATIONS

The set of analytical issues discussed above has direct and indirect policy implications in terms of the ability of network concepts and indicators to address some key policy issues and to allow for an evaluation of policies. Here we identify some implications for policy analysis.

- *Enhancing policy "intelligence".* Network indicators can expand the ability of governments and of individual agents to predict accurately future developments in markets and technologies. In theory at least, governments can use network indicators to devise "early warning systems" to create intelligence concerning changes in the technological and industrial landscape, thus allowing governments to maximize gain, or mitigate loss, from the fallout of those changes.
- *Understanding cohesion.* The extensive mapping of inter-organizational networks through strategic technology alliances,

scientific co-publications, co-patenting and patent citations allows analysts to illustrate the extent to which the networks in which European organizations participate have been transformed from national/regional to pan-European and global in scope. The formation of strong innovation networks across Europe can be considered an indication of the emerging European Research Area.

- *Promoting competition.* An important benefit from the creation of inter-organizational networks can be the improved ability of members to create and exploit technology options and opportunities. The formation of complex and partly overlapping networks, however, also has a dark side of increased potential for anti-competitive behaviour. What are the potential policy trade-offs between the improved ability to create and exploit technology options for members of a network, and the increased potential for anticompetitive behaviour as a result of the formation of complex and partly overlapping networks?

- *Perceiving competing constellations.* It is argued frequently that competition in certain industries (particularly those involving information and communication technology) takes place between constellations of companies rather than between individual companies. If so, this raises important implications for competition and industrial policies.

- *Avoiding unproductive lock-in.* Strategic networks may lock firms into unproductive relationships and preclude partnerships with more viable partners. In the case of industry-wide networks, one may perceive a lock-in situation in a specific technology or technological standard. When does the government have a role in intervening to disrupt such situations? When should the market be left without policy intervention?

- *Avoiding harmful lock-out.* The creation of tight networks around particular technologies may make it difficult for new entrants to participate. This may be particularly severe for new technology-based firms that lack commercial capital and social capital. Indeed, these may be the firms that need networks the most in order to access necessary social, technical and commercial resources. Is there a role for the government in terms of making these firms more attractive as partners? For example, by increasing their social capital?

- *Promoting effective network structure.* Different network structures are expected to vary in degree of effectiveness depending on the environment. Highly connected, strong-tie networks may be better suited for the diffusion and exploitation of existing knowledge, whereas weak-tie networks may be better suited for the exploration of new knowledge. How should a government structure incentives and criteria in programmes promoting new technologies in order to achieve the most effective network structures for experimentation and risk taking?

- *Benchmarking.* Inter-organizational networks are not new. Indeed, the literature has extensively discussed regional networks (clusters) in different parts of Europe. Rigorous network indicators can assist in the visualization and benchmarking of good practices for efficient communication and knowledge diffusion across geographical space.
- *Lowering management and coordination costs for new firms.* Alliance networks involve costs in terms of managerial resources. It is now being established that firms learn to manage alliances as experience accumulates. Conversely, the high expected costs for learning how to manage alliances may operate as a disincentive to inexperienced firms. Should this be a consideration for government agencies designing programmes targeting new technology-based firms and technology experimentation?
- *Promoting networks of learning.* When the knowledge base of an industry is complex and expanding and the sources of expertise are dispersed, the locus of innovation is expected to be found in networks of learning, rather than in individual firms. These inter-organizational networks sustain fluid and evolving communities of different kinds of agents including firms, universities and research institutes. Such a phenomenon points out the potential for differential policy approaches to complex and simple technologies. Alternatively, the characteristics of the knowledge base will affect the extent of success of policies promoting innovation networks in industry.
- *Additionality.* The additionality of a European Union effort to create and maintain inter-organizational networks in science, technology and innovation is always a concern. The answer will depend on the nature, characteristics and geographical spread of the supported networks. Significant additionality is expected when inter-organizational networks are increasingly international.
- *Labour market implications of network formation.* The growth and expansion of high-technology networks could have implications for labour market policies in various member countries. For instance, it is likely that worker mobility could be enhanced in the aftermath of network formation. Other concerns include whether firms have sufficient skills to join a network, and the role of skills development as a determinant of the performance of the network.

At the opening of this introductory chapter we argued that the proliferating literature on networks has just begun to address a multitude of challenging strategy and policy questions. We hope that this book adds a useful link in the long chain of policy-relevant network research.

## NOTE

1.  Complex technologies could be defined as related to products or processes that cannot be understood in full detail by an expert. Examples include aircraft and telecommunications equipment. These are contrasted with simple technologies that can be fully understood by an individual expert (e.g. chemicals, pharmaceutical compounds).

## REFERENCES

Breschi, Stefano, Franco Malerba and Luigi Orsenigo (2000) "Technological regimes and Schumpeterian patterns of innovation", *Economic Journal*, **110**, 388–410.

Dosi, G. (1988) "Sources, procedures, and microeconomic effects of innovation", *Journal of Economic Literature*, **26**, 1120–71.

Edquist, C. (ed.) (1997) *Systems of Innovation: Technologies, Institutions and Organizations*, London: Pinter.

Kogut, B. (2000) "The network as knowledge: generative rules and the emergence of structure", *Strategic Management Journal*, **21**, 405–25.

Lundvall, Bengt-Åke (ed.) (1992) *National Systems of Innovation: Towards a Theory of Innovation and Interactive Learning*, London: Pinter.

Malerba, Franco (2002) "Sectoral systems of innovation and production", *Research Policy*, **31**, 247–64.

Malerba, Franco (2004) "Sectoral systems of innovation: basic concepts", in F. Malerba (ed.), *Sectoral Systems of Innovation*, Cambridge: Cambridge University Press.

Malerba, Franco and Luigi Orsenigo (1996) "Schumpeterian patterns of innovation are technology-specific", *Research Policy*, **25** (3), 451–78.

Nelson, Richard R. (1995) "Recent theorizing about economic change", *Journal of Economic Literature*, **XXXIII**, 48–90.

Nelson, Richard R. and Nathan Rosenberg (1993) "Technical innovation and national systems", in Richard R. Nelson (ed.), *National Innovation Systems: A Comparative Analysis*, Oxford: Oxford University Press.

Teubal M, T. Yinnon and E. Zuscovitch (1991) "Networks and market creation", *Research Policy*, **20** (5), 381–92.

# PART I

# The current state of knowledge

# 2. Innovation networks in industry

**Nicholas S. Vonortas**

## 1. INTRODUCTION

It has become almost a cliché to argue that the behavior and performance of firms can only be understood fully by examining their social, technological, and exchange relationships with other economic agents. The image of atomistic agents competing for profits in impersonal markets has become increasingly inadequate in view of the explosion of inter-firm collaboration the past two to three decades, as well as the growing empirical evidence formally substantiating the influence of the social context in which firms are embedded on their conduct and performance (Gulati, 1998; Gulati et al., 2000).

Perhaps the most important aspect of the social context of an organization's environment is its social network of external contacts. A social network can be defined as a set of nodes linked by a set of social relationships of a specified type (Gulati, 1998). It is argued that the kind of networks in which the firm is embedded and its position in these networks affect the firm's behavior and performance. Reminiscent of the resource-based view of the firm – which emphasized the potential for enduring benefits to an organization from a collection of resources that is inimitable and not readily substitutable (Peteraf, 1993) – network scholars now argue that a firm's network relationships can themselves create unique and non-substitutable value and allow access to the inimitable resources and capabilities of other firms.

In other words, networks bestow the firm with "network resources," which are equivalent to the idea of "social capital" in an organizational setting (Gulati, 1999). The firm's stock of *relational* or *social capital* – network resources emanating from prior relationships with other organizations – is argued to qualify as a resource. Other resources joining with relational or social capital are *technical capital* – capabilities to create new technologies, products, processes – and *commercial capital* – complementary assets required to commercialize new technologies and obtain rents (Kale et al., 2000). Each of these asset stocks adds value, is accumulated over time, and, most importantly, is difficult to trade across markets. As such, each of these asset stocks becomes a potent, lasting source of competitive strength.

This chapter deals with the social context, the organizational aspects, and the strategic implications of inter-organizational networks for science, technology, and innovation – or innovation networks, for short. Innovation networks, the complex webs of relationships among firms, universities, and other research organizations associated with generating and sharing knowledge relevant to technological innovation, are considered a major new feature of the contemporary economy. In the presence of technological development involving an ever larger array of product and process systems, subsystems, and components, no single firm can deploy all of the required core capabilities and complementary assets at a reasonable cost. In this context, a network can serve as a locus for innovation because, for any network member, it can provide timely access to external knowledge and resources that are otherwise unavailable, while also testing internal expertise and learning abilities. Linkages within innovation networks are very complex, involving not only diverse kinds of formal contracts, but also informal exchanges of knowledge, thus increasing opportunities for knowledge transmission.

Such developments have created a proliferation of literature trying to explain incentives and results. Several special issues and individual papers on alliances and networks have appeared in the past decade and a half in journals such as the *Academy of Management Journal* (edited by Osborn and Hagedoorn, 1997), *Organization Science* (edited by Koza and Lewin, 1998), *Organization Studies* (edited by Grandori, 1998), *International Studies of Management and Organizations* (edited by Ebers and Jarillo, 1998), *Strategic Management Journal* (edited by Gulati et al., 2000), and *Journal of Technology Transfer* (edited by Arvanitis and Vonortas, 2000). In addition, several research projects in Europe have dealt with aspects of network formation and knowledge communication, including two we are more familiar with (Caloghirou and Vonortas, 2000; Caloghirou et al., 2001). There have been also review articles, such as Gulati (1998, 1999), Oliver and Ebers (1998), and Hagedoorn et al. (2000), as well as numerous books such as Nohria and Eccles (1992), Nooteboom (1999) and Vonortas (1997) that have tried to map the literature on alliances and networks.

Three concepts/analytical propositions have enjoyed widespread support in this literature and guide the discussion in this chapter (Kogut, 2000; Nooteboom and Gilsing, 2004; Rowley et al., 2000):

1.  The analysis of network influence on members' strategy must pay attention to both issues of cognition (information, learning) and governance.
2.  Network structure is an emergent phenomenon, very much a function of the context in which the network is called to operate.

3.  Optimality in network structure and an agent's position in it are determined, at least partly, by the purpose of the network and the strategic orientation of the agent.

The following sections of the chapter survey and synthesize important concepts of interest to the analysis of innovation networks. We draw on recent conceptual developments in the business and sociological literature regarding social capital/network resources, information/learning, network governance, network emergence, and network structure optimality and discuss their influence on firm strategy in industrial sectors characterized by rapidly changing technologies.

## 2. SOCIAL CAPITAL – NETWORK RESOURCES

Sociologists distinguish between social capital and human capital (Burt, 1992, 1997; Bourdieu and Wacquant, 1992; Coleman, 1990). Social capital is a quality created between people, whereas human capital is a quality of individuals. Social capital is, in a sense, the contextual complement to human capital: returns to human capital attributes such as intelligence, education, and seniority depend in part on the person's location in the social structure of a market or hierarchy. While human capital refers to individual ability, social capital refers to opportunity. Individuals with more social capital get higher returns to their human capital because they are positioned to identify and develop more rewarding opportunities. Consequently, the investments to build social capital are different from the investments that build human capital (Coleman, 1988, 1990).

Scholars have conceptualized social capital as a set of social resources embedded in relationships as well as the norms and values associated with social relationships (Burt, 1992; Coleman, 1990; Walker et al., 1997). The broad view of social capital encompasses many aspects of a social context, such as social ties, trust relations, and value systems that facilitate actions of individuals located within that context (Tsai and Ghoshal, 1998). Drawing on Granovetter (1992) and others, Nahapiet and Ghoshal (1997) have distinguished between the structural, the relational, and the cognitive dimensions of social capital. The structural dimension includes social interaction: the location of an actor's contacts in a social structure of interactions provides certain advantages to the actor. The relational dimension refers to assets that are rooted in these relationships, such as trust and trustworthiness. The cognitive dimension refers to attributes like a shared paradigm that facilitates a common understanding of collective goals and proper ways of acting in a social system. This dimension captures the essence of what Coleman (1990) described as "the public good aspect of social capital."

The three dimensions of social capital are interlinked (Tsai and Ghoshal, 1998). Social interaction ties (structural dimension) may stimulate trust and perceived trustworthiness (relational dimension). For example, an agent in a central network position can be perceived as more trustworthy by other agents. Common values and a shared vision of collective goals and aspirations (cognitive dimension) may also encourage the development of trust relationships. Finally, social interaction plays a critical role both in shaping a common set of goals and values and in the sharing of those goals and values among network members.

The social capital of individuals is akin to the network resources of firms (Walker et al., 1997). According to Bourdieu and Wacquant (1992, p. 119),

> Social capital is the sum of the resources, actual or virtual, that accrue to an individual or a group by virtue of possessing a durable network of more or less institutionalized relationships of mutual acquaintance and recognition.

And, according to Coleman (1988),

> social capital inheres in the structure of relations between actors and among actors. It is not lodged either in the actors themselves or in physical implements of production. Because purposive organizations can be actors ("corporate actors") just as persons can, relations among corporate actors can constitute capital for them as well.

Distinct from other firm-specific resources, network resources reside in the formal and informal inter-organizational networks in which firms are embedded and can be utilized by the firm for strategic conception and implementation. The available network resources can influence firms' strategic behavior by altering the opportunity set available to them. The investments necessary to create and maintain network resources are distinct from the investments to create and maintain firm-specific resources.

## 3. NETWORK INFLUENCE ON MEMBER ORGANIZATIONS

The literature has recognized two channels of network influence on members (Gulati, 1998). The first relates to informational benefits obtained through network ties and positioning. The second relates to control benefits that are generated by being more advantageously positioned in the network or by being part of a tightly knit network. Although analytically different, these two benefits also overlap significantly since the control benefits largely emanate from the possession and manipulation of information.

## Informational Benefits of Networks (Cognition)

The information benefits of network embeddedness have been summarized by Burt (1992) as access, timing, and referrals. Access refers to information about current and potential partners regarding their assets, capabilities, and trustworthiness. Timing means having the information at the right time. Referrals apply to information, passed through indirect links, about other organizations with which the firm has not had direct contact and about market or technological developments of interest. The location of a firm in a network is important for the referral component: advantageous location means that indirect referrals of partners and of their activities will flow faster and more reliably (through triangulation) than if the company was located in the network's fringes. The specific network location, in other words, confers different degrees of information.

Powell et al. (1996) argue that when knowledge that brings competitive advantage is widely distributed, inter-organizational collaborative networks become the locus of innovation. While internal capabilities, both for the creation of new knowledge and for the absorption of knowledge produced externally, are of vital importance, networks serve in such cases as innovation loci because they provide timely access to resources and to knowledge that are otherwise unattainable, and test internal learning capabilities. In addition to innovation-related knowledge, firms learn to operate synergistically and develop routines to that effect. They learn how to transfer technology across partnerships and how to locate themselves in advantageous network positions that enable them to keep abreast of pertinent scientific and technological developments. As stated in Powell et al. (1996) "collaboration is both an admission ticket to an information network and a vehicle for rapid communication of news about opportunities and obstacles".

Organizations learn which collaborations to pursue, how to function in the context of multiple collaborative ventures, and how to adapt their cooperative strategies in the midst of dynamically evolving network structures, a competency that becomes particularly important in high technology fields where frequent scientific and technological advances change the relative benefits of different forms of collaboration. Collaboration becomes, then, emergent (Kogut, 2000). Learning from prior experience makes collaboration between parties easier (cheaper) to uphold because of the continuous refinement of collaboration routines and the attainment of partnering reputations.

There are two channels for informational benefits to network members: direct ties (relational embeddedness); and through the positioning of partners in the network (structural embeddedness). Both channels are described below.

### Relational embeddedness

The concept of relational embeddedness (Rowley et al., 2000) can be traced back to the original definition of tie strength for individual actor networks proposed by Granovetter (1973, p. 1361): "[A] combination of the amount of time, the emotional intensity, the intimacy (mutual confiding), and the reciprocal services which characterize the tie." Extended to inter-organizational alliance networks, tie strength translates into broader and deeper commitment in terms of both actual investment and investment in the relationship. Traditional equity joint ventures may be considered as an example of strong inter-organizational ties.

Strong ties have been associated in the literature with the exchange of high-quality, complex information, as well as tacit knowledge. These ties imply a finer mutual understanding of partners' operations and deeper interpenetration of each others' organizational boundaries (Uzzi, 1996). In contrast, weak ties were proposed by Granovetter as the appropriate means for accessing new information. He argued that weak ties are more likely to serve as local bridges between relatively disconnected areas of the network and connect the agent with others that possess unique information (thus, implying more of a search activity than an exploitation activity).

Tie strength also relates to network structure and is discussed further in the relevant section below. Both tie strength and network structure are relevant also to network governance, the subject of which is addressed later on, as well.

### Structural embeddedness

Burt (1992) distinguished conceptually between tie strength and tie density. He argued that when the objective is to access new knowledge, tie density (strong network interconnection) creates redundancy. He suggested that efficiency in accessing knowledge improves by shedding redundant ties in favor of establishing selective ties that bridge "structural holes" (empty spaces in the network).

It is now well understood that the information passing through networks is influenced by each participant's position in the network structure (Powell et al., 1996). Differential location in a network results in firms having divergent capabilities for benefiting from information flows. Firms with more experience in collaborating can better locate themselves in information-rich positions in the network with access to a more diverse set of activities. More central positioning, locally or globally, generates visibility and reputation, and thus facilitates timely access to information and resources. Firms more centrally located should have more timely access to promising new opportunities and ventures. Their experience should also result in better capabilities to benefit from further relationships.

Put differently, the status of an organization in the network affects its reputation and visibility in the system. The signaling properties of status are particularly important in uncertain environments: if partner status enhances their own attractiveness, organizations will have a tendency to seek high-status partners (Podolny, 1993; Podolny and Page, 1998; Podolny et al., 1996).[1]

Research has shown that firms with larger sets of network ties and more central network locations are more likely to be part of new ties, and this seems to hold for various types of networks including partnerships, patent citation networks, and top management teams. Each network highlights a different underlying social process that enables central firms to enter alliances more frequently (Gulati, 1998; Wagner et al., 2004).

## Control Benefits of Networks (Governance)

Coleman (1988) proposed that a dense structure with strong ties enables a build-up of reputation and social capital in the form of trust and shared social norms across network members.[2] For the same reasons, Meyer and Rowan (1977) and Oliver (2001) argued that firms embedded in highly interconnected networks develop shared behavioral expectations. Consequently, like strong ties, dense networks create a mechanism of control of social relations in inter-organizational networks. According to Rowley et al. (2000), strong ties create trust at the dyadic level by producing goodwill between partners based on interdependence and a history of reciprocity and mutual forbearance. Dense structures also serve as mechanisms of norm creation at the network level as firms are confronted with established customs, higher collective ability to punish disobedience, and expectations that the network will produce effective incentives for cooperation, and facilitate collective monitoring and sanctioning.[3]

The above also agrees with posited concepts of organizational cognition and organizational culture (Nooteboom and Gilsing, 2004). Organizational culture is an institutional arrangement that enables and constrains actions and sense-making, and includes both relations of power and processes of exclusion (Contu and Wilmott, 2003). Kogut and Zander (1996) and Nooteboom (1992) have argued that organizations set cognitive frameworks for guiding attention, perception and interpretation, and for setting behavioral rules, constraining opportunism, building trust, and limiting and resolving conflicts of interest. Norms and values of behavior tend to be internalized by people as part of their tacit knowledge, and are assimilated, to a greater or lesser extent, in socialization and habituation. It is important to notice that the stronger the ties and the denser the set of relationships, the more tightly knit is the network and the more it resembles an organization. The more, then, it tends to create its own culture that both enables and constrains interpretations and actions, and that includes relations of power and processes of exclusion for deterrence of deviant behavior.

Governance and network control are important as they affect the cost of operating the network directly. Dense networks with strong ties and diffused norms and expectations project high degrees of built-up social capital. The cost of participation for incumbents is fairly low given the following characteristics: wide spread of information and significant trust among members; the low chance of opportunistic behavior as a result of lock-in in a relationship with high relation-specific investments; high switching costs; and the ability to control the damage from spillovers.

The dark side of dense (tight) networks is that they may lock in an organization with a group that may prove not to have been the best choice, in organizational or technological terms. More on this below.

## 4.   NETWORK STRUCTURE

In an eloquent paper, Kogut (2000) argued that network structure is emergent in the initial conditions of a specific industry, including the inherent characteristics of the relevant technologies, and the norms and institutional factors that help generate rules that guide the competitive/ cooperative behavior of firms in that industry. The argument runs on the elaboration of the characteristics of variety and specialization that are antithetical within the firm but complementary within the network. Using the parallelism of the market and the network, Kogut argues that they basically serve a similar purpose: achieving variety through specialization in the division of labor. The division of labor is the result of a dynamic learning process of individual agents (firms) who specialize (focus) in order to create competence. Firms can be considered social communities that enable specialization in the creation and replication of partly tacit, partly explicit organizing principles of work. The boundary between the firm and the network (market) is determined by the internal cost of production and management relative to the costs of market search and procurement (Coase, 1937). At some point, the internal management of variety in the firm becomes more expensive than sourcing variety from the external market/network.

> A network is, then, a collection of firms, each ensconced in an identity that supports specialization and a dynamic of learning and exploration. But the network, unlike the firm, does not consist of an authority relationship that can enforce an organizational structure on its members. (Kogut, 2000, p. 409)

Network structure emerges in a self-organizing process from the initial conditions of a specific industry, the characteristics of the relevant technologies, and the norms and institutional factors that help generate rules that guide firm behavior. Behavioral rules and network structure are embraced in an interactive relationship: as rules generate the structure of the network, network structure influences subsequent behavior. The emergent structure dissuades rule-breaking behavior. "The dynamic between internal capabilities, ensconced in specific identities and organizational structures, and the external knowledge in the market (network) drives a co-evolution between the emergent properties in the firm and the network" (Kogut, 2000, p. 412).

Herein lies a fundamental trade-off between organizational stability and variety in network structure. The emergent network properties, as discussed above, are the result of self-organization processes and the accumulation of social capital among partners. The accumulation of social capital is dependent on the maintenance and strengthening of the prevailing relationships. The requisite investment by individual organizations to build social capital naturally tends to create forces for the preservation and strengthening of the existing structures. Hence, a natural tendency emerges to freeze the structure of interactions into stable patterns. The more stable the patterns of interaction become, however, the more the characteristics of firm organization the network acquires; that is, the more it strives for specialization and the less capable it grows in achieving its fundamental objective: variety. Increasing coordination deprives individual partners of the ability to pursue potential avenues of exploration.

## 5. NETWORK STRUCTURE OPTIMALITY

Latching onto this fundamental trade-off, Walker et al. (1997) emphasized that it is exactly the tendency for preservation and reinforcement of network structures that generates opportunities for entrepreneurial agents to bridge across structures. In so doing, these agents profit individually, as well as alter the form of the network. The argument for network structure optimality is about balancing two opposing forces: the incentive to lower the operating cost in a network by facilitating information exchange and decreasing relational risk, versus the incentive of profit opportunities by breaking new ground to bridge stable but isolated regions of relationships in the network.[4]

This "entrepreneurial" activity is, of course, the selective establishment of information-rich ties across "structural holes" in the network, a concept that Burt (1992) has strongly advocated. Such ties are non-redundant in the sense that they connect previously unconnected nodes and, as a result, confer powerful brokerage positions. Firms positioned in structural holes are more powerful because they arbitrate the information flows between groups of firms with loose (or no) ties to each other. The rent in this situation accrues to the firm bridging the structural hole. Pushing the argument a bit further, it can be proposed that while there can be entrepreneurial agents from within the network that bridge the holes, it is more likely that there is an inverse relationship between network centrality and such entrepreneurship taking hold. The smaller the stake of an organization in a given network, the higher are its incentives to play the entrepreneurial role and bridge across. The highest possibilities for the entrepreneurial role thus rest with organizations at the network fringes or outside of the network altogether.

Such "entrepreneurial" activity contrasts with the style of networking involved in the closure argument for dense network structures based on solid amounts of social capital that Coleman (1988) had advocated earlier. In Coleman's world, redundant ties among firms resolve collective action problems and improve coordination. Here, the rent accrues to the group and is allocated among its members on the basis of relative market power and adjudication rules.

Seemingly contradictory, the two styles of networking may actually be complementary, as Burt (1998) has already suggested, providing different advantages to, and being used for different purposes by, firms and other actors. One could perceive the Burt style of networking as creating a counterbalance to the natural tendency for freezing patterns of inter-organizational ties in the Coleman style of networking. In other words, Burt's style of networking could play a safeguarding role against the progressive demise of variety in increasingly stable networks.

The question, then, becomes one of balance (optimality).[5] That is, a balance that allows for the advantages of stability, when it proves advantageous, and also allows for the recombination of information and (network) renewal, when that path has merits. Economists will quickly recognize the analogy with traditional market analysis: (network) entry and barriers to such entry become key factors for network structure and its rejuvenation, exactly as they do in markets where entrants dilute the strongholds of incumbents. Similarly to achieving optimality in markets, achieving balance in networks will be complex and will vary across activity areas (e.g. sectors).

Optimality in this sense is difficult to achieve, not least because of the "emergent" properties of network structure. The solution will, at least in part, depend on whether the predominant mode of operation in a sector concentrates on the better exploitation of existing technologies, skills, and information, or the exploration of emerging innovations and other changes (March, 1991). Generally speaking, exploitation signifies improvement of established practices whereas exploration signifies the development of new practices. Intimately related to the achievement of economic efficiency (lower cost for given output or more output for given cost), exploitation requires organizational routines that, in the case of networks, can be defined as "repetitive, recognizable patterns of interdependent actions, involving multiple actors" (Feldman and Pentland, 2003, p. 96). That is, exploitation involves the use of existing information to improve efficiency and returns from present strategies, competencies, and procedures. In contrast, routines are subject to change in exploration. Exploration involves searching for and experimenting with emerging innovations with good future prospects of profitability.

It is reasonable to anticipate that both processes are often needed, pursued simultaneously, and compete for limited resources within individual organizations (March, 1991).[6] The ensuing strategic trade-off is a classic one in economics. It pits short-term investment in the refinement of existing technologies for immediate, but relatively low-margin returns, against longer-term investment in radically new ideas and technologies for future, but potentially much higher-margin, returns. The optimal allocation of resources between the two will depend on the internal conditions of the firm (resources, capabilities, strategic inclination) and on environmental factors relating to both the demand side (conditions for market development) and the supply side (technological opportunity, appropriability, competitive conditions). Environmental uncertainty will tend to push for more exploration by increasing the need for innovation. According to this line of argument, then, the type and optimal amount of social capital for an organization to maintain will change in accordance with the distinct strategic mixtures of exploitation and exploration pursued by that organization in different environments (Nooteboom and Gilsing, 2004; Rowley et al., 2000).

On the basis of the different information requirements between exploitation and exploration, Rowley et al. (2000) have argued for high-density and strong ties for exploitation and for low-density and weak ties for exploration. Strong ties are said to facilitate rich exchanges of fine-grained information to assist firms in obtaining a deep understanding of a specific innovation in order to refine and improve it. Weak ties are said to be especially important for flexibility and low-density network structures preferable for broad searches in uncertain environments requiring relatively high investments in exploration.

Hagedoorn and Duysters (2002) reach the opposite conclusion: it is dense networks and redundant ties that may be conducive to experimentation and learning through contacts and not strict rules of network efficiency maximization. They reason on the basis of bounded rationality (Cyert and March, 1964; Nelson and Winter, 1982; Simon, 1957). In the context of dynamic environments with frequently changing conditions and continuous learning by companies, they argue, the efficiency of information transfer through bridges across existing local networks – while avoiding duplication of contacts – becomes less relevant as a realistic strategy. In dynamic environments characterized by rapid technological advance, openness of contacts, network density and tie redundancy are said to be preferable to efficiency-based behavior.

Nooteboom and Gilsing (2004) argue somewhere in between. Loose and non-redundant ties may be best for the identification of knowledge, whereas strong ties are needed for the transfer of complex and highly tacit knowledge. On the basis of bounded rationality and uncertainty concerning future dominant designs of technology, organization, and consequential configuration of future networks of exploitation, they expect dense networks and redundant ties in the case of exploration. Ties will be strong in some respects (scope, frequency, trust/mutual openness), show less strength in terms of relation-specific investments and duration, and little strength in terms of control. In contrast, less dense, more stable network structures and non-redundant ties are anticipated for exploitation. Increased specialization, reduced scope and reduced need for trust (more control) reduce frequency of interaction.

Moreover, Nooteboom and Gilsing (2004) discuss the important issue of the transition from exploration to exploitation with the development of a dominant design. They expect hybrid forms of networks to arise in transitions between, and through, combinations of exploration and exploitation. One theoretically possible form of hybrid network could be visualized as an intermediate network that links networks for exploitation and networks for exploration. Another form could be represented by a core network of exploitation connected to peripheral networks of exploration. Finally, exploration networks may be transformed into exploitation networks with larger scale organizations, elimination of redundancy, emergence of centrality, larger specific investments, less informality, fewer personalized relations, more distrust and more formal control.

# 6. SUMMARY AND CONCLUSION

Several important concepts for the strategic and policy analysis of inter-organizational innovation networks were discussed in this chapter. One relates to the network resources of firms. Like the social capital of individuals, network resources have a structural dimension determined by the location of an actor's contacts in a network, a relational dimension indicating their relationship assets such as trust/trustworthiness, and a cognitive dimension reflecting a shared paradigm that facilitates interaction in the network. Distinct from other firm-specific resources, network resources reside in the formal and informal inter-organizational networks in which firms are embedded and can be utilized by the firm to conceive of and implement its strategies. Available network resources can influence firms' strategic behavior by altering the opportunity set with which they are presented. The investments necessary to create and maintain network resources are distinct from the investments to create and maintain firm-specific resources. Organizations are typically embedded in more than one inter-locking network at any given point of time.

Networks confer informational benefits to their members that can be summarized as access, timing, and referrals. These informational benefits flow through two channels: the direct ties of the organization (relational embeddedness) and its positioning in the network (structural embeddedness). Strong ties have been traditionally associated in the network literature with the exchange of high-quality, complex information and tacit knowledge, whereas weak ties have been considered appropriate means for accessing new information. Weak ties are more likely to serve as local bridges between relatively disconnected areas of the network, and to connect the agent with others that possess unique information. Efficiency in accessing knowledge may improve by shedding redundant ties in favor of establishing selective ties that bridge "structural holes." Importantly, each participant's position in the network structure influences its capabilities for benefiting from the network: more central positioning (locally or globally) generates visibility and reputation and facilitates timely access to resources and information. This, in turn, raises the status of the organization in the network and makes it especially desirable as a partner. Such "preferential attachment" processes lead to skewed distributions of linkages in networks of all kinds, including innovation networks.

When the knowledge underlying competitive advantage is widely distributed, inter-organizational cooperative networks become the locus of innovation. Organizations learn which collaborations to pursue, how to function in the context of multiple collaborative ventures, and how to adapt their cooperative strategies in the midst of dynamically evolving network structures. Such competencies become particularly important in high technology fields where frequent scientific and technological advances change the relative benefits of different forms of collaboration.

Networks also confer control benefits for their members. Control benefits are generated when firms are more advantageously positioned in the network or are part of a tightly knit network. A dense network structure with strong ties enables firms to build reputation and social capital in the form of trust and shared social norms across network members. Strong ties create trust at the dyadic level, while dense structures serve as mechanisms of norm creation at the network level. Dense networks and strong ties decrease the cost of network operation. Moreover, the stronger the ties and the denser the set of relationships, the more tightly knit is the network and the more it resembles an organization. The more it then tends to create its own culture that both enables and constrains interpretations and actions, and that includes relations of power and processes of exclusion for deterrence of deviant behavior. The dark side of dense networks is in the form of fewer degrees of freedom for members because of lock-in.

An important concept in the literature is that network structure is emergent in the initial conditions of a specific industry, including the inherent characteristics of the relevant technologies, and the norms and institutional factors that help generate rules that guide the competitive/cooperative behavior of firms in that industry. In addition, it is now understood that the market and the network basically serve a similar purpose: achieving variety through specialization in the division of labor. In contrast, firms (hierarchies) enable specialization. The boundary between the hierarchy and the network is determined by transaction costs.

This points out a fundamental trade-off in network structure between organizational stability and variety. The accumulation of social capital is dependent on the maintenance and strengthening of the prevailing relationships; hence a tendency to freeze the structure of interactions into stable patterns. The more stable the patterns of interaction become, however, the more the characteristics of firm organization the network acquires; that is, the more it strives for specialization and the less capable it grows of achieving its fundamental objective of variety. Increasing coordination deprives individual partners of the ability to pursue potential avenues of exploration.

It is important to emphasize that network structure optimality will, at least in part, depend on whether the predominant mode of operation in an industry concentrates on the better exploitation of existing technologies, skills, and information, or the exploration of emerging innovations and other changes. Both processes are often needed, pursued simultaneously, and compete for limited resources within individual organizations. The optimal allocation of resources among the two will depend on the internal conditions of the firm (resources, capabilities, strategic inclination) and on environmental factors relating to industry characteristics, including both the demand side (conditions for market development) and the supply side (technological opportunity, appropriability, competitive conditions). The type and optimal amount of social capital for an organization to maintain will then change in accordance with the organization's strategic mixture of exploitation and exploration in different environments.

On the basis of the different information requirements between exploitation and exploration, analysts have argued for high-density and strong ties for exploitation and for low-density and weak ties for exploration. Others have reached the opposite conclusion by using bounded rationality arguments: in dynamic environments with frequently changing conditions and continuous learning by companies, the efficiency of transferring information through bridges in existing networks while avoiding duplication of contacts is argued to become less relevant than openness of contacts, network density and tie redundancy. Still others argue somewhere in between: dense networks, redundant ties, and variable tie strengths are expected in the case of exploration; less dense, more stable network structures and non-redundant ties are anticipated for exploitation. Moreover, hybrid network forms are anticipated in transitions from exploration to exploitation in the development of a dominant design.

We have thus come full circle: in order to determine the incentives (net benefits) of a firm to participate in a network, one needs to address network structure optimality and the firm's positioning in the network which, in turn, requires addressing the relationship between industry (activity) characteristics and firm strategy. This should not be surprising, given that networking is part of the more general strategic orientation of the firm, which itself is influenced by the characteristics of the economic activity in which the firm is engaged in the first place. In other words, network analysis must be complemented with more traditional investigations of market structure, technological advance, competitive behavior, and company performance. A particularly promising, in our view, avenue of investigation that can combine all these aspects would be the analysis of the co-evolution of industry and network structure, especially in sectors of rapid technological advance.

## NOTES

1. This process is often called preferential attachment. Let $P(k)$ be the probability that a randomly selected node has $k$ links (degrees). It is commonly found in the literature that,

for a sufficiently large $k$, the degree distribution of many networks follows the power law $P(k) \sim k^{\gamma}$, with $2.1 < \gamma < 4$, irrespective of the network origin (Barabási and Albert, 1999). This means that most network members have few links whereas a minority of members has disproportionately large numbers of links. Networks following a power law are referred to as scale-free networks since they lack a "typical" characteristic degree (Willinger et al., 2002).

2. Contrast this to Burt's (1992) argument for less dense structures in the previous section.
3. Rowley et al. (2000) then argue that dense networks and strong ties are, to some degree, substitutes for one another. A firm will gain much less from strong ties in a dense network than when its partners are sparsely connected. The structure itself in a dense network has produced behavioral norms to guide actions.
4. The analogy of the forces for preserving or altering the network structure to the incentives for maintaining the existing market structure or altering it through innovation should be obvious to economists.
5. This is not assumed as a static concept. Optimality evolves in time together with the factors responsible for an emergent network structure.
6. Evolutionary economics has offered extensive discussions on the use of organizational routines and their adaptation to new conditions, or abandonment, through time (Hodgson, 1993; Nelson, 1995; Nelson and Winter, 1982).

# REFERENCES

Arvanitis, R. and N.S. Vonortas (2000) "Introduction: symposium on technology transfer and learning through strategic technical alliances", *Journal of Technology Transfer*, **25**, 9–12.

Barabási, A.-L. and R. Albert (1999) "Emergence of scaling in random networks", *Science*, **286**, 509–12.

Bourdieu, P. and L. Wacquant (1992) *An Invitation to Reflexive Sociology*, Chicago, IL: University of Chicago Press.

Burt, R.S. (1992) *Structural Holes: The Social Structure of Competition*, Cambridge, MA: Harvard University Press.

Burt, R.S. (1997) "The contingent value of social capital", *Administrative Science Quarterly*, **42**, 339–65.

Burt, R.S. (1998) "The network structure of social capital", paper presented at the conference on social network and social capital, Duke University, Durham, NC.

Caloghirou, Y., N. Constantelou, and N.S. Vonortas (2001) "Innovation-related knowledge flows in European industry: extent, mechanisms, implications", Final Report of the KNOW Project, Targeted Socio-Economic Research Programme (TSER), European Commission, DG Research.

Caloghirou, Y. and N.S. Vonortas (2000) "Science and technology policy towards research joint ventures", Final Report of the STEP-TO-RJVs Project (SOE1-CT97-1075), Targeted Socio-Economic Research Programme (TSER), European Commission, DG Research.

Coase, R.H. (1937) "The nature of the firm", *Economica*, November, 386–405.

Coleman, J.S. (1988) "Social capital in the creation of human capital", *American Journal of Sociology*, **94**, 95–120.

Coleman, J.S. (1990) *Foundations of Social Theory*, Cambridge, MA: Belknap Press.

Contu, A. and H. Wilmott (2003) "Re-embedding situatedness: the importance of power relations in learning theory", *Organization Science*, **14** (3), 283–96.

Cyert, R.M. and J.G. March (1964) *A Behavioral Theory of the Firm*, Englewood Cliffs, NJ: Prentice Hall.

Ebers, M. and C.J. Jarillo (1998) "The construction, forms, and consequences of industry networks", *International Studies of Management and Organization*, **27** (4), 3–21.

Feldman M.S. and B.T. Pentland (2003) "Reconceptualizing organizational routines as a source of flexibility and change", *Administrative Science Quarterly*, **48** (1), 94–118.

Grandori, A. (1998) "Editorial: back to the future in organization theory", *Organization Studies*, **19** (4), I–xii.

Granovetter, M.S. (1973) "The strength of weak ties", *American Journal of Sociology*, **78**, 1360–80.

Granovetter, M.S. (1992) "Problems of explanation in economic sociology", in N. Nohria and R. Eccles (eds), *Networks and Organizations*, Boston, MA: Harvard Business School Press.

Gulati, R. (1998) "Alliances and networks", *Strategic Management Journal*, **19**, 293–317.

Gulati, R. (1999) "Network location and learning: the influence of network resources and firm capabilities on alliance formation", *Strategic Management Journal*, **20** (5), 397–420.

Gulati, R., N. Nohria, and A. Zaheer (2000) "Strategic networks", *Strategic Management Journal*, **21**, 203–15.

Hagedoorn, J, and G. Duysters (2002) "Learning in dynamic inter-firm networks: the efficacy of multiple contacts", *Organization Studies*, **23** (4), 525–48.

Hagedoorn, J., A. Link, and N.S. Vonortas (2000) "Research partnerships", *Research Policy*, **29** (4–5), 567–86.

Hodgson, G.M. (1993) *Economics and Evolution: Bringing Life Back into Economics*, Ann Arbor, MI: University of Michigan Press.

Kale, P., H. Singh and H. Perlmutter (2000) "Learning and protection of proprietary assets in strategic alliances: building relational capital", *Strategic Management Journal*, **21**, 217–37.

Kogut, B. (2000) "The network as knowledge: generative rules and the emergence of structure", *Strategic Management Journal*, **21**, 405–25.

Kogut, B. and U. Zander (1996) "What firms do? Coordination, identity, and learning", *Organization Science*, **7**, 502–14.

Koza, M.P. and A.Y. Lewin (1998) "The co-evolution of strategic alliances", *Organization Science*, **9** (3), 255–64.

March, J.G. (1991) "Exploration and exploitation in organizational learning", *Organizational Science*, **2** (1), 71–87.

Meyer, J.W. and B. Rowan (1977) "Institutionalized organizations: formal structure as myth and ceremony", *American Journal of Sociology*, **83**, 340–63.

Nahapiet, J. and S. Ghoshal (1997) "Social capital, intellectual capital and the creation of value in firms", *Academy of Management Best Paper Proceedings*, 35–9.

Nelson R.R. (1995) "Recent evolutionary theorizing about economic change", *Journal of Economic Literature*, **33** (1), 48–90.

Nelson, R.R. and S.G. Winter (1982) *An Evolutionary Theory of Economic Change*, Cambridge, MA: Belknap Press.

Nohria, N. and R. Eccles (eds) (1992) *Networks and Organizations*, Boston, MA: Harvard Business School Press.

Nooteboom, B. (1992) "Towards a dynamic theory of transactions", *Journal of Evolutionary Economics*, **2**, 281–99.

Nooteboom, B. (1999) *Inter-Firm Alliances: Analysis and Design*, London: Routledge.

Nooteboom, B. and V.A. Gilsing (2004) "Density and strength of ties in innovation networks: a competence and governance view", Working Paper, Rotterdam School of Management, Erasmus University, The Netherlands.

Oliver, A.L. (2001) "Strategic alliances and the learning life-cycle of biotechnology firms", *Organization Studies*, **22** (3), 467–89.

Oliver, A.L. and M. Ebers (1998) "Networking network studies: an analysis of conceptual configurations in the study of inter-organizational relations", *Organization Studies*, **19** (4), 549–83.

Osborn, R. and J. Hagedoorn (1997) "The institutionalization and evolutionary dynamics of interorganizational alliances and networks", *Academy of Management Journal*, **40**, 261–78.

Peteraf, M.A. (1993) "The cornerstones of competitive advantage: a resource-based view", *Strategic Management Journal*, **14** (3), 179–91.

Podolny, J.M. (1993) "A status-based model of market competition", *American Journal of Sociology*, **98** (4), 829–72.

Podolny, J.M. and K.L. Page (1998) "Network forms of organization", *Annual Review of Sociology*, **24**, 57–76.

Podolny, J.M., T.E. Stuart and M.T. Hannan (1996) "Networks, knowledge, and niches: competition in the worldwide semiconductor industry, 1984–1991", *American Journal of Sociology*, **102** (3), 659–89.

Powell, W.W., K.W. Koput and L. Smith-Doerr (1996) "Inter-organizational collaboration and the locus of innovation: networks of learning in biotechnology", *Administrative Science Quarterly*, **41**, 116–45.

Rowley, T., D. Behrens and D. Krackhardt (2000) "Redundant governance structures: an analysis of structural and relational embeddedness in the steel and semiconductor industries", *Strategic Management Journal*, **21**, 369–86.

Simon, H.A. (1957) *Organizational Behavior*, 2nd edn, New York: Macmillan.

Tsai, W. and S. Ghoshal (1998) "Social capital and value creation: the role of intrafirm networks", *Academy of Management Journal*, **41** (4), 464–76.

Uzzi, B. (1996) "The sources and consequences of embeddedness for the economic performance of organizations: the network effect", *American Sociological Review*, **61**, 674–98.

Vonortas, N.S. (1997) *Cooperation in Research and Development*, Boston, MA & Dordrecht, The Netherlands: Kluwer Academic Publishers.

Walker, G., B. Kogut and W. Shan (1997) "Social capital, structural holes and the formation of an industry network", *Organization Science*, **8**, 109–25.

Wagner, C.S., R. Thompson, T. Tesch and R. Perez (2004) "Evaluation of networks of collaboration between participants in IST research and their evolution to collaborations in the European Research Area (ERA)", Interim Report TR-220-EC, Directorate-Generale Information Society, European Commission.

Willinger, W., R. Govindan, S. Jamin, V. Paxson and S. Shenker (2002) "Scaling phenomena in the Internet: critically examining criticality", in N.R. Cozzarelli (ed.), *Proceedings of the National Academy of Science*, **99**, Washington, DC. National Academy of Sciences, pp. 2573–80.

# 3. The dynamics of networks and the evolution of industries: a survey of the empirical literature

**Lorenzo Zirulia**[1]

## 1. INTRODUCTION

The aim of this chapter is to review the empirical literature on interfirm technological agreements. Together with the phenomenon it describes, this literature has increased exponentially in recent years. Several suggestions on the rationale and effects of interfirm technological agreements have been proposed, receiving various degrees of confirmation by the empirical evidence. Interestingly, these efforts have been interdisciplinary, with contributions coming from disciplines such as economics, sociology and management (see Caloghirou et al., 2003; Gulati et al., 2000; Hagedoorn et al., 2000; Powell and Grodal, 2004, for previous recent surveys).

After a discussion of the empirical evidence, this chapter suggests a perspective that is relatively uncommon in the literature: interfirm technological agreements and R&D networks are seen as *structural elements* in the evolution and dynamics of industries. Our main point is that the existing empirical literature can constitute the basis for an appreciative theory of the role of R&D networks in industry evolution, which should be particularly appealing for economists interested in improving their knowledge of the fundamental link between technological progress and market structure. Furthermore, such a theory can be conceived of as a step towards further empirical analysis and formal modeling.

The chapter is structured as follows. Section 2 is introductory and preliminary: we define interfirm technological agreements, discuss the sources of data, and provide some basic evidence on the relevance and the evolution of the phenomenon over time, and on the broad motivations leading firms to collaborate. Sections 3 and 4 constitute the core of the chapter. Section 3 reviews the studies that consider the formation of technological agreements. First, we consider the characteristics at the firm, industry and dyadic levels that affect firms' propensity to enter into cooperative agreements. Second, we discuss the structural properties of the network resulting from the collaborations firms have in place. Section 4 surveys the studies that treat technological agreements as explanatory variables, considering the effects of agreements on firms' innovative and economic performance and on firms' technological profiles. This distinction is mainly adopted for expository reasons, since the two aspects are clearly interrelated. On the basis of the existing empirical evidence, section 5 proposes some themes for an appreciative theory of R&D networks and industry evolution. Finally, section 6 concludes.

## 2. DEFINITION, DATA AND STYLIZED FACTS

This section starts with the definition of interfirm technological agreements that we use in this chapter. This will help us in delimiting the object of this survey. Then, we discuss the main sources of data that have been used in the literature. This is done because the lack or limited availability of data has been a typical concern, weakening the reliability of results. Finally, we will present a number of "stylized facts" concerning the evolution of the phenomenon over time and its motivations.

### Definition

The definition of interfirm technological agreements is adapted from Hagedoorn (2002, p. 491):

> Interfirm technological agreements are defined as common interests between independent industrial partners, which are not connected through majority ownership, and in which R&D is at least part of the collaborative effort, through some arrangements for transferring technology or joint research.

This definition immediately excludes from the analysis all the agreements that are only concerned with production, such as standard, long-term buyer–supplier contracts or marketing joint ventures. Agreements that *also* have production or marketing elements, which are quite common in practice, are included. For instance, an agreement involving the joint development *and* production of a component to be used by the collaborating firms fits our definition. Not included in the definition is informal cooperation among firms, occurring, for instance, through information exchange among engineers or scientists (Von Hippel, 1987), or cooperation among firms and universities (Mowery and Sampat, 2004).[2]

The definition is broad enough to encompass several ways in which firms can collaborate. Cooperation can occur through various legal arrangements, implying different degrees of resources commitment, different levels and directions of technological flows, different coordination mechanisms, and different time horizons. Examples of interfirm technological agreements are: R&D joint ventures, where two or more firms constitute a new legal entity in order to perform R&D activities; joint R&D agreements, where firms share resources to undertake joint R&D projects; licensing and cross-licensing agreements; and research contracts, where one partner, usually a small R&D specialized firm, performs research activity for another firm.

**Data Sources**

The datasets used in the empirical analyses can be grouped into three classes:

1. *Literature-based datasets.* Several datasets have been collected by consulting specialized journals, financial newspapers and other publicly available sources of data. We discuss two of them in the following sections. The first one is the MERIT-CATI dataset, collected by John Hagedoorn and colleagues. Second is the SDC Platinum Joint Ventures and Strategic Alliances dataset collected by Thompson Financial.[3] Both of these datasets collect data for several sectors and are global in scope. At the same time, industry specific datasets have been collected as well, like the ARPA database developed at Politecnico di Milano for ICT sectors (Colombo and Garrone, 1996). Although the building of these datasets has greatly improved our knowledge of interfirm technological alliances, these types of data suffer from several limitations: agreements are known only if made public by the firms themselves; a general bias exists in favor of large, well-known firms, more fashionable technologies, and Anglo-Saxon countries; and information about the dissolution of agreements is less readily available than data on their formation.

2. *Surveys.* Some works have used data collected through questionnaires, in which firms are asked explicit questions about the extent of their collaborative activities, the motives behind them, and the types of collaborators (i.e. competitors, customers, suppliers or universities). In particular, a number of papers (for instance, Veugelers and Cassiman, 2002; Tether, 2002) used data from the Community Innovation Surveys (CIS), collected by the statistical offices of the EU member states according to a common European Standard, for the analysis of innovative inputs and outputs by European firms. The problems with these kinds of data are those that are usually

associated with survey analyses: results may depend on how questions are formulated; a degree of discretion in respondents' answers cannot be avoided; and a careful analysis for non-respondent biases must be performed.

3. *Data from public-funded R&D programs and antitrust authorities.* A third class of data concerns government-sponsored cooperative agreements and antitrust laws. In Europe, a cornerstone of technological policy rests on the programs (in particular, the Framework programs) promoted by the European Union to foster collaboration among firms (but also universities and research centers). Data on projects resulting from these programs have been collected recently and analyzed (see for instance Breschi and Cusmano, 2004). For the US, data have been collected using information from the Federal Register at the US Department of Justice (Vonortas, 1997). Under the National Cooperative Research Act, voluntary filings of R&D partnerships give firms benefits in case of anti-trust interventions. Finally, for Japan, Branstetter and Sakakibara (2002) have analyzed R&D consortia with a degree of government subsidization and intervention. These types of datasets may suffer from selection bias associated with the criteria according to which firms ask and obtain funds, or decide to register the partnership.

### Stylized Facts: Relevance and Trends

In order to give a flavor of the basic stylized facts concerning interfirm technological agreements, we refer to two datasets: the MERIT-CATI database and the SDC Platinum database. In MERIT-CATI, the references are given by the papers containing a descriptive account of the database (Hagedoorn, 1993, 2002). The dataset is composed of more than 10 000 technological agreements signed among more than 4000 firms worldwide, between the years 1960 and 1998. Data involve several sectors at different levels of R&D intensity. The dataset excludes from the analysis publicly funded agreements. The SDC Platinum dataset, instead, keeps track of all alliances announced between 1985 and 2002 in various media (e.g. newspapers, industry journals), which amounts to 95 329 alliances. These include both R&D and non-R&D related alliances and involve different types of organizations, such as firms, universities, and research centers. In the graphs we provide we restrict our attention to R&D agreements among publicly owned firms, and exclude pure licensing and cross-licensing agreements. The data provide 5485 agreements between 1985 and 2002.

Some basic stylized facts can be summarized as follows.

## Newly established agreements

In terms of the number of *newly established* agreements, worldwide and for all sectors, the CATI database shows that, after a limited growth in the 1960s and 1970s, the number of agreements exhibited highly significant growth rates in the 1980s, and since then it has been showing a cyclical behavior with a positive trend in the 1990s (see Figure 3.1). We observed no more than ten partnerships established each year during the 1960s, 160 at the end of the 1970s, and nearly 700 new partnerships at the peak in 1995.

If we look at SDC, we observe a slightly different behavior (see Figure 3.2). While the growth at the end of the 1980s is confirmed, we do not observe a cycle that starts in the 1990s. For the whole of the 1998–2002 period (which is not included in Figure 3.1), we observe a negative trend.

## Sectoral differences

*Sectoral differences* exist and are significant. Classifying sectors as high-tech, medium-tech and low-tech, according to their R&D intensities, we can see that the overall increase in the number of agreements has been accompanied by a significant increase of the high-tech industries' share. Figure 3.3, which refers to the CATI database, shows that, while in 1960 medium-tech sectors (instrumentation and medical equipment, automotive, consumer electronics and chemicals) accounted for about 70 percent of the total number of newly established agreements, with

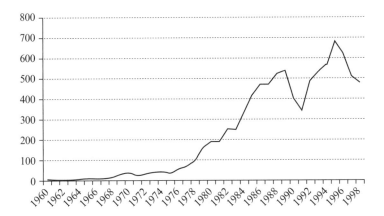

*Source:*   Hagedoorn (2002), MERIT-CATI database.

*Figure 3.1    Newly established R&D partnerships (1960–98)*

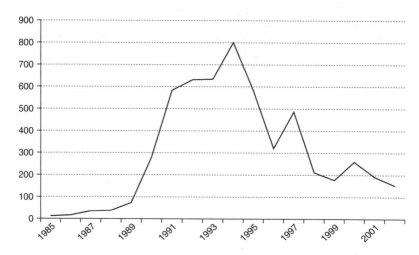

*Source:*   SDC Platinum, Thompson Financial.

*Figure 3.2    Newly established R&D agreements (1985–2002)*

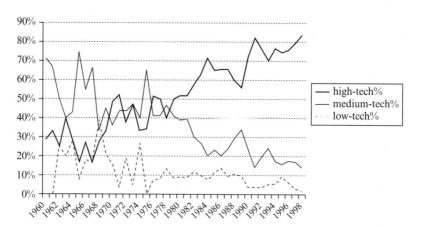

*Source:*   Hagedoorn (2002).

*Figure 3.3    New R&D partnerships, for low-, medium-, and high-tech
              industries (percentages)*

the remaining share composed of partnerships in the high-tech sectors
(computers, software, microelectronics, telecommunications), in 1998
the situation is reversed, with high-tech sectors accounting for more than
80 percent of the newly established agreements. At a more disaggregate

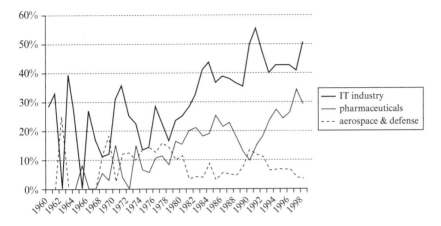

*Source:* Hagedoorn (2002).

*Figure 3.4* *Newly established R&D partnerships in high-tech industries (percentages)*

level, we observe that, within the high-tech sectors, the ICT industry plays a strikingly important role, constituting 50 percent of the total number of agreements at the end of the sample period. Pharmaceuticals, which includes biotechnology, also contributes in a significant way to the agreements in high-tech sectors, with approximately 30 percent of all newly established partnerships (Figure 3.4).

Using the SDC database as the source, Figure 3.5 reports the absolute number of new agreements in three sectors: semiconductors, pharmaceuticals, and biotech research. While semiconductors and pharmaceuticals exhibit a similar behavior, biotech research has undergone a boom in recent years, which is consistent with the increase in the percentage of alliances observed in the CATI database in pharmaceuticals (which includes biotech).

**Modes of cooperation**

Finally, it is possible to investigate the role of different *modes of cooperation*, in different sectors over time. For the CATI database, Hagedoorn (2002) divides the modes of cooperation into two broad categories: joint ventures and contractual arrangements (as R&D pacts, customer–supplier relations and licenses). Joint ventures are usually characterized by higher set-up costs and long-term orientation, as compared to the flexibility and generally shorter term orientation of contractual forms. Hagedoorn defines a relative contractual partnering index for each sector:

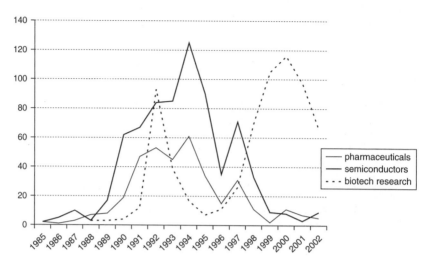

*Source:*  SDC, Thompson Financial.

*Figure 3.5   Newly established R&D agreements: selected sectors*

$$RCI_i = \frac{CP_i/JV_i}{TCP/TJV}$$

where $CP_i$ is the number of sectoral contractual partnerships, $JV_i$ the number of sectoral joint ventures, and $TCP$ and $TJV$ the total number of contractual partnerships and joint ventures, respectively. The value of the index across decades and sectors is reported in Table 3.1. The range for this index is $[0, \infty)$, where values larger than 1 denote a relative importance of contractual forms in that particular sector compared with the average value. We notice that, especially focusing on the last two decades, contractual forms are prevalent exactly in those industries in which partnerships are numerous (ICT and pharmaceuticals).

From the SDC database we report the percentage of joint ventures across all sectors in each year (Figure 3.6). The figure confirms the decrease in popularity of joint ventures coinciding with the upsurge of alliances in the second half of the 1990s. Interestingly, we observe a slight increase and then stabilization in the relative role of joint ventures in more recent years.

**Stylized Facts: Motivations**

Several industry case studies have emphasized the rationale for cooperation in specific cases. For a broader view, it can be useful to refer to the CATI

*Table 3.1*  *Relative contractual partnering index of selected sectors during 1960–98*

| Sectors | 1960–98 | 1970–79 | 1980–89 | 1990–98 |
|---|---|---|---|---|
| Pharmaceuticals | 2.65 | 2.48 | 2.29 | 1.48 |
| Information technology | 1.06 | 0.91 | 1.27 | 1.64 |
| Aerospace/defense | 7.94 | 5.34 | 3.57 | 0.58 |
| Automative | 1.32 | 3.16 | 0.46 | 0.57 |
| Chemicals | 0.38 | 0.26 | 0.35 | 0.24 |
| Instruments and medical equipment | 0.00 | 0.18 | 0.92 | 1.64 |
| Consumer electronics | 0.00 | 0.99 | 0.28 | 1.18 |

*Source:*  Hagedoorn (2002).

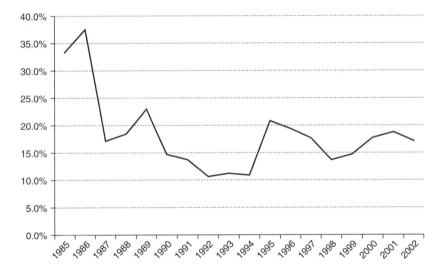

*Source:*  SDC Platinum, Thompson Financial.

*Figure 3.6*  *Percentage of joint ventures in newly established R&D agreements*

database. On the basis of the several and (partially) contrasting motives for cooperation – mainly put forth by business scholars using appreciative theoretical or empirically grounded considerations (see Hagedoorn, 1993, for references to relevant theoretical literature) – each agreement of the database is assigned to one or more of the following motives:

- Searching for complementarities, synergies, and cross-fertilization between technological and scientific fields, in sectors characterized by increased technological complexity, in which no firm can master all of the relevant knowledge required to innovate.
- Reducing costs and risks in R&D and exploiting economies of scale.
- Performing basic or "pre-competitive" R&D.
- Monitoring new technological opportunities, possibly followed by the development of new products and entry into new markets.
- Facing the shortening of the product life-cycle and the reduction of innovation time-span (i.e. the period between discovery and introduction into the market), which leads firms to cooperate to reduce the period of development.
- Market positioning; that is, modifying market structure in the firm's favor against rivals in domestic and international markets.
- Mostly "hidden" motives, like capturing a rival's tacit knowledge, technology transfer, and "technological leap-frogging."

Several alliances are assigned to more than one category, since some of these categories operate at different levels (i.e. market vs. technology level) and are not mutually exclusive. Hagedoorn (1993) provides a ranking of *importance* among the different motives across different sectors (see Table 3.2).

Two comments are necessary. First, although sectoral differences exist and are significant, nevertheless some motives exhibit a general prominence. Those motives are: searching for technological complementarities; shortening of the innovative time-span; and influencing market structure. Second, a general, broad view of the role of R&D partnerships is suggested by these data, which is consistent with a detailed account of specific industries. In high-tech industries, innovation is more and more complex, building on several technological fields. This is the case in pharmaceuticals, after the new discoveries in molecular biology in the mid-1970s, and in microelectronics, where innovation hinges on competencies in fields as different as solid physics, construction of semiconductor manufacturing and testing equipment, and programming logic. Firms cannot possess all the relevant knowledge required to innovate and, therefore, they look for partners with complementary capabilities to assist in an increased rate of introduction of new products and processes, to monitor new opportunities and enter new markets, and to sustain long-lasting competitive advantage.

**Stylized Facts: a Summary**

The stylized facts of technological agreements reported in this section can be summarized as follows. R&D agreements are a relatively recent phenomenon,

Table 3.2  Motives for cooperation, 1980–89, selected sectors (percentages)

| | Technological complementarities | Basic R&D | Lack of financial resources | Reduction innovation time span | Market access/ structure | High cost/ risks | Monitoring technology/ market entry |
|---|---|---|---|---|---|---|---|
| Pharmaceuticals | 35 | 10 | 13 | 31 | 13 | 1 | 15 |
| Computers | 28 | 2 | 2 | 22 | 51 | 1 | 10 |
| Software | 38 | 2 | 4 | 36 | 24 | 1 | 11 |
| Microelectronics | 33 | 5 | 3 | 33 | 52 | 3 | 6 |
| Aerospace/defense | 34 | 0 | 1 | 26 | 13 | 36 | 8 |
| Automative | 27 | 2 | 2 | 22 | 52 | 4 | 4 |
| Chemicals | 16 | 1 | 1 | 13 | 51 | 7 | 8 |
| Instruments and medical equipment | 35 | 2 | 4 | 40 | 28 | 0 | 10 |
| Consumer electronics | 19 | 0 | 4 | 19 | 53 | 2 | 11 |

Source:  Hagedoorn (1993).

having become significant only at the end of the 1980s. It is also remarkable that, after the boom in the first half of the 1990s, we observed a significant decrease in new technological agreements in more recent years. Since the data reported only covered newly established agreements, it is possible that an exhaustion effect (of partnering opportunities) has occurred. The agreements mainly concern flexible, short-term forms of cooperation in high-tech industries. In these industries, such agreements allow firms to access and acquire all the relevant knowledge required to innovate and exhibit an increased rate of introduction of new products and processes.

## 3.  THE FORMATION OF TECHNOLOGICAL AGREEMENTS

After the broad introduction to the general relevance and underlying motives of technological alliances, in this section we go more in depth to review the empirical studies that examine the formation of interfirm technological agreements. Using the terminology developed by Geroski (1995), in this section and in section 4 we provide a number of "stylized empirical results." Concerning the formation of technological agreements, we distinguish three levels of analysis:

1.  The first series of studies focuses on *the firm level*. Scholars have tried to identify firms' characteristics (size, age, technological capabilities, etc.) and industries' characteristics (concentration and appropriability of innovation) that affect firms' propensity to enter into collaborative agreements, the total number of agreements and the total number of partners.
2.  The second level of analysis is the *dyad* (i.e. the single pair of firms involved in an agreement). In this case, the studies investigate the characteristics of the firms that increase the probability of an agreement between them, and analyze how the choice of mode for cooperation is affected by firms' attributes, including their history of collaboration.
3.  The third level is the *network* of R&D alliances. Recent studies have investigated the structural properties of these networks, their evolution over time, and the relation between network measures at the firm level and the propensity to enter into new alliances.

**The Formation of Technological Agreements: the Firm and Industry Level**

Several studies have estimated logit or probit econometric models that link firm and industry characteristics to the propensity of setting up cooperative ventures. Other studies use Poisson and negative binomial regressions to discover the intensity of collaborative activities, measured by the number of technical agreements in which firms are involved or by the number of partners they have.

**The firm level**
Many empirical studies have found *positive* impacts of firm-level variables on firm-level collaborative activities. These variables are detailed below.

1.  *Size*. Firms that are active in interfirm technological agreements are typically large in size. This is one of the most robust findings of this literature. A positive relation between size and propensity to form interfirm alliances or between size and the number of technical agreements is found by Link and Bauer (1987), Kleinknecht and Reijen (1992), Hagedoorn and Schakenraad (1994), Colombo (1995), Colombo and Garrone (1996), Siebert (1996), Vonortas (1997), Ahuja (2000a), Fritsch and Lukas (2001), Bayona et al. (2001), Tether (2002), Veugelers and Cassiman (2002), Hernan et al. (2003), and Becker and Dietz (2004). This evidence is robust across time, sectors and countries.[4] Large firms are likely to engage in a wide range of economic activities, increasing the opportunities for cooperation. A "cost spreading" argument (Cohen and Klepper, 1996) may apply to technological agreements as it does to R&D in general: large firms can spread the gain from innovation over a larger base of economic activity, increasing their incentives towards cooperative agreements (as a form of R&D investment). Some forms of cooperative agreements, such as R&D joint ventures, entail high physical and legal set-up costs for which small firms lack financial resources. Finally, large firms can have significant bargaining power in contracting with their partners.

2.  *R&D intensity and technological capabilities*. Using data from the UK CIS 2 survey on 1275 innovating firms, Tether (2002) shows that performing R&D on a continuous basis and intensively has a significantly positive effect on firms' propensity to enter into collaborative ventures. Similar results are obtained by Fritsch and Lukas (2001) from a survey on German firms, and by Bayona et al. (2001) from a survey on Spanish firms. Link and Bauer (1987) find a positive value for *absolute* R&D in explaining cooperative activity. Ahuja (2000a), in his sample of 97 leading firms in the chemicals industry, shows that the stock of patents positively affects the number of agreements. Sakakibara (2002) introduces the variable "R&D capabilities," defined as the difference between firm and industry R&D intensity, and finds that this variable positively affects Japanese firms' participation in government

sponsored R&D consortia. Arora and Gambardella (1990) find that increasing the stock of biotechnology patents for large pharmaceuticals and chemicals firms increases the number of external linkages these firms have with specialized biotech firms.[5] In a similar vein, Stuart (1998) uses a sample of semiconductor firms to show that technologically "prestigious" firms (i.e. firms whose patents are highly cited) are more likely to form technological agreements.

The possibility that R&D intensity and the number of technical agreements are not strongly exogenous to each other has been successfully tested by Colombo and Garrone (1996). Their sample is composed of agreements by firms in the semiconductor, data processing and telecommunication sectors. Colombo and Garrone (1998) estimate a simultaneous two-equation structural model and find a significantly positive effect of R&D intensity on the number of technical agreements, while the coefficient for the reverse relation is not significant. A similar two-equation model is estimated by Becker and Dietz (2004), who find significantly positive effects in both directions.

These results suggest that internal and cooperative R&D should be seen as complementary rather than substitutes. The most common explanation for this result is the role of absorptive capacity (Cohen and Levinthal, 1989). In order to evaluate and fully absorb the outcomes from cooperative ventures, firms need to have pre-existing capabilities in those scientific or technological fields. This implies that firms lacking technological capabilities are not in a position to reap the benefits from cooperation. This view is confirmed by Stuart (1998), who shows that firms in more crowded technological areas are more likely to form new agreements. This outcome is explained by claiming that such firms have many potential partners for which they possess appropriate absorptive capacity.

3.  *Experience.* Firms that have more experience in managing collaborative ties (usually measured by the cumulative number of past alliances or by the number of partners in previous years) are more likely to enter collaborative agreements. This is the result obtained by Gulati (1995a), Powell et al. (1996), Ahuja (2000a), Sakakibara (2002), Hernan et al. (2003), and Okamura and Vonortas (2004). In the business literature, this result is usually explained by referring to the notion of "cooperative capability" (Gulati, 1998). With experience, firms learn how to manage their collaborative ties, to develop interfirm knowledge-sharing routines, to funnel results inside the organization, to govern contractual arrangements where there is room for moral hazard and incompleteness, and to initiate necessary changes in the partnership as it evolves over time. Possessing this experience increases returns from

technical agreements. A second, complementary explanation points at the role of previous partners as an important information source about new opportunities for agreements and new potential partners. We will come back to this point in the second and third parts of section 3, discussing the dyadic and the network level.

The relevance of these variables (size, R&D intensity, and experience in managing ties) is already shedding light on the "strategic" nature of cooperative agreements. Interfirm technological alliances are an important, persistent part of the innovative strategies of large and technologically leading firms, rather than a defensive tactic by small firms lacking the ability to innovate alone.[6] This perspective is confirmed by the results of surveys (Fritsch and Lukas, 2001; Tether, 2002) which show that firms' propensity to enter into collaborative agreements is higher when they aim at introducing breakthrough innovation (e.g. radically new products).

**The industry level**
Concerning industry level factors, section 2 showed that the intensity of the phenomenon of interfirm strategic alliances varies across sectors, while a positive relationship exists between sectoral R&D intensity and the number of R&D alliances in that sector. In other words, technological agreements are particularly common in high-tech sectors (Hagedoorn, 1993). More rigorously, Hernan et al. (2003) confirm this evidence, finding a significantly positive coefficient for R&D intensity on firms' participation in R&D joint ventures in the Eureka and Framework programs.[7] We focus in this section on two other industry-specific variables: concentration and appropriability. It is worth noting, however, that the number of cross-industry studies has been restricted by the limited availability of large data sets. For this reason, this evidence seems less robust than that presented in the previous paragraphs.

1.  *Concentration.* Link and Bauer (1987), Sakakibara (2002), and Hernan et al. (2003) find that R&D cooperation is more likely to occur in concentrated industries. It is argued that in oligopolistic markets it is easier to find the appropriate partners or convince other firms to cooperate. Furthermore, market power associated with such structures allows firms to appropriate returns from the cooperative investment. This result also emerges in a pioneering study by Pfeffer and Nowak (1976), who found a positive relation between concentration and the number of joint ventures at the industry level in US manufacturing firms.[8] It is worth mentioning that the opposite result (a negative relation between concentration and the rate of formation of strategic alliances) is found

by Eisenhardt and Schoonhoven (1996). These authors used a sample of 102 new US firms in the semiconductor sector, and found that the number of competitors in the segment in which the firm operates positively affects the rate of alliance formation. The authors relate this to gains enabled through access to external resources, when market conditions are difficult. Eisenhardt and Schoonhoven's results can be seen as complementary to the previously discussed findings if one considers that, while Eisenhardt and Schoonhoven focus on new (and typically small) firms, the papers we previously discussed are concerned with large, established firms. This suggests that the cooperative strategies of new and established firms may differ significantly, as they are differently affected by industry characteristics.

2.  *Appropriability.* Several authors inspired by the economic theories of R&D cooperation have tested the link between the degree of appropriability of R&D investments and R&D cooperation. Indeed, models of R&D cooperation in the IO tradition (d'Aspremont and Jacquemin, 1988; Kamien et al., 1992) identify in the internalization of R&D spillovers one of the main rationales for R&D cooperation.[9] When sectoral measures of R&D appropriability are introduced as explanatory variables for firms' propensity to cooperate, the sign of the corresponding coefficient turns out to be negative, in accordance with the theory. Thus, higher spillovers lead to more cooperation (Hernan et al., 2003; Sakakibara, 2002, Okamura and Vonortas, 2004).[10]

**The Formation of Technological Agreements: the Dyadic Level**

The studies considering the characteristics of the dyad and the probability of cooperation have focused on two main dimensions: technological and social/relational.

1.  The first dimension is technological. One concern of the literature has been to assess the probability of two firms forming a collaborative link, as a function of their technological distance, empirically measured on the basis of their patent portfolios. A first argument claims that firms need to be close in technological space in order to be good partners. This is related, again, to an absorptive capacity argument. As long as firms use technological alliances in order to learn, they need to have pre-existing knowledge in the partner's field of expertise to better absorb its capabilities. At the same time, cognitive proximity is required for effective communication to occur. This hypothesis is confirmed by the works by Stuart (1998) and Okanamura and Vonortas (2004). Stuart (1998) defines firms' technological positions using

patent citations for a sample of semiconductor firms, and finds that proximity in such a space increases the likelihood of alliance formation. Okanamura and Vonortas (2004) find that an increase in technological proximity, measured by the similarity of patent portfolios, has a positive effect on link formation for US research joint ventures.

However, if firms are technologically too close, opportunities for learning decrease. Firms need to be sufficiently dissimilar for technological complementarities to be exploited through collaboration. Mowery et al. (1998) find evidence to support this idea. In a sample of 151 international joint ventures in several sectors, they find an inverted U relationship between partners' technological overlap (measured by the cross-citation rate and common citation rate in patent portfolios) and the probability of alliance formation. In other words, firms need to be "not too distant nor too close" from a technological point of view (Nooteboom, 1999).

2.  The second dimension of dyad relationships can be defined as "social" or "relational." Technological alliances are usually complex arrangements for which uncertainty and investment appropriability are relevant issues. For the particular nature of the transaction involved, there is significant room for opportunistic behavior, and, conversely, there is a role for trust building among partners.

    A quite robust result in this stream of literature is that firms tend to ally with previous partners (Gulati, 1995a; Stuart, 1998; Gulati and Gargiulo, 1999, Okamura and Vonortas, 2004). Firms, with familiarity, can build trust, lowering transaction costs and limiting the risk of opportunistic behaviors. They can also choose organizational forms that are more flexible (Gulati, 1995b). At the same time, they can develop routines and codes in order to increase the effectiveness of communication with the partner and control the flows of knowledge.

    Indirect links among firms are important as well. Common previous partners play two main roles: first, they constitute sources of information about potential partners for new collaborative opportunities; second, they can reduce the asymmetric information among the potential partners, providing an indirect reputation effect. Gulati and Gargiulo (1999) find that the number of indirect links (common partners) has a positive effect on the probability of link formation at the dyadic level.

### The Formation of Technological Agreements: the Network Level

In recent years, there has been a substantial shift of attention from the dyadic to the network level, spurred by sociology's massive contributions to the field. The structure of the overall network of alliances resulting from firms' (uncoordinated) choices matters for two reasons. First, theoretical contributions emphasize that the network structure has an impact on the level of efficiency of the industry (Cowan and Jonard, 2003 and 2004). In other words, the structure of the network of alliances is a factor that may explain cross-sectional variation in the rate of technological progress. Second, firms' positions in the network can affect not only their economic and innovative performance, but also their propensity to enter into new alliances, in general and at the dyadic level.

The first structural characteristic of networks that has been extensively considered is the existence of *cliques*, or, more generally, cohesive sub-groups of firms within the network.[11] There are two main reasons for which we should expect cliques to emerge in networks of technological alliances. Both reasons are related to the contributions that cliques give to the building of "social capital," defined as the sum of resources that accrue to a firm by virtue of possessing a durable network of relationships.

The first reason for clique emergence can be labeled as "cognitive." Firms that share many common partners can develop a common language for cooperation, practices and routines, which favors the creation of new knowledge and its transmission among the firms in the clique. The second reason can be labeled as "reputational," and in turn can be divided into ex post and ex ante motivations. *Ex post* (once the link is formed) participation in a clique can favor cooperation in a context of contractual incompleteness, because in presence of opportunistic behavior, the information about a "deviation" by a firm can spread among the partners, increasing the cost of opportunistic behavior. *Ex ante* (before the alliance is formed) common partners can reduce the degree of information asymmetry about firms' competencies and trustworthiness, thus creating conditions favorable to the formation of links.

The existence of cohesive sub-groups has been shown in a number of sectors. Nohria and Garcia-Pont (1991) consider 35 leading firms in the automobile industry, and 133 alliances those firms formed in the 1980s. They detect six "strategic" blocks. It turns out that strategic blocks are composed of firms with complementary capabilities, and are such that firms in each block have access to a similar set of capabilities. The analysis of Gomes-Casseres (1996) shows that competition in the personal digital assistants market has been characterized, since its inception, by alliance groups of firms coming from different sectors (computer hardware and software, telecommunications and consumer electronics).

This view of social capital as "closure" (Coleman, 1988), which emphasizes the benefits of clustering in networks, is often set against the "structural holes" argument (Burt, 1992). Burt considers players (individuals or organizations) in a competitive arena (for instance, a market). Such a competitive arena is characterized by a "social" context, defined as a social network among the players.

The theory suggests that the players' position in the network should help explain their performance in the competition. In particular, a player's performance should be positively correlated with the extent to which the player manages non-redundant contacts in its network. Contacts are defined as redundant if they are connected by a strong relationship (cohesion criterion), or when they have, in turn, the same contacts (redundancy by structural equivalence). Whenever two contacts are non-redundant, a structural hole is assumed to exist between them. Players that occupy structural holes can enjoy higher rates of return from their investments. Non-redundant contacts are more likely to give them timely access to diverse sources of information (being the players exposed to more rewarding opportunities), as well as to give control over such information, in order to secure more favorable terms in the opportunities they choose to pursue.

In the case of technological alliances, the network among firms is mostly seen as a conduit of information about technology (for instance, about more or less promising technological directions). In this perspective, firms in a clique have by definition redundant links, and according to this view, an inefficient structure of the ego-network.[12] Burt's argument clearly has a normative flavor. Firms should fill structural holes, because this allows them a higher rate of return. We will mention in the next section studies that test this hypothesis.

A study by Walker et al. (1997) uses a sample of biotech firms from the period 1984 to 1988 to examine how the rate of alliance formation depends on the structure of the networks in which firms are embedded. They find that firms endowed with "social capital" (located in dense areas of the network) form more links than firms active in less dense areas (full of structural holes). At the same time, new links tend to increase the level of social capital.

The social capital and structural holes views are not incompatible. If we assume the existence of advantages (at the firm level) of being located in a clique and having (some) non-redundant contacts, we could expect firms in a cliquish network to have some "long-distance" connections. Watts and Strogatz (1998) show that networks with these characteristics exhibit a "small world" property (low average distance, even in a cliquish, sparse network), because some "short-cuts" among otherwise disconnected areas dramatically reduce the average distance among actors. Theoretical models (Cowan and Jonard, 2003 and 2004) have shown that "small world networks" (networks exhibiting both high cliquishness and low average distance) are the most efficient in the process of knowledge creation and diffusion.

From the above considerations, it is natural to ask if firms' innovative networks are "small worlds." The answer from existing studies is generally yes. Verspagen and Duysters (2004) find a "small world" network for the alliances of the two sectors they analyze: chemicals and food (639 firms in their sample) and electronics and ICT (837 firms). Cowan and Jonard (2003) find a small world in the network of firms participating in the BRITE/EURAM program and the network of research institutes from the TSER program. Breschi and Cusmano (2004) find high clustering and low average distance for the network of firms, universities and research institutes participating in the third and fourth Framework programs.

A question that has not been addressed by the empirical literature on technological networks is the identity of firms that activate "short cuts" between separated cliques. From a methodological point of view, it is worthwhile to mention the work by Baum et al. (2003) whose research question is concerned with the formation of "small world" networks. Their theory is that a small world structure emerges from a cliquish network, through clique-spanning ties. Baum et al. (2003) want to understand the identity of the actors that activate such ties and propose three alternative explanations: (1) chance, in that while firms add new links, this increases the probability that some of them will be outside the cliques; (2) insurgent partnering, activated by peripheral firms in the network that aim to improve their status; and (3) control partnering, activated by central firms that attempt to preserve their privileged position. Baum et al. consider the network of Canadian investment banks, emerging from underwriting syndicates over the period from 1952 to 1990. They find support for all three explanations, but especially for the chance and insurgent partnering motives.

This kind of exercise would be worthy of being replicated on interfirm technological alliance networks. It seems interesting to study if the characteristics of the information that circulates in the network (information on technology vs. other kind of information) may affect firms' incentives towards clique-spanning ties.

Finally, the distribution of collaborative links across firms has been studied. Typically, we observe a *hierarchy* within the firms in the network: a few firms have many links and many firms have a few links. The distribution of links typically follows a power law distribution ($P(k) = k^{-\gamma}$, where $k$ is the firms' number of links, and typically $\gamma \approx 2$): these structures are defined as scale-free networks. Barabasi and Albert (1999) show that this structure can emerge in a growing network if a preferential attachment mechanism is at work: the probability of a new connection at time $t + 1$ positively depends on the number of connections a firm has at time $t$. We have seen in section 3 that this property is found at the firm level. Studies that find evidence of scale-free networks are those by Krebs (2004) for the Internet industry, Breschi and Cusmano (2004), and Riccaboni and Pammolli (2002) for networks in life sciences and ICT. Typically, large firms take the role of highly connected firms, or "hubs."

# 4. TECHNOLOGICAL AGREEMENTS AND FIRMS' PERFORMANCE AND TECHNOLOGICAL CAPABILITIES

This section surveys the studies that treat several dimensions of firm R&D cooperative activity as explanatory variables. The first sub-section considers the fundamental question of the causal relationship between technological agreements and economic and innovative performance. The second sub-section considers the effects of technological alliances on firms' technological specialization.

**Technological Agreements and Economic and Innovative Performance**

Firms enter technological agreements because it is felt that they will increase their *expected* performance. However, two issues remain relevant: first, the distribution of returns from cooperative ventures; second, a more precise quantitative assessment of such effects in general, and the factors that positively or negatively affect their magnitude.

In general, assessing the success or the failure of a cooperative venture is not an easy task. Often, the true goal of cooperation is not known either to the public or to the partners. Unpredictable side effects and externalities may also have significant impacts on success or failure. When the termination date of an agreement is not fixed ex ante, its dissolution is both consistent with failure (i.e. the objective of cooperation has not been reached and cannot be reasonably reached in the future), and with success (i.e. the goal has been reached) (Kogut, 1988).

However, it is less problematic to assess the relationship between the different dimensions of a firm cooperative strategy and a firm's overall economic performance (measured in terms of rate of profits, sales growth, market shares, productivity or survival). In some cases, the object of study has been the link between innovative output and technological agreements (Sampson, 2003; Cusmano, 2005).

Several dimensions of cooperative strategy have been considered in assessing partnership success or failure. These dimensions, and relevant literature, are detailed below.

1. A positive relationship is usually found between firms' participation in cooperative ventures, number of agreements and number of partners, and firms' performance. A number of studies with a policy orientation have aimed at estimating the effects on firms' performance of their participation in government sponsored agreements. Benfretello and Sembenelli (2002), in their sample of firms from several sectors participating in the Eureka and third and fourth Frameworks programs sponsored by the European Union, find a significantly positive effect on the ex post firm performance measured in terms of total factor productivity, labor productivity, and price cost margin. With a similar sample, Cusmano (2005) finds a positive effect from participation in research joint ventures on innovative output in the medical and biotechnological sector, but not in the information technology sector. Studying the performance of R&D in Japanese consortia, Branstetter and Sakakibara (2002) show that participation in the consortia increases the productivity of firms in terms of innovative output. Similar results have been obtained for non-government sponsored partnerships. For example, Siebert (1996) shows that the elasticity of profit margins to R&D is higher for firms participating in research joint ventures filed at the US Federal Register.

   The intensity of cooperative activities (measured by the number of technical agreements) usually has a positive effect on a company's performance. Hagedoorn and Schakenraad (1994) find a positive effect of the intensity of strategic alliances with an R&D orientation on firms' profitability for a sample of large firms in different sectors and countries. Mitchell and Singh (1996) show a positive effect for the number of technical agreements on firm survival in a sample of US firms in the hospital software systems industry. In a sample of 85 biotech firms, Shan et al. (1994) show that commercial ties have positive effects on innovative output.

   Some studies have considered the number of partners of a firm (termed the degree of centrality of the firm in the innovative network in the social network analysis terminology) and their characteristics as explanatory variables of that firm's performance. A positive relation between sales growth and the degree centrality in the network is found by Powell et al. (1996) in a sample of 225 dedicated biotech firms. For plant biotechnology, Debackere et al. (1998) find a positive relationship between the number of partners and innovative output, measured by scientific publications. Stuart (2000), in a sample of semiconductor firms, shows that partners' innovativeness has a greater impact on a firm's patenting rate and sales growth, than the simple count of technical agreements, and finds that partners' sales matter for growth especially if firms are small or young (this is explained with reference to the status-enhancing effect of these alliances). Baum et al. (2000) consider a sample of 142 start-ups in biotechnology, and show a positive effect on firms' performance (measured by revenues, employment, and patents) of the number of alliances with pharmaceutical firms, the variety in the type of partners (pharmaceutical firms, universities, biotech firms, etc.), and the number of alliances with rivals with a narrower product scope. As indirect evidence for the same effect, Singh and Mitchell (1996) show that a firm's likelihood of survival in the hospital software system industry decreases if a partner shuts down and the firm does not form a new partnership.

2.  A small group of studies have tried to assess the impact of characteristics at the dyadic level (or more, generally, at the project level) on a firm's innovative performance. Consistent with the evidence on alliance formation, the results generally show that technological proximity has a positive and significant effect, with evidence of an inverted U relationship. Branstetter and Sakakibara (2002), in their sample of R&D Japanese consortia, find that technological proximity among consortium members has a positive effect on a firm's ex post patenting activity. Sampson (2003) finds an inverted U relationship between technological distance and ex post innovation output (measured by citation weighted patent count) in a sample of 463 alliances in the international telecommunications equipment industry.

3.  Finally, recent papers have studied how the structure of the ego networks impact firm performance. The main question concerns the tension between a notion of a social capital *à la* Coleman and Burt's structural holes argument.

    Ahuja (2000b) considers a sample of 107 chemical firms, and investigates the roles of direct ties, indirect ties, and structural holes in explaining innovation output measured by patents. His findings show that: direct ties (more concerned with knowledge creation) have a strong positive effect on innovation output; indirect ties (concerned with information diffusion) have a positive effect but smaller than direct ties; filling structural holes has a negative effect on innovative output; and the coefficient for the interaction of direct and indirect ties is negative, indicating a substitution effect between the two. This result supports the "social capital as closure" perspective.

    Hagedoorn and Duysters (2002) consider 88 firms in the computer industry, and they use patent intensity (computer patents/size) as a measure of technological performance. They find that having non-redundant contacts and bridge ties has no significant effect on a firm's performance (which contrasts with Burt's view), while multiple, repeated links with the same partner have a positive effect on a firm's innovative output. They claim that this result is consistent with a learning view of alliances, while it contrasts with the static, efficiency-based view of Burt.

**Technological Agreements and Firms' Technological Capabilities**

Together with the effects of cooperation on firms' performance, some interest has been raised by the effect of technological alliances on firms' technological profiles. An empirical assessment of this issue is relevant for two main reasons. First, such exercises can be seen as an empirical test for the hypothesis of technological alliances as sources of learning. Ex post technological convergence among partners would be consistent with such a hypothesis. Second, these results have implications for a dynamic theory of partnership formation, as long as the resulting technological positions affect the probability of firms to form links in subsequent periods (see the second part of section 3).

There is evidence that strategic alliances are significant factors in explaining firms' movement in the technological space. Stuart and Podolny (1996) consider a small sample of ten Japanese semiconductor firms, and they characterize their technological positions using patent citations. They find that alliances are part of the strategies of firms that want to move from a peripheral to a core position in the technological space. However, there is evidence of an ambiguous effect of alliances on technological positions. Mowery et al. (1996) consider a sample of 792 alliances in several sectors. They measure firms' technological overlap by cross-citation rates in patent portfolios and test the hypothesis of an increase in the technological overlap after collaboration. They reject this hypothesis, but do find a significant and positive effect of collaboration in the absolute value of variation in cross-citation rate. This result leads the authors to distinguish between alliances through which firms acquire new capabilities, causing technological convergence (191 alliances in their sample), and alliances in which firms aim at accessing new capabilities, leading to divergent technological positions (601 alliances in their sample). The authors do not investigate the factors (at the level of industry, technology, or mode of organization of the alliance) that lead to one outcome or the other, and we are not aware of studies that consider this issue. This seems an interesting line of research to pursue.

## 5. INTERFIRM TECHNOLOGICAL AGREEMENTS AND INDUSTRY EVOLUTION

As the previous sections have shown, the evidence on interfirm technological agreements is becoming very rich, although some aspects still wait for a satisfactory analysis. In this section we argue that the existing empirical literature can constitute the basis for an "appreciative theory" (Nelson and Winter, 1982) that links the self-organization of R&D networks to the rate and direction of technological progress, to the actors involved in the innovative process, and, through these, to the evolution of industries. The formation of R&D networks is a self-organizing process because such networks are the result of uncoordinated firm choices over time, as a function of technological variables (i.e. a firm's technological position) and economic variables (i.e. firm's size) (section 3). In turn, these variables change over time as a function of the network (section 4), so that the dynamics of the system are characterized by several feedbacks, mostly positive (self-reinforcing) in nature (for instance, the "preferential attachment" mechanism). Such an appreciative theory, whose elements have been at least partially put forth by some authors (Gomes-Casseres, 1996), should be of obvious interest to economists. Furthermore, it can be conceived as a step towards further empirical analysis and formal modeling, which are currently lacking.

There are at least three interrelated themes that emerge as being important in the relationships among technological collaborations, R&D networks, and industry evolution. The first is the role of *path dependency*. At the firm level (see the first part of section 3) we saw that experience in managing ties is an important variable in explaining firms' cooperative activities. At the dyadic level (second part of section 3), we gave account of several studies that show how firms tend to ally with previous partners. Furthermore, the history of alliances by a firm explains the formation of its technological capabilities (second part of section 4), which in turn affect the selection of its partners (second part of section 3). If firms that are active in the network in the early stages are more likely to be central actors in subsequent periods, and this is reflected in firm performance, events at the beginning of an industry (or network) life cycle can have long-lasting effects on firm competitiveness. Such events can be a result of initial, significant differences in capabilities or can consist of "historical accidents," such as geographical location or pre-existing social contacts among entrepreneurs. Theories of industrial dynamics with an evolutionary flavor (such as the industry life cycle theory, Klepper, 1997) frequently emphasize the importance of first-mover advantages in explaining both the prosperity of firms and some stylized facts of industry evolution, such as shake-outs (i.e. the drastic reduction in the number of firms that often occurs in an industry in the early stages of its life cycle). R&D networks seem to work in this direction, and their role of providing first-mover advantages deserves further empirical and theoretical analysis.

The second theme, which directly refers to the first theme of path dependency, is related to the role of networks as both mechanisms of technological knowledge diffusion for firms within the network and exclusionary mechanisms for firms outside the network. This has clear implications for the evolution of industries.

If no firm possesses all the relevant technological capabilities to innovate, it is the network that acts as the "locus of innovation" (Powell et al., 1996). This tends to favor competition, since no firm can control the market via distinctive technological capabilities. However, as we just mentioned, path dependency and self-reinforcing mechanisms, both at the firm and at the dyadic level, tend to limit over time the number of actors that actively participate in the network. An oligopolistic market structure emerges, where a core of large firms (first part of section 3) controls the rate and the direction of technological progress, erecting barriers to entry and to survival against firms outside the network ("knowledge-based networked oligopoly," in the terminology of Delapierre and Mytelka, 1998). This view is consistent with the so-called Schumpeter Mark II paradigm for the link between market structure and technological progress (Schumpeter, 1942): incumbent, "networked" firms are the main actors of innovation. In a policy perspective (for antitrust authorities and governments that subsidize technological cooperation) this logic suggests that anti-competitive effects may be more dynamic than static, and these must be traded off with the dynamic gains from increased technological progress. Finally, the network can be composed of different cohesive subgroups, so that competition occurs among groups, rather than at the firm level (third part of section 3). From an industrial dynamics perspective, belonging to different groups can explain interfirm differences in exit rates, growth, economic performance, and innovativeness (Gulati et al., 2000).

A third theme is related to the role of networks in affecting the "collective" direction of technological change in industries. This is probably the theme for which most of the work is still to be done. The extent to which collaborations lead to technological convergence or technological divergence among firms in the network (second part of section 4) is important for two main reasons. First, from the society point of view, a certain degree of experimentation at the technological level must be preserved. Using evolutionary terminology, variety generation mechanisms must be present. Firms need to explore different routes in environments characterized by substantive uncertainty, a distinctive feature of Schumpeterian competition. If firms in a network explore collectively the same areas of technological space, risks of technological "lock-in" are possible. Indeed, some authors have argued that advantages of the network form of organization compared to more integrated forms lie in the capacity of preserving variety at the technological level (Kogut, 2000). An important role in this respect can be played by the existence of different cliques. Even if lock-in exists at the level of the single sub-group of firms, this can be counterbalanced by different groups exploring different technological directions. Similarly, as argued in the third part of section 3, variety and access to novel information can be guaranteed by short-cuts or clique-spanning ties in a "small world" network.

The second reason for studying the effect of collaborations on technological convergence or divergence is that networks matter when firms face technological discontinuities. A traditional distinction here is between competence-enhancing discontinuities, favoring incumbent firms versus new entrants, and competence-destroying discontinuities, favoring new entrants versus incumbents (Tushman and Anderson, 1986). This distinction has been adapted to networks by Madhavan et al. (1998). These authors define structure-reinforcing events as those discontinuities that favor incumbent firms in the network, leading to an increase in their centrality, and structure-loosening events as those discontinuities that favor more peripheral agents, reducing the degree of centralization in the network. Similarly, Rosenkopf and Tushman (1998) discuss the link between network intensity and the stages of technological life cycles. They show that in the flight simulation industry the rate of founding of technical agreements is high during discontinuities, and cliques emerge in mature phases. In general, there are opportunities, both at the theoretical and the empirical level, for studying the role of network structures in mediating between technological discontinuities and their consequences on industry evolution. When we can distinguish between different cliques, their internal structure, and the capabilities to which firms have access it may then be possible to determine what influences the way they react to environmental shocks.

## 6.  CONCLUSION

This chapter has surveyed the streams of empirical literature on interfirm technological alliances. As we tried to show, the evidence is rich, coming from several disciplines whose theoretical frameworks are sometimes radically different.

First, this survey has proposed a number of stylized facts concerning the relevance of the phenomenon, its evolution over time, the differences across sectors, and the most common motivations that lead firms to cooperate. Second, we have produced some stylized results concerning the formation of technological alliances, the structural properties of the networks, and the effects of firm cooperative activity on performance and technological capabilities.

The broad picture that emerges is one in which interfirm technological agreements are structural elements of the evolution of high-tech sectors. Cooperation is part of the innovative strategies of large firms, the main actors in the network, which perform R&D in alliances and on an individual basis and look for partners with complementary capabilities to introduce new products and processes. The network, which becomes the "locus of innovation," is strongly driven by path dependent mechanisms, in which the central actors tend to increase their prominence, and significantly affects firms' innovative and economic performance.

These results notwithstanding, there are still promising lines of research, both at the empirical and theoretical level. First, we need theories and empirical studies that identify more precisely the general mechanisms that drive the formation and evolution of alliances and networks. These studies would surely benefit from a more unified framework, where insights from transaction cost economics, game theory, evolutionary economics, sociology, and managerial sciences are considered. Second, clear sectoral specificities exist, in the form of intensity of alliances, their content and their mode of organization. This, presumably, may be reflected in the structure of the network at the sectoral level. All these characteristics depend on the technological regimes, which are specific to industries (Malerba, 2004). In this respect, we need detailed case studies of network evolution, taxonomies, and theories for specific mechanisms of collaboration in specific contexts.

Given the relevance of the phenomenon, its complexity and multidimensionality, these are surely exciting opportunities for future research.

## NOTES

1. I thank Franco Malerba, Lorenzo Cassi, Nicoletta Corrocher and Roberto Fontana for very useful and detailed comments on a preliminary version of this chapter. The usual disclaimers apply.
2. Nevertheless, some of the studies we survey consider datasets including both formal and informal cooperation, and interfirm and firm–university technological agreements.
3. The dataset has been made available to us by Nicholas Vonortas.
4. For exceptions, see Shan (1990) (who found a negative sign), Pisano (1990) and Arora and Gambardella (1990) (who found size as non-significant) and Burgers et al. (1993) (who found a non-monotonic relationship). However, Shan focuses on small biotech

firms, Pisano and Arora and Gambardella on large pharmaceutical firms, Burgers et al. on the world's largest car producer. All these studies focus on a relatively small number of size classes. This would explain the results.

5. However, Pisano (1990) finds that biotech experience decreases the propensity of pharmaceuticals firms to start external projects with specialized biotech firms.
6. See for instance IBM's webpage dedicated to partners for a practical example (www. pc.ibm.com/ww/alliances).
7. However, Becker and Dietz (2004) found that technological intensity has a *negative* impact on the likelihood of cooperation.
8. On the contrary, Becker and Dietz (2004) find that the concentration is not significant as an explanatory variable of cooperation.
9. R&D spillovers constitute a form of externality, whose relevance is inversely related to the degree of appropriability.
10. This result partially contrasts with Veugelers and Cassiman (2002). These authors find that the relevance of outgoing spillovers *at the firm level* negatively affects cooperation. These are related, but do not coincide, with the inverse of the degree of appropriability at the industry level, because they are also affected by firms' strategic considerations.
11. See Wasserman and Faust (1994), ch. 7, for a general discussion on the different notions of cohesive sub-groups.
12. Ego (-centered) networks (Wasserman and Faust, 1994) are defined as networks consisting of a focal actor (ego), a set of alters who have ties to the ego, and measurements of the ties among these actors. Extensively, some authors have considered an ego network as comprising the focal actor, all the actors at a finite distance from the ego, and all the ties among them.

# REFERENCES

Ahuja, G. (2000a), "The duality of collaboration: inducements and opportunities in the formation of interfirm linkages", *Strategic Management Journal*, **21**, 317–43.

Ahuja, G. (2000b), "Collaboration networks, structural holes, and innovation: a longitudinal study", *Administrative Science Quarterly*, **45**, 425–55.

Arora, A. and A. Gambardella (1990), "Complementarity and external linkages: the strategies of the large firms in biotechnology", *Journal of Industrial Economics*, **38** (4), 361–79.

Barabasi, A. and R. Albert (1999), "Emergence of scaling in random networks", *Science*, **286**, October, 509–12.

Baum, J.A.C., T. Calabrese and B.S. Silverman (2000), "Don't go it alone: alliance network composition and start-ups' performance in Canadian biotechnology", *Strategic Management Journal*, **21**, 267–94.

Baum, J.A., A.V. Shipilov and T.J. Rowley (2003), "Where do small worlds come from?", *Industrial and Corporate Change*, **12** (4), 697–725.

Bayona, C., T. Garcia-Marco and E. Huerta (2001), "Firms' motivations for cooperative R&D: an empirical analysis of Spanish firms", *Research Policy*, **30**, 1289–307.

Becker, W. and J. Dietz (2004), "R&D cooperation and innovation activities of firms – evidence for the German manufacturing industry", *Research Policy*, **33**, 209–23.

Benfretello, L. and A. Sembenelli (2002), "Research joint ventures and firm level performance", *Research Policy*, **31**, 493–507.

Branstetter, L.G. and M. Sakakibara (2002), "When do research consortia work well and why? Evidence from Japanese panel data", *American Economic Review*, **92** (1), 143–59.

Breschi, S. and L. Cusmano (2004), "Unveiling the texture of a European Research Area: emergence of oligarchic networks under EU Framework Programmes", *International Journal of Technology Management. Special Issue on Technology Alliances*, **27** (8), 747–72.

Burgers, W.P., C.W. Hill and W.C. Kim (1993), "A theory of global strategic alliances: the case of the global auto industry", *Strategic Management Journal*, **14** (6), 419–32.

Burt, R.S. (1992), *Structural Holes: The Social Structure of Competition*, Cambridge, MA: Harvard University Press.

Caloghirou, Y., S. Ioannides and N. Vonortas (2003), "Research joint ventures: a critical survey of theoretical and empirical literature", *Journal of Economic Surveys*, **17** (4), 541–70.

Cohen, W. and S. Klepper (1996), "A reprise on size and R&D", *Economic Journal*, **106**, 925–51.

Cohen, W. and D. Levinthal (1989), "Innovation and learning: the two faces of research and development", *The Economic Journal*, **99**, 569–96.

Coleman, J.C. (1988), "Social capital in the creation of human capital", *American Journal of Sociology*, **94**, 95–120.

Colombo, M.G. (1995), "Firm size and cooperation: the determinants of cooperative agreements in information technology industries", *International Journal of the Economics of Business*, **2** (1), 3–29.

Colombo, M.G. and P. Garrone (1996), "Technological cooperative agreements and firms' R&D intensity. A note on causality relations", *Research Policy*, **25**, 923–32.

Colombo, M.G. and P. Garrone (1998), "A simultaneous equation model of technological agreements and inframural R&D", in M.G. Colombo (ed.), *The Changing Boundaries of the Firm*, London: Routledge.

Cowan, R. and N. Jonard (2003), "The dynamics of collective invention", *Journal of Economic Behavior and Organization*, **52** (4), 513–32.

Cowan, R. and N. Jonard (2004), "Network structure and the diffusion of knowledge", *Journal of Economic Dynamics and Control*, **28** (8), 1557–75.

Cusmano, L. (2005), "Self-selection and learning in European Research Joint Ventures: a microeconometric analysis of participation and patenting", in Y. Caloghirou, N. Constantellou and N. Vonortas (eds), *Knowledge Flows in European Industry: Mechanisms and Policy Implications*, London: Routledge.

d'Aspremont, C. and A. Jacquemin (1988), "Cooperative and noncooperative R&D in duopoly with spillovers", *American Economic Review*, **78**, 1133–37.

Debackere, K., B. Clarysse and M. Rappa (1996), "Dismantling the ivory tower: the influence of networks on innovative output in emerging technologies", *Technological Forecasting and Social Change*, **53**, 139–54.

Delapierre, M. and L. Mytelka (1998), "Blurring boundaries: new inter-firm relationships and the emergence of networked, knowledge-based oligopolies", in M.G. Colombo (ed.), The Changing Boundaries of the Firm, London: Routledge.

Eisenhardt, K.M. and C.B. Schoonhoven (1996), "Resource-based view of strategic alliance formation: strategic and social effects in entrepreneurial firms", *Organization Science*, **7** (2), 136–50.

Fritsch, M. and R. Lukas (2001) "Who cooperates on R&D?", *Research Policy*, **30**, 297–312.

Geroski, P.A. (1995) "What do we know about entry?", *International Journal of Industrial Organization*, **13**, 421–40.

Gomes-Casseres, B. (1996), *The Alliance Revolution*, Cambridge, MA: Harvard University Press.

Gulati, R. (1995a), "Social structure and alliance formation patterns: a longitudinal analysis", *Administrative Science Quarterly*, **40**, 619–52.

Gulati, R. (1995b), "Does familiarity breed trust? The implications of repeated ties for contracual choice in alliances", *Academy of Management Journal*, **38**, 85–112.

Gulati, R. (1998), "Alliances and networks", *Strategic Management Journal*, **19**, 293–317.

Gulati, R. and M. Gargiulo (1999), "Where do interorganizational networks come from?", *American Journal of Sociology*, **104** (5), 1439–93.

Gulati, R., N. Nohria and A. Zaheer (2000), "Strategic networks", *Strategic Management Journal*, **21**, 203–15.

Hagedoorn, J. (1993), "Understanding the rationale of strategic technology partnering: interorganizational modes of cooperation and sectoral differences", *Strategic Management Journal*, **14**, 371–85.

Hagedoorn, J. (2002), "Inter-firm R&D partnerships: an overview of major trends and patterns since 1960", *Research Policy*, **31**, 477–92.

Hagedoorn, J. and J. Schakenraad (1994), "The effect of strategic technology alliances on company performance", *Strategic Management Journal*, **15** (4), 291–311.

Hagedoorn, J., A.N. Link and N.S Vonortas (2000), "Research partnerships", *Research Policy*, **29**, 567–86.

Hagedoorn, J. and G. Duysters (2002), "Learning in dynamic inter-firm networks – the efficacy of multiple contacts", *Organization Studies*, **23**, 525–48.

Hernan, R., P.L. Marin and G. Siotis (2003), "An empirical evaluation of the determinants of research joint venture formation", *Journal of Industrial Economics*, **LI** (1), 75–89.

Kamien, M., M. Mueller and I. Zang (1992), "Research joint ventures and R&D cartels", *American Economic Review*, **82**, 1293–306.

Kleinknecht, A. and J.O.N. Reijen (1992), "Why do firms collaborate on R&D?", *Research Policy*, **21**, 347–60.

Klepper, S. (1997), "Industry life cycles", *Industrial and Corporate Change*, **6**, 156–81.

Kogut, B. (1988), "Joint ventures: theoretical and empirical perspectives", *Strategic Management Journal*, **9**, 319–32.

Kogut, B. (2000), "The network as knowledge: generative rules and the emergence of structure", *Strategic Management Journal*, **21**, 405–25.

Krebs, V. (2004), available at: www.orgnet.com.

Link, A.N. and L.L. Bauer (1987), "An economic analysis of cooperative research", *Technovation*, **6**, 247–60.

Madhavan R., B.R. Koka and J.E. Prescott (1998), "Networks in transition: how industry events (re)shape interfirm relationships", *Strategic Management Journal*, **19**, 439–59.

Malerba, F. (2004), "Sectoral systems: how and why innovation differs across sectors", in J. Fagerberg and D.C. Mowery and R. Nelson (eds), *The Oxford Handbook of Innovation*, Oxford: Oxford University Press.

Mitchell, W. and K. Singh (1996), "Survival of business using collaborative relationships to commercialise complex goods", *Strategic Management Journal*, **17** (3), 169–95.

Mowery, D.C., J.E. Oxley and B.S. Silverman (1996), "Strategic alliances and interfirm knowledge transfer", *Strategic Management Journal*, **17**, Winter Special Issue, 77–91.

Mowery, D.C., J.E. Oxley and B.S. Silverman (1998), "Technological overlap and interfirm cooperation: implications for the resource-based view of the firm", *Research Policy*, **27**, 507–23.

Mowery, D.C. and B. Sampat (2004), "Universities in national innovation systems", in J. Fagerberg and D.C. Mowery and R. Nelson (eds), *The Oxford Handbook of Innovation*, Oxford: Oxford University Press.

Nelson, R. and S. Winter (1982), *An Evolutionary Theory of Economic Change*, Cambridge, MA: Harvard University Press.

Nohria, N. and C. Garcia-Pont (1991), "Global strategic alliances and industry structure", *Strategic Management Journal*, **12**, 105–34.

Nooteboom, B. (1999), *Inter-Firm Alliances: Analysis and Design*, London: Routledge.

Okamura, K. and N. Vonortas (2004), "Choosing a partner", paper presented at the Schumpeter conference, Milan, 9–12 June.

Pfeffer, J. and P. Nowak (1976), "Joint venture and interorganizational interdependence" *Administrative Science Quarterly*, **21**, 398–418.

Pisano, G.P. (1990), "The R&D boundaries of the firm: an empirical analysis", *Administrative Science Quarterly*, **35** (1), 153–76.

Powell, W.W. and S. Grodal (2004), "Networks of innovators", in J. Fagerberg and D.C. Mowery and R. Nelson (eds), *The Oxford Handbook of Innovation*, Oxford: Oxford University Press.

Powell, W.W., K.W. Koput and L. Smith-Doerr (1996), "Interorganizational collaboration and the locus of innovation: networks of learning in biotechnology", *Administrative Science Quarterly*, **41**, 116–45.

Riccaboni, M. and F. Pammolli (2002) "On firm growth in networks", *Research Policy*, **31**, 1405–16.

Rosenkopf, L. and M. Tushman (1998) "The coevolution of community networks and technology: lessons from the flight simulation industry", *Industrial and Corporate Change*, **7**, 311–46.

Sakakibara, M. (2002), "Formation of R&D consortia: industry and company effects", *Strategic Management Journal*, **23**, 1033–50.

Sampson, R. (2003), "R&D alliances and firm performance: the impact of technological diversity and alliance organization on innovation", mimeo, University of Maryland.

Schumpeter, J. (1942), *Capitalism, Socialism and Democracy*, New York: Harper & Row.

Shan, W. (1990), "An empirical analysis of organizational strategies by entrepreneurial high technology firms", *Strategic Management Journal*, **11**, 129–39.

Shan, W., G. Walker and B. Kogut (1994), "Interfirm cooperation and startup innovation in the biotechnology industry", *Strategic Management Journal*, **15** (5), 387–94.

Siebert, R. (1996), "The impact of research joint venture on firm performance: an empirical assessment", Discussion Paper FS IV 96-13, Wissenschaftszentrum Berlin.

Singh, K. and W. Mitchell (1996), "Precarious collaboration: business survival after partners shut down or form new partnerships", *Strategic Management Journal*, **17**, 99–115.

Stuart, T.E. (1998), "Network positions and propensities to collaborate: an investigation of strategic alliance formation in a high-technology industry", *Administrative Science Quarterly*, **43**, 668–98.

Stuart, T.E. (2000), "Interorganizational alliances and the performance of firms: a study of growth and innovative rates in a high-technology industry", *Strategic Management Journal*, **21**, 791–811.

Stuart, T.E. and J.M. Podolny (1996), "Local search and the evolution of technological capabilities", *Strategic Management Journal*, **17**, 21–38.

Tether, B. (2002), "Who co-operates for innovation, and why. An empirical analysis", *Research Policy*, **31**, 947–67.

Tushman, M. and D. Anderson (1986), "Technological discontinuities and organizational environments", *Administrative Science Quarterly*, **31**, 439–65.

Verspagen, B. and G. Duysters (2004), "The small worlds of strategic technology alliances", *Technovation*, **24** (7), 563–71.

Veugelers, R. and B. Cassiman (2002), "R&D cooperation and spillovers: some empirical evidence", *American Economic Review*, **92** (4), 1169–84.

Von Hippel, E. (1987), "Cooperation between rivals: informal know-how trading", *Research Policy*, **16**, 291–302.

Vonortas, N.S. (1997), *Cooperation in Research Development*, Boston, MA: Kluwer Academic Publishers.

Walker, G., B. Kogut and W. Shan (1997), "Social capital, structural holes and the formation of an industry network", *Organization Science*, **8** (2), 109–25.

Wasserman, S. and K. Faust (1994), *Social Network Analysis*, New York: Cambridge University Press.

Watts, D.J. and S.H. Strogatz (1998), "Collective dynamics of 'small-world' networks", *Nature*, **393**, June, 440–42.

# PART II

# Variety of networks in industries and sectoral systems

# 4. Measuring the corporate web of science: research and partnership networks within the European pharmaceutical industry

**Robert J.W. Tijssen**

## 1. INTRODUCTION

Many innovative R&D-intensive companies are in the business of applying and creating knowledge and skill bases to achieve or sustain a competitive advantage. Leading innovative firms are engaged in a continual search for applicable knowledge and first-rate partners. Analysts and commentators often look at such companies from a resource-based view, in which the efficient building and utilization of corporate resources and R&D capabilities is the prime consideration (e.g. Teece et al., 1997). Another approach focuses on corporate structure, often introducing a proximity-based distinction between local and multinational firms, or domestic and foreign subsidiaries and affiliations (e.g. Pavitt and Patel, 1999). A third perspective, the knowledge-based view, conceptualizes these firms as possessing a certain knowledge and skill base that is different from their competitors (e.g. Grant, 1996; Mowery et al., 1996). This chapter merges elements from these three perspectives in its analysis and discussion of research cooperation.

This analysis is presented against the backdrop of a growth of business sector investments in public sector research (e.g. OECD, 2002), and the fact that the numbers of *public–private* research partnerships, involving for-profit firms and not-for-profit public research organizations (PROs), has become quite significant in enhancing competitive advantages of innovative R&D-intensive companies. Despite the growing interest and increasing resources invested in this type of public–private partnership, the actual dynamics and results of these collaborative arrangements are poorly understood. Even with an abundance of anecdotal information about these pervasive developments within R&D-intensive industries, and the plethora of case studies in the academic and professional literature, there is still a striking lack of a generally accepted analytical framework to collect internationally comparative empirical evidence on research arrangements, networks and research joint ventures. Other than the available statistical data on numbers of R&D alliances, very little internationally comparable data exists on the magnitude, intensity and distributional properties of corporate research partnerships – neither between firms, nor between firms and PROs. Nor do we have economic models or firm-level indicators to inform us whether these investments have been effective and have paid off in terms of positive rates of return.

In order to collect systematic and comprehensive evidence on research networks one could conduct large-scale nation-wide surveys among firms, such as the European Union's *Community Innovation Survey*, or one could undertake sector-based sampling of collaborative agreements. Both methods have their pros and cons, the latter in terms of methodological drawbacks such as sampling biases, non-response rates and confidentiality issues. Alternatively, researchers could focus on one of the key outputs of these cooperative arrangements: the occurrence of joint research publications in the open literature. This source produces quantitative data on several key properties of research networks at various levels of analysis, including the firm level. This output-oriented approach is introduced in sections 2 and 3 within a general discussion of corporate R&D and research networks. Sections 4 and 5 describe general features of the pharmaceutical sector and its research publications. A case study dealing with research partnership profiles of Europe's top ten "Big Pharma" firms is described in section 6. Section 7 concludes by summarizing results and offering some ideas for ways to extend the approach for producing strategic intelligence on research networks in the pharmaceutical sector.

## 2. RECENT TRENDS IN CORPORATE R&D COOPERATION

Most science-based firms are engaged in a variety of R&D partnerships, ranging from small-scale networks[1] dealing exclusively with basic research,[2] to large alliances dealing with technological development. The main rationale for engaging in R&D cooperation is that research-based information, knowledge and skills ("know-how") are among the primary inputs to the process of building innovative capacity in R&D-intensive technology firms, especially those business enterprises that are active in highly competitive global industries where future survival and success depend increasingly on collaboration and the exchange of resources with partners. As a result, many companies are now also embarking on the novel R&D paradigm of "open innovation" (e.g. Chesbrough, 2003) to optimize the effectiveness and efficiency of in-house research endeavours. Large, high-tech, science-dependent firms are gradually opening up their research laboratories to foster cooperation with external partners, a population composed of both firms and public research organizations.[3] Traditionally, the firm's most strategic "proprietary" research activities were concentrated in a central research laboratory, usually located in the "home" country of the corporate headquarters. Nowadays, more elaborate organizational structures exist to promote research collaborations and to improve access to local knowledge and expertise. This pervasive development is part of the ongoing rise of institutionalized cooperative structures (such as inter-firm joint research ventures, university–industry strategic research partnerships, and regional clustering) that has taken root during the last 10–15 years in most advanced industrial nations (e.g. Hagedoorn et al., 2000). Driven by the dynamics of the globalizing "techno-economic geography", many firms, both multinational enterprises (MNEs) and small and medium enterprises (SMEs), show an ever-growing propensity to relocate their R&D facilities, or establish new ones, in other countries or continents. Geographical proximity is also often no longer the main criterion for selecting a suitable research partner: high-tech businesses are now more inclined to cooperate on the basis of "value for money", engaging with the most appropriate or best-performing PROs regardless of their physical location.

Several forces are influencing science-based technology companies to engage in alliances and partnerships to access external knowledge, skills and technologies. In an era in which even the largest of companies lack the required resources to stay abreast of all potentially significant developments in science, the nature of the knowledge-generation process itself seems to be evolving towards a more network-embedded and interdisciplinary process, characterized by a stronger emphasis on the interplay between knowledge demand and knowledge supply, and involving a heterogeneity of partners (firms, public research organizations, intermediate organizations, and government regulators). A second determinant is the globalization of high-profit markets, often coupled with the regionalizing of R&D on innovative applications for local markets. The large multinational firms have developed various organizational and management models to balance the R&D agenda of central research laboratories with the needs of business groups. An increasingly large share of the funding for those laboratories now comes from (local) business groups and product divisions through contractual agreements centred on programmes and costs.

Dependence on the input from external sources comes at a price. Knowledge absorption and accumulation can occur in firms only if there

---

## BOX 4.1   CORPORATE INCENTIVES TO ENGAGE IN "DISCOVERY" RESEARCH

### Research, development and innovations

- Explore new avenues of scientific investigation.
- Open possibilities for research cooperation with external partners.
- Source for developing new ideas, methods, technologies and systems.
- Better understanding of presently used methods and technologies.
- Find new concepts and scientific support for new technologies.
- Monitor and evaluate the value of external research.
- Evaluate options for applied research.

### Business strategies

- Gain first-mover advantages or maintain lead position.
- Improve competitive position.
- Create new long-term investment options.

### Public relations and marketing

- Interaction with governments, regulators and consumers (product safety and efficacy).
- Gain goodwill and influence decision makers and external stakeholders.

---

is sufficient corporate competence that can be used to maintain or build innovative capabilities in the first place. Companies need to conduct in-house research to benefit from external research, and they must also invest – sometimes heavily – to acquire or access additional resources, capabilities and assets (researchers, engineers, patent licences, or entire biotechnology companies). Science-based technology companies need a research base – either in-house or external – that covers all resources from which new scientific and engineering knowledge can be drawn. The optimum level of internally generated research knowledge and skills versus externally sourced knowledge and technologies, and the related optimum level of protection versus publication of internally generated knowledge, will depend on the networking strategy and level of R&D activities of the firm. However, all firms are users of the existing global stock of scientific and technical knowledge, regardless of the flow into that stock for which they are responsible. So even for the most developed and sophisticated "leading" firms, R&D networking capacity will remain a significant concern. Knowledge derived from scientific research or engineering research provides an invaluable understanding and theoretical base for the distributive power of innovation-oriented corporate R&D activities. Thus, the benefits of research are derived not only from in-house applied research, but also from basic research with a longer time-horizon.

Basic research is usually a costly activity with uncertain strategic benefits or monetary gains and has therefore always been a small part of corporate R&D. On average, some 10 per cent of business R&D expenditures are devoted to research with a long-term orientation, and these expenditures are traditionally confined to the large R&D-active technology companies and their central laboratories. There are many good reasons why companies might want to engage in scientific research and seek external partners. Box 4.1 provides a summary, non-exhaustive overview of the motives that may apply to science-based companies in general.

## 3.   PARTNERSHIPS IN DISCOVERY RESEARCH

In order to reap economies of scale and scope, many large and (some) smaller firms have increasingly outsourced and sub-contracted risky, long-term research to private or university laboratories. R&D managers in science-dependent industrial sectors try to encourage and foster lasting and productive cooperation between private firms and PROs that may be used as sources of person-embodied information and experience (tacit knowledge), a gateway to access leading-edge explicit (codified) knowledge, or a partner to generate new required research-based resources through a collaborative arrangement. The transfer of knowledge within these arrangements is often a person-to-person process, where the tacit knowledge offers great potential for competitive advantage since it is often customized for the partner and not available to other interacting parties.

Naturally, the private sector engages in networking only when expected (longer term) private returns from such activities rise above a minimum level. Companies may act on a variety of incentives to achieve a sufficient rate of return to engage in joint research partnerships and R&D networks with other business enterprises. Box 4.2 lists three broad categories of incentives.

---

## BOX 4.2   CORPORATE INCENTIVES FOR CONDUCTING JOINT SCIENTIFIC RESEARCH

**R&D driven**

- Share R&D costs and pool R&D risks to enlarge economies of scale and scope, and reduce uncertainties.
- Standardization of technical parameters (e.g. testing equipment, protocols for clinical trials).

**Resource driven**

- Resource dependency.
- Access complementary resources (to exploit own resources).
- Capture knowledge of suppliers and users.
- Apply cooperation and networking as a learning vehicle to access, accumulate and deploy new knowledge, capabilities, techniques and skills.
- Increase efficiency and synergy through networking.
- Minimize transaction costs associated with tacit knowledge and intangible assets.
- Accelerate return on R&D investments.
- Avoid high costs of internalizing R&D outputs.

**Market driven**

- Cope with short life-cycles of products.
- Avoid opportunistic market behaviour amongst competitors.
- Co-opt competition.
- Create new investment options.
- Increase market power.
- Improve competitive position or gain first-mover advantages.
- Respond to government funding initiatives.

---

Research-oriented partnerships are often complex organizational entities, which can take on many sizes and shapes depending on the kind of scientific or technical research objectives ("basic", "applied", or "strategic"), and the quantity and diversity of participants. Some partnerships are designed to create infrastructures for informal sharing of information, skills or facilities, while others include large numbers of firms joining together to set industry standards. Focusing on research partnerships and networks dedicated to cooperation in discovery-oriented "up-stream" research, the production and transfer of scientific knowledge within these cooperative arrangements usually emerges as a result of an interactive and collective process within a web of personal and institutional linkages that evolve over time.

Being engaged in joint research activities implies the existence of knowledge flows that connect different nodes in the network and different sources of scientific and technological information. Researchers contribute and exchange experience, information and facilities resources, the form of which ranges from equipment, instruments and other physical artefacts, to knowledge in a written "codified" form, and person-embodied non-codified "tacit" knowledge or skills. These elements are exchanged most effectively in networks based on long-term relationships between experts that involve close collaboration (OECD, 2002). There are many communication channels and routes in which these connections and knowledge flows may materialize. Some key features of these research partnerships, and their knowledge transfer processes, are made visible through co-authored research articles published in the open literature. A large chunk of co-authored research articles lists the names and affiliations of researchers employed by business enterprises. The science-based companies in the pharmaceuticals sector are among the biggest contributors to the worldwide output of public–private, co-authored research articles.

## 4.   THE PHARMACEUTICALS SECTOR

The discovery of penicillin in the 1920s is widely regarded as the birth of modern pharmaceuticals, in that the development of prescription drugs and large scale production were made possible by a combination of systematic scientific approaches, understanding of human biology and advanced manufacturing techniques. Of all chemical compounds investigated for use in humans, only a small proportion are eventually approved, and only after a long process of pre-clinical development, clinical trials, and monitoring undertaken in order to determine the safety and efficacy of a compound. The conventional chemical-based model for drug development is gradually shifting toward an "industrialized R&D" paradigm of drug discovery that rests on a target-based selective approach where systematic studies reveal cellular and molecular mechanisms and biochemical pathways that underlie common disorders, illnesses and diseases.[4] This science-based deductive method focuses on searching for new target receptors, and molecules that inhibit the target, in order to design drugs to carry out precise missions at the molecular level. Many of the recent successes in medical and pharmaceutical research are a result of progress in the fields of immunology and molecular biology. Further breakthroughs can be expected from basic research in the field of genomics and the neurosciences. Work in other fields of the life sciences, especially the discovery of restriction enzymes, has provided biotechnological tools in the form of "molecular scissors". Recent developments in biotechnology are also offering new possibilities for the future. The first generation of "biologic" therapies is already in use, especially in cancer. Vaccines are a renewed focus of interest as a better understanding of genetics offers new ideas on how diseases might be prevented. Through the emerging science of pharmacogenomics, future possibilities are emerging to tailor medicines to each individual.

Most major pharmaceutical companies were founded in the late nineteenth and early twentieth centuries, though the industry remained relatively small-scale until the scientific advancements and breakthroughs in biomedicine and genomics, occurring from the 1970s to today, elevated some companies to become among the most profitable and productive in the world. The industry has delivered significantly improved treatment for patients worldwide, and morbidity/mortality rates across developing countries continue to fall as a result, in no small part, of the innovation of research-based pharmaceutical companies.

Drug development is a research-intensive and costly process. The large research-based pharmaceutical companies invest huge sums in generating, accumulating and applying scientific knowledge and technical know-how to produce breakthrough technologies. A pharmaceutical company spends upwards of $800 million and takes ten years or more to get a drug from lab bench to bedside (DiMasi et al., 2003).[5] On average, about 25 per cent of their R&D investments are devoted to pre-clinical research and another 40-45 per cent on clinical development in phases I, II and III (PhRMA, 2006). The pharmaceutical sector in the USA and Europe (excluding the biotech companies) invested an estimated $45 billion in R&D in 2004 (EFPIA, 2006). In the pharmaceutical sector, the most research-intensive economic sector of all, many of the largest research-based companies spend, approximately, up to 15 per cent of their sales on R&D, and in some cases their annual R&D costs amount to billions of dollars/euros. In Europe, the share of these investments amounts to 12.5 per cent of sales, making this sector the second largest R&D-intense sector (EC, 2005).

Generally, these firms prosper only in this market because most of their customers have extreme needs (i.e. high-quality medicine and medical care), and their R&D investments are protected by strong intellectual property rights (IPR) regimes. These extreme medical needs also justify the high risk of failure, and consequent high gross margins from 60 per cent to 90 per cent of revenues. Although annual R&D investments have increased from $1 billion to $45 billion since 1975, the annual new drug approvals have remained flat at between 20 and 30. Thus, drug development today is less efficient than 30 years ago, which partly explains the continual rise in drug costs. A considerable fraction of the enormous expense of drug discovery is a result of the cost of attrition along this path from basic research to marketing, including marketing costs hidden under the guise of pre- and post-marketing trials. Since so many individual R&D projects yield no exploitable product (i.e. a newly approved prescription drug on the market), gross profits will be as much as 90 per cent of the sales cost, with R&D, manufacturing, and marketing costing only 10 per cent of the product price. These economic pressures are forcing pharmaceutical companies toward greater R&D productivity. The costs of research, testing, production and marketing of ever more sophisticated medicines grows every year and the tension between the affordability of new medicines and their benefits looks certain to be a continuing concern. The net outcome of the rising costs and dwindling efficiency of the industrial drug discovery process is an increasing reliance of big drug companies on external sources to keep the industrial drug discovery pipeline filled with (potential) blockbuster medicines. External source use involves, on the one hand, outsourcing of "front end" discovery research to universities and public research organizations for longer-term future competitiveness,[6] and on the other hand working with smaller biotechnology or biopharmaceutical companies to feed them the most promising drug candidates, usually through patent licensing agreements. So far, these biotech companies have not been able to significantly improve the productivity of the drug development pipelines of the pharmaceuticals industry as a whole (Pisano, 2006).

Considering the dynamics and complexity of contemporary cutting-edge R&D, and the fierce competition in local and global markets, it is impossible to think of science-based companies carrying out all R&D activities in isolation, let alone longer-term scientific research, an undertaking with uncertain outcomes and results that are often difficult to appropriate and commercialize. Even in the case of the most innovative firms, R&D strategies and research portfolios dealing with discovery research are increasingly subject to constraints in terms of cost effectiveness and risk aversion. As a consequence, the pharmaceutical sector is now one of the most globalized industrial sectors in terms of collaborative activities and R&D alliances, as well as in the geographical distribution of research laboratories and technical support centres.

## 5. CORPORATE RESEARCH ARTICLES IN THE SCIENTIFIC LITERATURE

Apart from technical reports or contributions to in-house reports series, a range of publication outlets can be used for disseminating findings originating from discovery research. These outlets include scientific journals, engineering and technical research journals, trade journals, and conference proceedings. This analysis is focused exclusively on the peer-reviewed international scientific and technical journals, most of which are in English and target an international readership. The majority of the research articles that are published in these journals represent results of successful (by academic standards) scientific research focusing on "pre-competitive" topics far removed from immediate commercial applications or strategic business objectives. General trends in the output of basic research efforts within large science-intensive technology firms, or for that matter, entire science-based industries, can be gauged from statistical analyses of the quantity of papers published in these journals. These data enable comparisons between (parent) companies, while aggregation of firm-level data allow for comparisons between associated industrial sectors. Although recent empirical data suggest that the corporate contribution to the open scientific literature is in gradual decline (Tijssen, 2004), researchers at corporate labs are still producing many thousands of research articles in scientific and technical journals each year.

There exists a wide range of reasons for corporate researchers to publish (selected) results in those journals. Box 4.3 summarizes the incentives for research-intensive business enterprises and other private sector organizations to publish research findings in the open scientific and technical literature. One of the prime reasons is simply because corporate researchers are active members of a research community and want to be regarded as scientific peers in leading edge research. Their publications signal command of codified and tacit knowledge and the ability to produce high-quality research, all of which may act as an entry ticket to scientific networks and obtaining access to technical opportunities in the public science base (including the recruitment of skilled graduates).[7] These publications in peer-reviewed journals may arise from internal pressures and reward systems within corporate labs to assure international levels of quality by subjecting papers on research methods and findings to journal peer-review processes. Moreover, public authorities and agencies involved in (co-) funding of corporate research expect solid proof of scientific achievements, and research papers in journals of acknowledged scientific quality would serve as such evidence. In those cases where corporate researchers

---

# BOX 4.3 CORPORATE INCENTIVES FOR PUBLISHING RESULTS OF RESEARCH IN THE OPEN LITERATURE

**Contacts and sourcing**

- Improve contacts with universities or other public research organizations.
- Establish domestic or international research cooperation and alliances.
- Participate in domestic or international research networks and alliances.
- Joint appointments of corporate researchers at public research institutions.

**Public relations and marketing**

- Signal scientific knowledge, research themes and R&D capabilities.
- Attract customers and inform suppliers.
- Enhanced credibility for doing high-quality (basic) research.
- Enhanced credibility for independent testing and using research facilities at universities.
- Corporate image improvement, gaining reputation and credibility.

**Human resources**

- Setting and evaluating internal scientific quality standards.
- Facilitating personnel/human resource management.
- Condition of recruitment, employment and job satisfaction.

**Funding**

- Attract capital and public research funding.

---

are actively cooperating with academics, one would also expect joint research articles in view of the reward systems at universities and other public research institutions that emphasize the necessity to publish in peer-reviewed journals. Also, along the same lines, one would expect to see research publications from (senior) corporate researchers who are part-time or temporarily employed by public research institutions.

The scientific articles in research journals in this study were extracted from the CWTS *Corporate Research Papers* (CRP) database, a subset of research articles published in international scientific and technical journals that are covered by the CWTS-licensed version of the *Web of Science* (WoS) database produced by Thomson Scientific.[8, 9] This international multidisciplinary bibliographical database indexes some 9000 journals and it is generally considered to be the most comprehensive and reliable source of information on basic research activity across all countries and fields of science.[10] The WoS provides an excellent representation of internationally accepted, high-quality, "mainstream" biomedical and pharmacological research.

The bibliographic records of research articles published in WoS-listed journals include, among many other items, all author names and all their affiliate addresses. Each publication is treated equally, regardless of the number of authors, the position of authors, or the position of institutional affiliations in the list of author addresses. In some papers, the corporate author(s) are listed as first "lead" authors, while in other instances they are at the end of the list, or somewhere in between. A co-authored paper is fully credited to all firms and other organizations listed in the author address information. Co-authoring is the clearest link to informal networking that can be made. These co-publications are the building blocks for measuring research cooperation and networking. Box 4.4 displays a random example of a public/private internationally co-authored research article.

The underlying assumption is that co-publication data are a reasonably good, albeit partial, indicator of collaborative research activity and of flows of both tacit and codified knowledge. Joint research papers reflect successful scientific cooperation between individual researchers and research teams. Co-publication statistics is, in fact, one of the very few sources of quantitative information that enables comparative analysis and longitudinal overviews.[11] Joint public–private undertakings with shared resources that are primarily aimed at developing new basic knowledge and know-how are more prone to generating jointly authored papers, especially when these collaborative projects include contributions from academics who are particularly focused on producing international research papers to enhance visibility and prestige. However, literature-based performance statistics and indicators should be handled with due care as a reliable source of conclusive empirical evidence on genuine scientific cooperation and networking. For instance, articles in biomedical journals may list up to ten or more companies in the author affiliate list, many of which refer to the dissemination of scientific or technical standards (e.g. protocols for clinical trials) rather than results of joint research activities.

---

## BOX 4.4 BIBLIOGRAPHIC ITEM OF A CORPORATE CO-AUTHORED PHARMACEUTICALS RESEARCH ARTICLE*

**Journal**
*European Journal of Pharmaceutics and Biopharmaceutics*, vol. 59, pp. 283–8, 2005
**Title**
*"Studies on a new device for drug delivery to the eye"*
**Authors**
*Pijls R.T.; Sonderkamp T.; Daube G.W.; Krebber R.; Hanssen H.H.L.; Nuijts R.M.M.A.; Koole L.H.*
**Author addresses**
*Univ Maastricht; Fac Med, Ctr Biomat Res; NL-6200 MD Maastricht; Netherlands*
*Eindhoven Univ Technol; Fac Biomed Engn; NL-5600 MB Eindhoven; Netherlands*
*Bayer Healthcare AG; Div Anim Hlth, Clin R&D Antibiot; Germany*
*Bayer Crop Sci AG; Dev ROCS; Germany*
*MCTEC bv; Netherlands*
*Acad Hosp Maastricht; Dept Ophthalmol; Netherlands*

* Random sample extracted from the CWTS/Thomson *Web of Science* database (edition September 2006).

---

## 6. RESEARCH COOPERATION PROFILES WITHIN THE EUROPEAN PHARMACEUTICAL INDUSTRY

Over the last two decades, the pharmaceutical industry has been the subject of many empirical studies incorporating statistics extracted from the research literature, mostly on a case study basis and often dealing with the US pharmaceutical industry (e.g. Koenig, 1983; Narin and Rozek, 1988; Gambardella, 1995; McMillan and Hamilton, 2000; Tijssen, 2004). This case study focuses on Europe's R&D-intensive "Big Pharma" companies – that is, those with their corporate headquarters in a European country and R&D expenditures in excess of $500 million in 2004. These ten research-based drug companies are presented in Table 4.1. Many of

*Table 4.1    Selected European "Big Pharma" companies and their R&D profiles*

| Company* | Country of corporate headquarters (2005) | Worldwide health-related R&D expenditure (2004, US$ mil.)* | R&D centres (2006)** home country/ | abroad |
|---|---|---|---|---|
| GlaxoSmithKline | United Kingdom | 5204 | 7 | 7 |
| Sanofi-Aventis | France | 4927 | 13 | 12 |
| Novartis | Switzerland | 4207 | 2 | 9 |
| Roche | Switzerland | 4098 | 2 | 10 |
| AstraZeneca | United Kingdom | 3803 | 2 | 8 |
| Boehringer Ingelheim | Germany | 1532 | 2 | 5 |
| Bayer*** | Germany | 1299 | 1 | 2 |
| Schering | Germany | 1143 | 1 | 7 |
| Novo Nordisk | Denmark | 727 | 1 | 2 |
| Merck | Germany | 611 | 1 | 5 |

*Notes:*
 * Source: Top 50 pharmaceutical companies, *MedAdNews*, September 2005.
 ** R&D centres located in the same country as the corporate headquarters and those located in other countries. Excludes technological support centres and production facilities, but includes supporting sites of research institutes and centres of research excellence. Excludes majority-owned biopharmaceuticals companies (such as Genentech and Chugai Pharmaceuticals in the case of Roche). Source: Company websites, accessed 16 October 2006.
 *** R&D centres relate exclusively to Bayer Healthcare (Bayer Pharma).

them are highly internationalized, having R&D labs and research facilities scattered across Europe, as well as overseas (in the USA in particular). Each of these companies is very actively involved in basic scientific research (both pre-clinical and clinical). They produce large numbers of research articles in the international scientific literature, typically in the range of a few hundred to more than 1000 per year. The publication output is often concentrated in a few large and specialized research labs, rather than spread evenly across all R&D centres. Most of those labs are located in the company's home country or in the USA. Earlier studies of research publication output by pharmaceutical companies indicate that the big pharma firms predominately publish institutionally co-authored papers, the majority of which are public–private co-authored research papers with academic partners (Tijssen, 2004). In many cases, the university researchers are the main partner and also take the lead in producing peer-reviewed research articles.

The bibliographic information in the research papers about institutional affiliation and geographical location of the authors provides a range of comparative statistics about the research cooperation profile of each firm. In this case study, the analysis concerns aggregate-level statistics at the firm level, which are used to examine and compare distributional characteristics of their research partnership patterns. These patterns provide an external source of quantitative indicators of firm-level *research partnership profiles* (RPPs). The information on institutional affiliations of the researchers enables a relatively straightforward breakdown of research partners along two institutional divides: inside or outside the company, and public or private sector. Note that all publication output statistics displayed in Tables 4.2–4.4 refer to publications produced by researchers based in the "home" country of the corporate headquarters, and do not cover a company's worldwide publication output.

The findings presented in Table 4.2 indicate a remarkable overall similarity in RPP profiles but also some noteworthy differences. For instance, the within-company co-publications with researchers with affiliations

*Table 4.2   Research partnership profiles of European Big Pharma companies: organizational distribution indicators (2005)\**

| Percentage authors from: | Within company | | Outside company | |
|---|---|---|---|---|
| | Headquarters | Other countries | Public sector | Private sector |
| GlaxoSmithKline | 37 | 6 | 53 | 4 |
| Sanofi-Aventis | 24 | 4 | 66 | 6 |
| Novartis | 31 | 5 | 61 | 3 |
| Roche | 27 | 3 | 60 | 10 |
| AstraZeneca UK | 33 | 1 | 61 | 5 |
| Boehringer Ingelheim | 36 | 6 | 49 | 9 |
| Bayer\*\* | 40 | 4 | 49 | 7 |
| Schering | 29 | 3 | 60 | 8 |
| Novo Nordisk | 28 | 2 | 67 | 3 |
| Merck | 30 | 2 | 62 | 6 |

*Notes:*
  \* Consists of all "home country" company research articles including institutionally co-authored articles – i.e. publications that list the corporate headquarters or the R&D headquarters, or any other corporate affiliations within this home country.
\*\* Bayer HealthCare, Bayer CropScience, and Bayer MaterialScience.

*Source:*   CWTS/Thomson Science *Web of Science* database (edition September 2006); publication year 2005.

from outside the home country, where companies such as Sanofi Aventis and Roche have comparatively low shares of such publications, indicate that major research labs are located in the home country and they tend to co-publish with external partners. Less significant, but nonetheless interesting to observe, are the shares of authors from the public sector, ranging from 49 per cent in the case of Boehringer Ingelheim and Bayer to a share as high as 67 per cent in the Novo Nordisk research publications.

These differences suggest that some firms are more reliant on public sector research than are others. Reliance on external sources extends to the private sector, where some companies (Roche, Boehringer Ingelheim and Schering) produce two to three times as many research papers with other companies compared to competitors like Novartis and Novo Nordisk. Several of those business sector partners are dedicated biotechnology companies, which have become increasingly important during the last 20 years (Roijakkers and Hagedoorn, 2005). Many of those biotech firms are in fact spin-offs of universities or other public sector research organizations, and help fill the drug development pipeline of the big pharmaceutical companies by licensing the patents they hold on new technologies or new chemical compounds. Although these inter-firm research partnerships appear to be relatively rare compared to the large quantities of public–private partnerships, the co-publication data also provide a unique window on both intra-firm and inter-firm research networking propensities. The first results of these studies suggest that some companies adopt "centralized" inter-firm collaboration models across the globe, focusing on the central lab in the home country as a "hub", whereas others have implemented decentralized systems (Calero et al., 2007).

Increasing R&D internalization within the biomedical drug-discovering research community, combined with the widespread distribution of clinical trials to test candidate drugs, means that big pharma's research partners are now scattered across the globe. As for the geographical distribution of research partners, Table 4.3 reveals to what degree these developments have taken a firm hold on the European pharmaceutical industry. Although "home base" partners still represent a (slim) majority in most firms, in three cases we find that most of the partners are based in other countries. The Swiss companies Roche and Novartis show the most pronounced "multinational" RPP profiles: more than half of the papers (58 per cent) involving Roche's researchers based in Switzerland list partners from other European countries; almost half of the Novartis Switzerland's papers (45 per cent) involve partners outside Europe.

The order of authorship is usually indicative of the formal status of the corresponding organizations within the collaborative arrangements. Some 40 per cent of all publications produced by the ten firms in this case study

*Table 4.3    Research partnership profiles of European Big Pharma
companies: geographical proximity indicators (2005)*

| Percentage external authors from: | Country of headquarters | Other European countries* | Non-European countries |
|---|---|---|---|
| GlaxoSmithKline | 50 | 22 | 27 |
| Sanofi-Aventis | 37 | 31 | 32 |
| Novartis | 10 | 44 | 45 |
| Roche | 8 | 58 | 34 |
| AstraZeneca UK | 46 | 20 | 34 |
| Boehringer Ingelheim | 32 | 28 | 40 |
| Bayer** | 39 | 29 | 32 |
| Schering | 48 | 27 | 26 |
| Novo Nordisk | 43 | 34 | 23 |
| Merck | 42 | 33 | 24 |

*Notes:*
 * EU-25 member states and Switzerland.
** Bayer HealthCare, Bayer CropScience, and Bayer MaterialScience.

*Source:*   CWTS/Thomson Science *Web of Science* database (edition September 2006);
publication year 2005.

have corporate researchers acting as first author. Our analysis focuses on the co-publications with external partners, where the first authors usually belong to the leading organizations (either as primary investigator, coordinator and/or sponsor) within the partnership that produced these joint papers. The data in Table 4.4 reveal that the vast majority of the corporate research papers, on average about 97 per cent, include one or more external partners. The remaining 3 per cent are "single-firm" publications without external partners ("in-house" partnerships between researchers included). Researchers at Sanofi-Aventis top the list with a 6 per cent share of single-firm research publications. Overall, the share of these publications is remarkably low, in some cases as low as 2 per cent.

The numbers of co-authoring external organizations on research publications are indicative of the size and scale of the associated research networks. This information offers the possibility to gauge the propensity of firms to engage in collaborative arrangements with several partners simultaneously. Here, the occurrence of different institutional addresses listed on each publication is used as a proxy for the number of institutional partners involved: one address reflects a single-firm research paper without any institutional partnerships; a few addresses are likely to

*Table 4.4    Research partnership profiles of European Big Pharma companies: network indicators (2005)*

| | Number of institutional research partners* | | | | Firm as lead partner in network (%)** |
|---|---|---|---|---|---|
| | 2–3 | 4–5 | 6–10 | >10 | |
| GlaxoSmithKline | 47 | 35 | 14 | 1 | 29 |
| Sanofi-Aventis | 32 | 32 | 24 | 5 | 20 |
| Novartis | 45 | 30 | 17 | 3 | 17 |
| Roche | 38 | 31 | 19 | 8 | 19 |
| AstraZeneca UK | 54 | 47 | 15 | 4 | 25 |
| Boehringer Ingelheim | 47 | 33 | 13 | 3 | 21 |
| Bayer*** | 53 | 31 | 11 | 3 | 15 |
| Schering | 43 | 27 | 26 | 2 | 20 |
| Novo Nordisk | 46 | 30 | 19 | 1 | 26 |
| Merck | 43 | 34 | 17 | 1 | 24 |

*Notes:*
  * Number of institutional addresses on corporate co-authored research articles (per cent of all company articles).
 ** Share of papers co-authored with external partners where company researchers are first author.
*** Bayer HealthCare, Bayer CropScience, and Bayer MaterialScience.

*Source:*   CWTS/Thomson Science *Web of Science* database (edition September 2006); publication year 2005.

represent "one-to-one" or small-scale partnerships; while many partners tend to reflect large-scale "network" arrangements. Note that different affiliate addresses may still refer to one and the same company or main organization (see the example of Bayer in Box 4.4).

Table 4.4 provides a breakdown according to the following crude and arbitrary categorization of external partnerships: 2–3 and 4–5 addresses represent small-sized external partnerships or networks; 6–10 addresses reflect medium-sized networks; more than 10 addresses are indicative of large networks, which usually span across national borders. Also indicated is the share of papers per company in which their researcher is first author, thereby reflecting their propensity to act as the "core" or "hub" in these knowledge generating networks.

On the whole, the distributive characteristics of the ten firms are again remarkably similar, which suggests that these research cooperation patterns within the large companies are predominantly sector-specific, rather than company-specific. This degree of similarity most likely is affected also by "natural laws of cooperation" in which partnership configurations, and the number of institutional partners, are kept at manageable, efficient and cost-effective levels. The "managerial optimum", also defined as the most frequently occurring number of partners, is, in this case, somewhere between three or four co-authoring organizations (i.e. the firm and two or three partners), and accounts for 24 per cent and 20 per cent of all research papers, respectively. Nonetheless, the data reveal that some companies appear to be significantly more network oriented than others. Roche, for example, participates in many research articles with relatively large numbers of co-authoring organizations (large networks), whereas Sanofi-Aventis and Schering authors are often found in research papers reflecting medium-sized networks.

On the whole, the results presented in Table 4.4 are affected by a range of firm, sector, and field-specific determinants, not least of which are the R&D objectives of partnerships, and the kind of research stage to which these papers refer. As for the latter, collaborative pre-clinical "drug discovery" research projects are more likely to involve fewer partners and be concentrated in just a few locations, especially in the case of longer-term arrangements that involve research and licensing agreements between firms and PROs, or between big pharma companies and small dedicated biotechnology companies. Research papers dealing with the results of clinical trials, however, will list many authors and affiliate addresses, as these trials involve a range of institutes and small companies working in collaboration with hospitals and medical centres scattered across multiple sites in different countries.

## 7.   FROM MEASUREMENTS TO STRATEGIC INTELLIGENCE

Given the overwhelming significance of pre-clinical "discovery-oriented" research and successive clinical "development-oriented" research for drug development pipelines, and the resulting numbers of scientific papers that are produced annually, the open scientific literature obviously constitutes a very useful source of empirical information on research cooperation patterns within the pharmaceutical sector. External measurements derived from this source are likely to produce reasonably reliable estimates in the case of research cooperation, particularly on industry–university partnerships. There are, of course, well-known limitations to the use of co-authored publications as proxies for successful research cooperation arrangements, notably the fact that publication propensities are often field-specific and firm-specific, and results of applications-oriented research are less likely to find their way into scientific journals. Nonetheless, the sheer quantity of research publications offers a source large enough for reliable indicators to be estimated for the largest science-based firms, and even at higher aggregate levels, such as the entire pharmaceutical industry in Europe, the USA or worldwide.

Not only does the quality of measurement tools depend on adequate information sources, it also hinges on a host of other methodological and technical parameters, ranging from the choice of proper measurement concepts, commonly accepted criteria, and appropriate metrics and quantitative indicators. Carefully chosen and well-designed indicators are a bridge between interesting statistics and useful evidence-based knowledge for strategic analysis, debate and decision-making. For example, the results that emerge from this case study of ten European pharmaceutical companies enable a certain degree of aggregate-level benchmarking. The indicators in Tables 4.2 to 4.4 produce a one-year snap-shot of the aggregate firm-level research partnership profiles, in which several interesting features can be observed. The various statistics reveal differences in research cooperation propensities, but the most striking feature is probably the degree of similarity between the RPPs of these ten companies. That said, the pronounced international orientation of the two Swiss companies, Novartis and Roche, with many labs outside their home countries, highlights the impact of corporate strategies for locating R&D centres. This outcome raises questions of how and why these firm-level RPP features come about. Are they mainly determined by global, sector-specific R&D processes or by competitive pressures impacting on corporate R&D strategies, or are they still very much rooted in the traditional practice of proximity-driven preferences for partners? Can these internally driven partnering mechanisms be redirected and become more effective by introducing additional incentive systems and imposing new collaborative frameworks from the outside? For example, to what degree will new European policy initiatives like the *Innovative Medicines Initiative*, one of the seventh Framework's Joint Technology Initiatives, impact these partnering profiles in terms of strengthening and broadening European research partnerships and R&D networks?

Even though these partnership indicators and statistics produce a novel and unique window of research cooperation within the European pharmaceutical industry, and help unravel the web of research networks involving pharmaceutical companies, this measurement model cannot provide conclusive evidence as to the significance of the outcomes, nor can it provide explanations. A truly convincing interpretation of these findings requires a global perspective and sector-wide frame of reference. What does it mean for a specific European company to be near the bottom of a ranking, or to have an average score, in terms of participation in co-authored research articles? And without an "expected" or "optimum" value for levels of research cooperation within the pharmaceutical sector worldwide, it is impossible to characterize a measure of European companies as either low, high or average.

Providing answers to such questions not only requires technical expertise on the ins and outs of the information sources and an in-depth understanding of the underlying metrics and statistical properties of the data, but, above all, answers require a thorough grasp of the relevant economic environments and geo-political contexts in which these European multinational companies operate (e.g. Pammolli et al., 2004). We still know precious little about the detailed and hard-to-observe mechanisms and organizational conditions that are driving these research partnerships. It stands to reason that the various types of linkages are driven by different environments, which are strongly affected by the prevailing R&D objectives and constraints, IPR, and knowledge appropriation regimes. Moreover, each type of research partnership and network is likely to operate according to its own managerial models and organizational structures, with different milestones and deliverables.

Clearly, more work is also needed to develop a comprehensive analytical framework and an associated typology of research partnerships that incorporate their key characteristics and their performance in terms of efficiency, effectiveness and efficacy. For this, we obviously need further in-depth analysis of research publication data coupled with conclusive information from other sources on inter-organizational research networks. Also needed is information on R&D alliances in conjunction with case studies to unearth R&D objectives and business strategies that drive and shape these partnerships. Further statistical analyses of the underlying relational patterns within the joint research publications of these firms might also disclose more details about how they organize models. Recent exploratory studies by Calero et al. (2007) of these co-publication patterns, using "two-dimensional" network graphs rather than "one-dimensional" statistics, indicate that the large pharmaceutical firms may adopt different organizational structures for managing within-company research networks. Case studies of specific research networks or pharmaceutical companies, such as recent studies conducted by Criscuolo and Narula (2005) or Criscuolo (2005), constitute the obvious complementary step to help gain inside information on the reasons for engaging in research cooperation. Ultimately, the mixture of comparative measurements and qualitative case studies may allow us to develop an analytical framework to assess and monitor scientific, economic, and healthcare impacts of collaborative research within the pharmaceutical industry.

## ACKNOWLEDGEMENT

The author is grateful to Erik van Wijk for research assistance. This chapter is based on research that was partially funded by the European Commission/DG RTD, Sixth Framework Programme ("Improving Human Potential and Socio-Economic Knowledge Base" Programme – project "STI-NET" and "Analysis, Studies, Statistics and Indicators on Science and Technology" – project "Regular Collection of Bibliometric Indicators").

## NOTES

1. A "network" is defined as "an evolutionary mutual dependency system based on resource relationships in which their systemic character is the outcome of interactions, processes, procedures and institutionalization" (see Tijssen, 1998)
2. The generic term "basic research" is usually referred to within pharmaceutical industry as "discovery", "front end", "front line", or "pre-project" research. The research goals are usually of a "pre-competitive" nature and not related to current corporate products or services. The research agenda is often driven by a strategic vision of market developments with a 3–5 year time horizon. Nonetheless, the research projects and programmes themselves may have schedules of no more than two or three years, and short-term objectives and deliverables.
3. The PRO category includes universities and other education institutions, public research institutes and laboratories, as well as other (virtual) research centres and networks, and "hybrid" (public–private) funded public sector research organizations.
4. This new approach is a major shift from the medical chemistry's "trial-and-error" "one-molecule-at-a-time" approaches in drug discovery that were prevalent in the pharmaceuticals industry up to the 1980s.
5. Details about these calculations or estimates were never disclosed by the authors. It is believed that substantial shares of this amount are marketing costs and costs for the development of all unsuccessful drugs.
6. University research presents the highest "upstream" stage in the R&D process, preceding "project research" within industry itself, which is targeted towards drug discovery and further developing of drug candidates. The "pre-project" biomedical research activities involving academics often focus on the search for emerging opportunities.
7. Another possibility of strategic publishing is to introduce "prior art" that prevents others from patenting the knowledge, or restricting the scope of their patent claims (i.e. "defensive publishing").
8. Formerly, *Thomson ISI* and its predecessor the *Institute for Scientific Information* (ISI).
9. The current edition of the CRP includes some 350 000 research papers published in 1996–2005 and (partially) assigned to business enterprises and private sector organizations. The coverage extends across all countries and fields of science and some 40 000 different main organizations are covered. Foreign branches and foreign subsidiaries of multinational companies are labelled with the consolidated name of the parent company. Companies that were added to the parent company through mergers and acquisitions were renamed to the current (ultimate) parent company to ensure backwards and forwards compatibility in trend analyses.
10. The distinction between basic research and applied research is becoming increasingly blurred, especially in the corporate sector where creation of new knowledge and its

application often go hand in hand. Hence, not all publications in these journals arise from "basic research" in the traditional sense, and irrespective of the definition of the term, but may also relate to applied scientific and technical research.

11. Being actively involved in (joint) research is not the only linking mechanism between PROs and pharmaceutical companies, nor are co-authored scientific publications the only measure of research-related interaction and cooperation. The transfer of researchers, or their skills, tacit knowledge and other less tangible assets, is probably of greater importance in terms of cementing and sustaining long-lasting and mutually rewarding cooperative arrangements. We can only assume that the research papers are a reasonably representative "tip of the iceberg".

# REFERENCES

Calero, C., T.N. Van Leeuwen and R.J.W. Tijssen (2007), "Research cooperation within the bio-pharmaceutical industry: network analyses of co-publications within and between firms", *Scientometrics*, **71** (1), 87–99.

Chesbrough, H. (2003), *Open Innovation: The New Imperative for Creating and Profiting from Technology*, Cambridge, MA: Harvard Business School Press.

Criscuolo, P. (2005), "On the road again: researcher mobility inside the R&D network", *Research Policy*, **34**, 1350–65.

Criscuolo, P. and R. Narula (2005), "Using multi-hub structures for international R&D: organizational inertia and the challenges of implementation", DRUID Working Papers 05-13, DRUID, Copenhagen Business School, Department of Industrial Economics and Strategy/Aalborg University, Department of Business Studies.

DiMasi, J.A., R.W. Hansen and H.G. Grabowski (2003), "The price of innovation: new estimates of drug development costs", *Journal of Health Economics*, **22**, 151–85.

EC (2005), *The 2005 EU Industrial R&D Investment Scoreboard Data*, Vol. II, Brussels/Seville: European Commission.

EFPIA (2006), *The Pharmaceutical Industry in Figures*, Brussels: European Federation of Pharmaceutical Industries and Associations.

Gambardella, A. (1995), *Science and Innovation. The US Pharmaceutical Industry during the 1980s*, Cambridge: Cambridge University Press.

Grant, R.M. (1996), "Towards a knowledge-based theory of the firm", *Strategic Management Journal*, **17**, 109–22.

Hagedoorn, J, A. Link and N. Vonortas (2000), "Research partnerships", *Research Policy*, **29**, 567–86.

Koenig, M.E.D. (1983), "A bibliometric analysis of pharmaceutical research", *Research Policy*, **12**, 15–36.

McMillan, G.S. and R.D. Hamilton (2000), "Using bibliometrics to measure firm knowledge: an analysis of the US pharmaceutical industry", *Technology Analysis and Strategic Management*, **12**, 465–75.

Mowery, D.C., J.E. Oxley and B.S. Silverman (1996), "Strategic alliances and interfirm knowledge transfer", *Strategic Management Journal*, **17**, 77–91.

Narin, F. and R.P. Rozek (1988), "Bibliometric analysis of U.S. pharmaceutical industry research performance", *Research Policy*, **17**, 139–54.

OECD (2002), *Benchmarking Industry–Science Relationships*, Paris: Organisation for Economic Co-operation and Development.

Pammolli, F., M. Riccaboni and L. Magazzini (2004), *European Competitiveness in Pharmaceuticals*, Report for DG Enterprise, Brussels: European Commission.

Pavitt, K. and P. Patel (1999), "Global corporations and national systems of innovation: who dominates whom?", in D. Archibugi, J. Howells, and J. Michie (eds), *Innovation Policy in a Global Economy*, Cambridge: Cambridge University Press, pp. 94–119.

PhRMA (2006), *Annual Membership Survey 2006*, Pharmaceuticals Research and Manufacturers of America: Washington DC.

Pisano, G. (2006), *Science Business: The Promise, the Reality, and the Future of Biotech*, Cambridge, MA: Harvard Business School Press.

Roijakkers, N. and J. Hagedoorn (2005), "Inter-firm R&D partnering in pharmaceutical biotechnology since 1975: trends, patterns, and networks", *Research Policy*, **35**, 431–46.

Teece, D.J., G. Pisano and A. Shuen (1997), "Dynamic capabilities and strategic management", *Strategic Management Journal*, **18**, 506–33.

Tijssen, R.J.W. (1998), "Quantitative assessment of large heterogeneous R&D networks: the case of process engineering in the Netherlands", *Research Policy*, **26**, 791–809.

Tijssen, R.J.W. (2004), "Is the commercialisation of scientific research affecting the production of public knowledge? Global trends in the output of corporate research articles", *Research Policy*, **33**, 709–33.

# 5. Knowledge search and strategic alliance: evidence from the electronics industry

**Stefano Breschi, Lorenzo Cassi and Franco Malerba**

## 1. INTRODUCTION

The idea that searching for new knowledge is at the basis of firms' innovative performance underlies the evolutionary perspective on industrial innovation. A central tenet is that search activities are highly "local" and path dependent, meaning that firms tend to search for new knowledge in areas closely related to the their established knowledge base and competencies. According to this view, far from emerging in isolation, current innovations build upon past innovations and may themselves become foundations for future innovations. In other words, it is assumed that technological development is a cumulative process. Viewed from the perspective of organizations, this process of knowledge accumulation may take place by building on the internal stock of knowledge of a firm or accessing novel and different domains of knowledge that reside just beyond firms' immediate boundaries.

The aim of this chapter is to provide an empirical investigation of firms' knowledge search strategies in crowded technological areas. In particular, we argue that processes of competition and collaboration have to be taken into account when exploring impacts on innovative performance. On the one hand, competition from other firms that build on a firm's knowledge base may hamper innovation in that the innovating firm finds reduced effectiveness in a local and cumulative search strategy and finds a more exploratory strategy increasingly attractive. On the other hand, forming alliances with competitors is a means to internalize the potential negative effects arising from competitors exploiting a firm's knowledge base. In this case, we also expect R&D alliances to be formed among partners that perform searches in the same knowledge base and along similar lines, rather than among companies searching in different directions.

The chapter combines patent citations and strategic alliances data for a sample of publicly traded companies operating in the electronics industry. In particular, patent co-citation data are used to investigate the extent to which the pattern of search for new knowledge overlaps across companies. The chapter is organized as follows. Section 2 discusses the notions of cumulativeness and the different knowledge search strategies followed by firms. Section 3 presents the methodology adopted based mainly on patent citations data, while section 4 illustrates the sources of data and the sample used. Section 5 presents the basic results of our empirical estimates, and section 6 concludes.

## 2. CUMULATIVENESS AND KNOWLEDGE SPILLOVERS

A central tenet of evolutionary economics is that search activities are highly "local" and path dependent: past searches become the natural starting point for new searches, thereby generating highly contextual and cumulative learning processes at the organizational level. The cumulative nature of organizational learning implies that the generation of new knowledge builds on current knowledge and that past knowledge not only constrains current research, but may also be exploited to generate new questions and new knowledge. Several reasons have been advanced in the literature to explain why search activities are likely to be local. The economics and organizational literature has pointed out that in uncertain environments, boundedly rational decision makers tend to rely on established organizational routines and practices in the search for new knowledge (Nelson and Winter, 1982). Also, searching in areas in which firms have prior experience and competencies may increase the likelihood of successful innovation. Following this argument, one should expect firms exploiting their own established knowledge base in a cumulative way to exhibit a relatively higher innovative performance. At the same time, it has been recognized that a search strategy too heavily based on the exploitation of the existing knowledge resources, while potentially increasing a firm's innovativeness because of returns from specialization, is fraught with risks. In particular, the literature has often emphasized that the path dependent nature of firms' capabilities may lead to technical obsolescence, locking them out of new areas of development and preventing them from adjusting their technological strategies to handle "competence destroying" technical changes (Tushman and Anderson, 1986).

In this chapter, we argue that a further negative effect of a search strategy based upon the exploitation of a firm's own reservoir of ideas and knowledge is related to competition coming from other organizations, which try to build on that focal firm's knowledge base. To the extent that other firms benefit from spillovers generated by a focal firm's stock of knowledge, opportunities for cumulative innovation are relatively diminished and one should expect a negative impact on that focal firm's innovative performance. Summarizing, we expect search strategies based on the cumulative exploitation of a firm's own stock of knowledge to be positively related to the firms' rate of innovation. Yet, we also expect such a positive effect to be moderated by the negative effect arising from competition from other organizations trying to exploit the same knowledge base of the focal firm.

The potential competition effect generated when firms' search activities overlap to a large degree has been discussed recently in a series of papers by a few scholars in the sociology tradition (Stuart, 1999, 2000; Podolny and Stuart, 1995; Stuart and Podolny, 1996; Podolny et al., 1996). They introduce the notion of *crowding* to characterize the position of companies in the knowledge search space. In particular, a firm is said to be located in a crowded position to the extent that the focus of its search activities overlaps to a large degree with that of other organizations. In other words, crowded positions correspond to contested areas of technology in the sense that firms pursue similar lines of research and are engaged in the refinement of very similar ideas. From this perspective, a relevant question concerns the likely impact of crowdedness on firms' innovative performance. According to the proponents of this notion, crowding is most likely to incite organizational search and therefore should positively affect a firm's innovation rate. The most fundamental reason behind this prediction is that firms in crowded positions have greater incentives to invest in organizational search in order to differentiate themselves from other firms pursuing similar lines of research and enjoy the rewards from being the winner in the technological race (Stuart, 1999).

Although we think that the notion of crowding and the basic methodology to assess it provide a powerful interpretative tool, we argue in this chapter that the meaning of such a concept, and the most likely effect on firms' innovative performance, are more complex than has been presumed in the sociological literature. In particular, our claim is that crowding may arise in two different circumstances with sharply different implications. A first case already has been discussed above and refers to the instance of a firm that builds cumulatively on its own antecedent ideas and knowledge base. In this case, the search space of the firm may be crowded to the extent that other organizations also draw on its knowledge base. In these circumstances, we expect that the incentives for the focal firm to invest in search activities are likely to be reduced, as the probability of being first to invent declines as crowding around its knowledge base increases.

A second case arises when crowdedness derives from the fact that a focal firm is building on the antecedent ideas and knowledge bases of other firms and, at the same time, other organizations are also drawing upon the same knowledge bases and ideas. In such circumstances, we also expect crowding to lead to a higher intensity of organizational innovation, albeit for quite different reasons. In one scenario, the fact that companies crowd around certain technological areas signals the existence of rich and possibly unexploited opportunities. One may argue that technological areas become crowded precisely because firms are attracted to domains where the returns from innovative search are likely to be substantial. Another scenario shows that even when firms build upon a common pool of external ideas and knowledge, it is also the case that each firm recombines such elements with firm specific knowledge and competencies. In such circumstances, one may expect that any direct competition effect among companies for the same set of innovations is offset by the recombinatory effect that widens the set of possible innovations.

The distinction discussed above introduces a novel way to look at R&D alliances. Most of the evolutionary approach and the innovation systems literature has rightly and effectively emphasized that in uncertain and changing environments networks emerge not because agents are similar, but because they are different, and that networks may integrate complementarities in knowledge, capabilities and specialization (see Lundvall, 1993; Edquist, 1997). Following this line, the management literature has pointed out that collaboration among firms allows them to overcome local search (Rosenkopf and Almeida, 2003) because alliances allow firms to get access to complementary knowledge, and thus recombine knowledge in various new ways and overcome the constraints and context of local search. Such recombination could be seen as a different role of R&D collaboration. In this chapter, we advance a different point, related to the knowledge bases of the various firms and the degree of competition among those firms. We claim that R&D collaborations by a firm that has its knowledge set crowded by too many competitors searching in its technological space, aim to reduce the intensity of competition. This type of collaboration increases the rate of technological innovation, and will be examined here.

## 3. MEASURING KNOWLEDGE SPILLOVERS AMONG OVERLAPPING FIRMS

In this chapter, we use patent citations to measure the extent to which firms cumulatively build on their own knowledge base, as well as to capture the extent of overlap and similarity in the search profile of different organizations. The use of patent citations to track knowledge flows has recently gained legitimacy. Here, we adapt the approach proposed by Podolny et al. (1996). In particular, we view patent citations as providing evidence of a knowledge link between a firm's present search activities and the results of past searches. Looking at the whole set of patent citations made in a firm's current patent portfolio, it is possible to examine the type of knowledge that a company has used in its search activities and to characterize its search strategy.

Figure 5.1 illustrates the basic idea behind the approach proposed. The example focuses upon a specific organisation, i.e. firm A. The white box identifies firm A's current inventions, while arrows departing from it represent knowledge building relationships. The arrows are directed from firm A's current inventions to technological antecedents (i.e. previous patents), which are marked with black boxes. The label below the black boxes identifies the organisation responsible for the development of such antecedent knowledge. Looking at the solid lines reveals that, in the example reported, organisation A exhibits a highly cumulative and local pattern of search, as all current inventions draw upon knowledge embodied in firm A's past inventions.

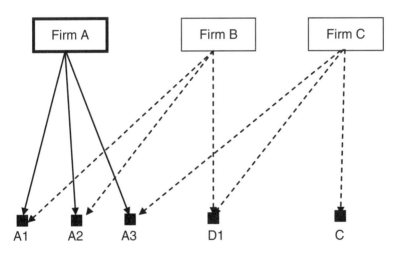

*Note:* White boxes represent firms' current inventions (i.e. patents). Black boxes represent technological antecedents (i.e. cited patents) upon which current inventions build. Arrows identify a knowledge link (i.e. citation) between current and past inventions. Labels in white boxes represent organizations responsible for the current inventions. Labels below black boxes identify organizations responsible for past inventions.

*Figure 5.1 Firm A's pattern of search*

In this respect, a natural way to measure the extent of cumulativeness in a firm's search for new knowledge is to calculate the self-citation rate; that is, the ratio between the number of citations to a firm's own previous patents and the total number of citations made by that firm's current patents. Formally, this is given by:

$$S_{it} = \frac{\sum_{p_i} s_{ip_it}}{\sum_{p} s_{ipt}} \tag{5.1}$$

where, $p_i$ indexes firm $i$'s previous patents, $p$ indexes all previous patents, $s_{ip_it}$ is coded 1 if a patent of firm $i$ cites patent $p_i$ at time $t$, and 0 otherwise, and $s_{ipt}$ is coded 1 if a patent of firm $i$ cites patent $p$ at time $t$, and 0 otherwise. With reference to the example reported above, the self-citation rate is equal to one (i.e. 3 citations to own previous patents divided by a total of 3 citations), thereby indicating that all of firm A's citations are made to firm A's own patents. Of course, the self-citation rate may take values lower than 1 (and greater than or equal to zero). In the case of firms B and C, for example, the self-citation rate is respectively equal to 0 and 1/3.

The self-citation rate indicates the degree of cumulativeness in a firm's innovative activities, but it does not tell anything about the extent to which a firm's pattern of search overlaps with that followed by other firms. This aspect may be captured by using information on patent co-citations. This is also illustrated in Figure 5.1, where dotted lines represent citations from firm B's and firm C's current patents to previous patents. In the example reported, we note that not only does firm A build cumulatively on its own knowledge base, but that other firms also draw on firm A's stock of antecedent ideas, thereby "crowding" its search space. Out of three citations made by firm A's patents to its own previous patents (self-citations), two are matched by citations by firm B's patents and one by citations made by firm C's patents.

To study this phenomenon, we propose to use an index that captures the extent to which the self-citations made by a company to its own previous patents match with the citations made by other organizations. The index is formally defined as follows:

$$\sigma_{ijt} = \frac{\sum_{p_i} s_{ip_it} s_{jp_it}}{\sum_{p} s_{ipt}} \qquad i \neq j \tag{5.2}$$

*Table 5.1     Crowding on a firm's own knowledge base*

|        | Firm A | Firm B | Firm C |
|--------|--------|--------|--------|
| Firm A | 1      | 2/3    | 1/3    |
| Firm B | 0      | 0      | 0      |
| Firm C | 1/3    | 0      | 1/3    |

where $s_{jp,t}$ is coded 1 if a patent of firm $j$ cites patent $p_i$ at time $t$, and 0 otherwise, while all other symbols have the same meanings discussed above. The numerator of the above expression moves in increments of 1 any time that patents of firms $i$ and $j$ cite a common patent of firm $i$, while the denominator is simply a count of all firm $i$'s patent citations.

Two things are worth noting. First, the index captures the pairwise degree of overlap in the pattern of search between organizations. Second, the index is asymmetric; that is, in general $\sigma_{ijt} \neq \sigma_{jit}$. In the hypothetical case of Figure 5.1, the value of the index for each pair of organisations is reported in the following matrix (Table 5.1).

Note that the elements on the main diagonal of the matrix in Table 5.1 are simply the self-citation rates of each company. The off-diagonal elements report instead the value of the pairwise overlap index. Thus, looking at the second cell on the first row suggests that the search space of firm A is "crowded" by the presence of firm B, which builds on firm A's knowledge base. A summary index of the extent to which a firm's knowledge base is crowded by other organizations is therefore given by the row summation of the off-diagonal elements of the matrix:

$$\sigma_{it} = \sum_j \sigma_{ijt} \qquad i \neq j \tag{5.3}$$

In our example, the value of this index is equal to 1 for firm A, 0 for firm B, and 1/3 for firm C.

The hypothetical case reported in Figure 5.1 suggests that organizations may follow radically different search strategies. Whereas firm A's strategy may be characterized as a highly cumulative search pattern, firm B's strategy seems to rely more on the acquisition of external knowledge and possibly on the recombination of such external knowledge with internal capabilities. To put it another way, despite firm A and firm B both citing three antecedent patents and having two citations in common, there is a fundamental asymmetry between the two companies. One is following a strategy of incremental exploitation of internal knowledge, and the other is taking advantage of spillovers from knowledge produced beyond its immediate boundaries. Our prediction is that such an asymmetry may translate into sharply different implications for firms' innovative performance. In particular, the likelihood that firm A develops a successful invention is reduced by the competition of other companies that draw on the same set of ideas. This negative effect is less likely to be felt by firms B and C as they are able to benefit from spillovers generated by firm A and recombine such knowledge with their own firm-specific knowledge assets. The extent to which a firm is able to draw on externally generated knowledge and recombine it with its own specific knowledge assets may be captured by the following index:

$$\varepsilon_{ijt} = \frac{\sum\limits_{p \neq i} s_{ip_{\neq i}t} s_{jp_{\neq i}t}}{\sum\limits_{p} s_{ipt}} \qquad i \neq j \qquad (5.4)$$

where $p_{\neq i}$ indexes previous patents *not* made by firm $i$, $s_{ip_{\neq i}t}$ is coded 1 if a patent of firm $i$ cites a previous patent of another company, and 0 otherwise, $s_{jp_{\neq i}t}$ is coded 1 if a patent of firm $j$ cites a previous patent not produced by company $i$, and 0 otherwise, and all other symbols have the same meaning discussed before. For the example used here, the value of the index is reported in the following matrix (Table 5.2).

The value of the index increases to the extent that a focal company cites patents of other organizations and such citations are matched by citations made by other firms. As before, we may calculate a summary index for firm $i$ by performing row summations of the values contained in the matrix:

$$\varepsilon_{it} = \sum_{j} \varepsilon_{ijt} \qquad i \neq j \qquad (5.5)$$

It is worth noting that $\alpha_{ijt} = \sigma_{ijt} + \varepsilon_{ijt}$ corresponds to the share of *all* citations made by firm $i$ that are matched by citations made by firm $j$. In other words, this represents what Podolny et al. (1996) have called the overall "crowding" of firm $i$'s search space. As we argued here, however,

*Table 5.2    Crowding on other firms' knowledge bases*

|        | Firm A | Firm B | Firm C |
|--------|--------|--------|--------|
| Firm A | –      | 0      | 0      |
| Firm B | 0      | –      | 1/3    |
| Firm C | 0      | 1/3    | –      |

a problem with this index is that it is unable to discriminate between the identities of the firms responsible for the cited patents, and therefore it is also unable to tell whether crowding occurs on a firm's own knowledge base, which we posit to have a negative effect on its innovative performance, or on other firms' knowledge bases, which we posit instead to have a positive effect on its innovative performance.

As we argued in section 2, high levels of crowding on a firm's own knowledge base are likely to hinder its innovative performance because of the competition effect resulting from other organizations trying to exploit spillovers leaking out from its stock of ideas. In such circumstances, a way to internalize these potentially negative externalities is to form strategic alliances with direct competitors. To capture this phenomenon, we have further divided the index $\sigma_{it}$ by distinguishing cases in which crowding on a firm's knowledge base takes place with allied firms, from cases in which crowding occurs with competing firms. We expect a negative effect on firm's innovative performance to arise only in the latter scenario, and not in the former. Formally, we have:

$$\sigma_{ijt}^{A} = \frac{\sum_{p_i} s_{ip_it} s_{jp_it}^{A}}{\sum_{p} s_{ipt}} \qquad i \neq j \qquad (5.6)$$

$$\sigma_{ijt}^{NA} = \frac{\sum_{p_i} s_{ip_it} s_{jp_it}^{NA}}{\sum_{p} s_{ipt}} \qquad i \neq j \qquad (5.7)$$

where symbol $A$ indicates that company $j$ has formed a strategic alliance with firm $i$, while symbol $NA$ indicates the opposite case, and all other symbols have the same meaning already discussed above. Of course, we have that $\sigma_{ijt} = \sigma_{ijt}^{A} + \sigma_{ijt}^{NA}$.

In what follows, we present the data and the network variables used to test these propositions and we report on the main results obtained.

## 4.   DATA AND VARIABLES

### Sample Selection and Data Sources

We examine firm innovativeness for a sample of firms operating in three industrial sectors: computers, telecommunications and semiconductors.

The sample of firms has been drawn from the COMPUSTAT file and includes all publicly traded firms reporting the corresponding SIC codes as the main sector of activity. For each firm in the sample we have collected data on patent applications to the European Patent Office from 1978 (the founding date of the EPO) to 1998. For each firm, patents of subsidiaries have been consolidated using *Who Owns Whom* as of 1998. In addition to patent data, for each company in the sample we have collected data on the strategic alliances in which they are involved. To this purpose, we have matched the companies in our sample with the companies reported in the MERIT-CATI dataset on cooperative technology agreements (Hagedoorn and Schakenraad, 1994). This database contains information on the most important strategic technology alliances between independent industrial partners over the period of 1985 to 1998.

We have considered all publicly traded companies operating in three industries – computers, telecommunications and semiconductors – as reported by Datastream. The sample consists of 345 firms, of which 104 are in the computer industry, 126 in the telecom industry and 115 in the semiconductor industry.[1] For each company, we have collected data about sales, employees and R&D expenditures over the period 1990–98 and the year of foundation. However, the dataset is unbalanced since there are some missing data.

For each company in our sample we also have extracted information on the patent applications to the European Patent Office over the period 1985–99. Patent applications in the following fields have been included: audiovisual technology, ICT, telecommunications, semiconductors, optics and instruments. Patents of subsidiaries have been consolidated using *Who Owns Whom*. Of the 345 firms in our sample, 272 (79%) reported at least one patent in the period 1990–98, while 73 (21%) of them did not report any patents. The 272 firms reporting patents in our sample account for 44 per cent of all patents in electronics, and more specifically: 29 per cent of all patents in audiovisual technology, 51 per cent in ICT, 52 per cent in telecommunications, 48 per cent in semiconductors, and 33 per cent in optics in the period 1990–98.

For each company, we have extracted information on the strategic alliances in the electronics field in which it was involved over the period 1990–98, using the MERIT-CATI database. Of the 345 firms in our sample, 154 (45%) had at least one alliance, while 191 (55%) did not report any alliances. The 154 companies reporting at least one alliance in our sample represent only around 8 per cent of all companies (1931) involved in the alliance network in electronics in the period 1990–99, but they participate in 63 per cent of the 2542 alliances signed in that period.

*Table 5.3   Firm sample breakdown by patenting activity and alliance participation*

| Frequency *Per cent* | | Patents | | Total |
|---|---|---|---|---|
| | | NO | YES | |
| Alliances: | NO | **59** | **132** | **191** |
| | | *17.1* | *38.3* | *55.4* |
| | YES | **14** | **140** | **154** |
| | | *4.1* | *40.5* | *44.6* |
| Total | | **73** | **272** | **345** |
| | | *21.1* | *78.9* | *100* |

Considering jointly alliances and patents, 140 (around 51%) of all companies reporting patents had at least one alliance (see Table 5.3).

Firms with both patents and alliances are on average older and larger than the other firms (see Tables 5.4 and 5.5). Firms with no patents and no alliances are on average smaller, but not younger than the other firms.

The difference in terms of intensity of R&D expenditure is not significantly relevant between firms with both patents and alliances and firms patenting but not participating in any alliance (see Table 5.6).

From now on, we focus on firms that do have patents.

The fact that firms with a larger portfolio of patents are more likely to engage in strategic alliances (or perhaps to be reported in specialized journals) is confirmed by comparing the average number of patents of firms with and without alliances (see Table 5.7). The difference in the mean number of patents is statistically significant at the 99 per cent level, even if the standard deviation is very high for firms with patents and alliances because of the presence of some outliers.

These findings suggest that the sample of companies typically included in alliance databases like MERIT-CATI is likely to be biased; that is, the sample comprises mostly large companies in terms of patents and number of employees.

**Variables and Descriptive Statistics**

The performance variable used to test the hypotheses above is the count of the number of new patents applied for by each organization in the sample in each year from 1991 to 1999. The use of the priority year to date the patent documents ensures that they are counted as close as possible to the actual time of the invention. The merits and limitations of patent data are well known and we will not review them here.

*Table 5.4   Age – average age in 1998*

|                             | Mean  | Standard deviation |
| --------------------------- | ----- | ------------------ |
| No patents – no alliances   | 27.8  | 23.42              |
| No patents – alliances      | 20.21 | 9.54               |
| Patents – no alliances      | 25.31 | 23.41              |
| Patents – alliances         | 34.46 | 30.56              |

*Table 5.5   Size – annual average number of employees (1990–98)*

|                             | Mean    | Standard Deviation |
| --------------------------- | ------- | ------------------ |
| No Patents – no alliances   | 1 400.4 | 2 212.75           |
| No Patents – alliances      | 1 954.4 | 2 560.12           |
| Patents – no alliances      | 3 922.9 | 11 491.85          |
| Patents – alliances         | 27 754.8| 57 878.23          |

*Table 5.6   R&D intensity – annual average of R&D share of sales (1990–98)*

|                             | Mean  | Standard Deviation |
| --------------------------- | ----- | ------------------ |
| No Patents – no alliances   | 11.57 | 17.25              |
| No Patents – alliances      | 9.37  | 7.79               |
| Patents – no alliances      | 12.81 | 13.12              |
| Patents – alliances         | 11.32 | 10.13              |

*Table 5.7   Innovativeness – annual average of number of patents (1990–98)*

|                          | Number | Mean  | Min | Max   | Standard Deviation |
| ------------------------ | ------ | ----- | --- | ----- | ------------------ |
| Patents – no alliances   | 132    | 5.06  | 0,1 | 68.1  | 7.33               |
| Patents – alliances      | 140    | 47.76 | 0,1 | 544   | 101.19             |

The main independent variables are the measure of crowding described in section 3. In order to calculate those variables, we have built up the co-citation network for each year of the analysed period (i.e. 1990–98). For constructing the co-citation network in any specific year (e.g. 1990), we have considered all the patents with primary IPC classification in any

*Table 5.8   Descriptive statistics*

| Variable | Obs. | Mean | Std. Dev. | Min | Max |
|---|---|---|---|---|---|
| logSales | 1791 | 13.24027 | 2.217095 | 2.564949 | 19.12249 |
| logRD | 1566 | 11.43059 | 2.855093 | 4.75359 | 20.57027 |
| Selfcit | 2065 | 9.697154 | 14.39138 | 0 | 100 |
| Age | 2325 | 27.04086 | 27.47699 | 0 | 147 |
| Crowding | 1950 | 1.302139 | 1.070211 | 0 | 9.75 |
| Crowding I | 1950 | 0.0910617 | 0.2099892 | 0 | 3 |
| Crowding non I | 1950 | 1.214414 | 1.051722 | 0 | 9.75 |
| Crowding I with partners | 1950 | 0.0048599 | 0.0173368 | 0 | 0.1428571 |
| Crowding I with others | 1950 | 0.0862018 | 0.2072617 | 0 | 3 |

of the six technological classes described above and having a priority date occurring in the previous five years (e.g. 1986–90).

We consider also a more traditional measure of cumulativeness: the share of citation to own patents (i.e. *selfcit*). Also, we have considered all citations done in a period of five years (e.g. 1986–1990). Other explanatory variables considered are the logarithm of sales (i.e. *logSales*) that captures the size of the firm, and the logarithm of R&D expenditure (i.e. *logRD*). We consider also the *age* of firms measured as the difference between year *t* and the year of foundation of the company.

Tables 5.8 and 5.9 provide descriptive statistics and correlations for all variables for the observations of our sample.

## 5.   ECONOMETRIC ESTIMATION

In Tables 5.10 and 5.11, we report the results of the regression analysis using negative binomial regression estimators. Table 5.10 reports the regressions assuming random effects, while Table 5.11 reports the estimates when fixed effects are considered.

The first specification (equation 5.8) presents the base model with only the control variables.

$$INNOVATION_{i,t}+_1 = \exp(\alpha + \beta_1 * log(Sales_{i,t}) + \beta_2 * Selfcit_{i,t} + \gamma' X + e_{i,t})$$
$$(5.8)$$

We have considered a common measure of cumulativeness: the share of citations for firm $i$ that refer to its own patents (i.e. *Selfcit*). Second, we

Table 5.9  *Correlation matrix (1325 observations)*

| | logSales | logRD | Selfcit | Age | Crowding | Crowding I | Crowding non I | Crowding I with partners | Crowding I with others |
|---|---|---|---|---|---|---|---|---|---|
| logSales | 1 | | | | | | | | |
| logRD | 0.8141 | 1 | | | | | | | |
| Selfcit | 0.1165 | 0.1523 | 1 | | | | | | |
| Age | 0.4884 | 0.5251 | 0.2599 | 1 | | | | | |
| Crowding | 0.0796 | 0.0775 | -0.0917 | -0.0280 | 1 | | | | |
| Crowding I | 0.0558 | 0.0518 | 0.3904 | 0.0893 | 0.2755 | 1 | | | |
| Crowding non I | 0.0693 | 0.0680 | -0.1892 | -0.0506 | 0.9729 | 0.0459 | 1 | | |
| Crowding I with partners | 0.4495 | 0.4270 | 0.1972 | 0.3260 | 0.0757 | 0.1975 | 0.0311 | 1 | |
| Crowding I with others | 0.0148 | 0.0128 | 0.3776 | 0.0603 | 0.2724 | 0.9958 | 0.0437 | 0.1075 | 1 |

*Table 5.10    Dependent variable: INNOVATION (number of patents),*
*negative binomial, random effects*

|  | (1) | (2) | (3) | (4) |
|---|---|---|---|---|
| CROWDING | | 0.112 | | |
| | | [0.035]*** | | |
| CROWDING I | | | −0.349 | |
| | | | [0.171]** | |
| CROWDING NON I | | | 0.147 | 0.146 |
| | | | [0.037]*** | [0.037]*** |
| CROWDING I WITH | | | | 2.119 |
| PARTNERS | | | | [1.232]* |
| CROWDING I NOT | | | | −0.435 |
| WITH PARTNERS | | | | [0.181]** |
| SALES (log sales) | 0.265 | 0.251 | 0.250 | 0.242 |
| | [0.025]*** | [0.025]*** | [0.026]*** | [0.026]*** |
| SELF CITATION | 0.014 | 0.018 | 0.021 | 0.021 |
| (per cent of) | [0.003]*** | [0.003]*** | [0.003]*** | [0.004]*** |
| AGE (years from | 0.001 | 0.001 | 0.002 | 0.002 |
| foundation) | [0.002] | [0.002] | [0.002] | [0.002] |
| y91 | 0.072 | 0.051 | 0.053 | 0.042 |
| | [0.098] | [0.098] | [0.097] | [0.096] |
| y92 | 0.102 | 0.085 | 0.099 | 0.095 |
| | [0.097] | [0.097] | [0.096] | [0.095] |
| y93 | 0.183 | 0.152 | 0.160 | 0.151 |
| | [0.095]* | [0.094] | [0.094]* | [0.093] |
| y94 | 0.264 | 0.245 | 0.252 | 0.245 |
| | [0.093]*** | [0.092]*** | [0.092]*** | [0.091]*** |
| y95 | 0.262 | 0.222 | 0.224 | 0.227 |
| | [0.092]*** | [0.092]** | [0.092]** | [0.091]** |
| y96 | 0.251 | 0.234 | 0.241 | 0.234 |
| | [0.091]*** | [0.091]** | [0.091]*** | [0.090]*** |
| y97 | 0.235 | 0.199 | 0.206 | 0.199 |
| | [0.091]*** | [0.091]** | [0.091]** | [0.089]** |
| y98 | 0.320 | 0.284 | 0.292 | 0.283 |
| | [0.090]*** | [0.090]*** | [0.089]*** | [0.088]*** |
| Constant | −3.353 | −3.336 | −3.362 | −3.250 |
| | [0.331]*** | [0.332]*** | [0.334]*** | [0.339]*** |
| Observations | 1571 | 1508 | 1500 | 1500 |
| Number of id | 259 | 255 | 255 | 255 |

*Note:*   Standard errors in brackets; * significant at 10%; ** significant at 5%;
*** significant at 1%

*Table 5.11*   *Dependent variable: INNOVATION (number of patents),*
               *negative binomial, fixed effects*

|                        | (1)          | (2)          | (3)          | (4)          |
|------------------------|--------------|--------------|--------------|--------------|
| CROWDING               |              | 0.093        |              |              |
|                        |              | [0.040]**    |              |              |
| CROWDING I             |              |              | −0.413       |              |
|                        |              |              | [0.182]**    |              |
| CROWDING NON I         |              |              | 0.138        | 0.136        |
|                        |              |              | [0.042]***   | [0.042]***   |
| CROWDING I WITH        |              |              |              | 1.792        |
| PARTNERS               |              |              |              | [1.322]      |
| CROWDING I NOT         |              |              |              | −0.490       |
| WITH PARTNERS          |              |              |              | [0.192]**    |
| SALES (log sales)      | 0.202        | 0.190        | 0.187        | 0.178        |
|                        | [0.030]***   | [0.030]***   | [0.030]***   | [0.031]***   |
| SELF CITATION          | 0.012        | 0.015        | 0.019        | 0.018        |
| (per cent of)          | [0.004]***   | [0.004]***   | [0.004]***   | [0.004]***   |
| AGE (years from        | 0.002        | 0.002        | 0.002        | 0.002        |
| Foundation)            | [0.002]      | [0.002]      | [0.002]      | [0.002]      |
| y91                    | 0.095        | 0.077        | 0.077        | 0.069        |
|                        | [0.103]      | [0.102]      | [0.102]      | [0.101]      |
| y92                    | 0.124        | 0.109        | 0.125        | 0.122        |
|                        | [0.101]      | [0.101]      | [0.101]      | [0.100]      |
| y93                    | 0.215        | 0.188        | 0.196        | 0.188        |
|                        | [0.099]**    | [0.099]*     | [0.098]**    | [0.098]*     |
| y94                    | 0.323        | 0.308        | 0.314        | 0.309        |
|                        | [0.097]***   | [0.097]***   | [0.096]***   | [0.096]***   |
| y95                    | 0.338        | 0.300        | 0.302        | 0.306        |
|                        | [0.097]***   | [0.097]***   | [0.097]***   | [0.096]***   |
| y96                    | 0.322        | 0.307        | 0.312        | 0.307        |
|                        | [0.096]***   | [0.096]***   | [0.096]***   | [0.095]***   |
| y97                    | 0.310        | 0.279        | 0.283        | 0.279        |
|                        | [0.096]***   | [0.096]***   | [0.096]***   | [0.095]***   |
| y98                    | 0.396        | 0.364        | 0.369        | 0.365        |
|                        | [0.096]***   | [0.096]***   | [0.095]***   | [0.095]***   |
| Constant               | −2.523       | −2.482       | −2.494       | −2.376       |
|                        | [0.388]***   | [0.392]***   | [0.394]***   | [0.401]***   |
| Observations           | 1503         | 1426         | 1419         | 1419         |
| Number of id           | 230          | 219          | 219          | 219          |

*Note:*   Standard errors in brackets; * significant at 10%; ** significant at 5%;
*** significant at 1%

have controlled for firm size to account for scale effects in the production of patents, using the value of sales (i.e. *logSales*).[2] Third, the model includes a year dummy variable to account for a variety of economic factors that could vary over time, but have a common effect on the propensity of organizations to patent (i.e. $X$ is a matrix of the annual dummies, and $\gamma'$ is the vector of parameter estimates). Finally, we control for firm hetero-geneity using its age (i.e. *AGE*). Both *logSales* and *Selfcit* coefficients are significant and they have a positive sign. Firms of greater size innovate more, and the cumulative strategy of knowledge search gives better results in terms of number of patents.

Model 2 (equation 5.9) adds the measure of crowding as defined by Stuart and colleagues.

$$\text{INNOVATION}_{i,t}+_1 = \exp\,(\alpha + \beta_1 * log(Sales_{i,t}) + \beta_2 * Selfcit_{i,t}$$

$$+ \beta_3 * AGE_{i,t} + \beta_4 * C_{i,t} + \gamma'X + e_{i,t}) \qquad (5.9)$$

$C_{i,t}$ is the crowding of organization $i$'s niche in the technological network at time $t$. As in Stuart (1999), we get a significant positive sign of *crowding*.

In the third model specification equation 5.10, the variable crowding has been separated into the two parts as were described in section 3. In this way, it is possible to discriminate between the identities of the firms responsible for the cited patents, and therefore to discriminate whether crowding occurs on a firm's own knowledge base (i.e. variable $I$) or on other firms' knowledge bases (i.e. variable $NI$).

$$\text{INNOVATION}_{i,t}+_1 = \exp\,(\alpha + \beta_1 * log(Sales_{i,t}) + \beta_2 * Selfcit_{i,t}$$

$$+ \beta_3 * AGE_{i,t} + \beta_3 * I_{i,t} + \beta_4 * NI_{i,t} + \gamma'X + e_{i,t})\,(5.10)$$

As we expected, the former coefficient, $\beta_3$, is negative while $NI_i$ has a posi-tive effect on firm $i$'s innovative performance. Higher levels of crowding on a firm's own knowledge base are likely to hinder its innovative perform-ance because of the competition effect resulting from other organizations trying to exploit spillovers leaking out from its stock of ideas.

Finally, the fourth specification equation 5.11 considers if the crowd-ing on firm $i$'s technological base (i.e. variable $I_i$ of previous specification) involves firms that are partners in some strategic alliance (i.e. $IA_i$) or not (i.e. $INA_i$).

$$\text{INNOVATION}_{i,t}+_1 = \exp\,(\alpha + \beta_1 * log(Sales_{i,t}) + \beta2 * Selfcit_{i,t}$$

$$+ \beta3 * AGE_{i,t} + \beta4 * NI_{i,t} + \beta5 * IA_{i,t} + \beta6 * INA_{i,t} + \gamma'X + e_{i,t})\,(5.11)$$

As we expected, we found a negative effect on a firm's innovative performance only when the overlap occurs with competing firms, while the impact
is positive when overlap takes place with allied firms.[3]

## 6.   CONCLUSIONS

This chapter inquires empirically about different knowledge search strategies in crowded technological sectors, taking into account competitive
effects and cooperative behaviour. Furthermore, we relate this analysis
with the R&D collaboration activities of the examined firms.

In order to do that, the chapter combines patent citations and strategic
alliances data for a sample of 272 publicly traded companies operating in
the electronics industry in the 1990s. In particular, patent co-citation data
are used to investigate the extent to which the pattern of search for new
knowledge overlaps across companies.

The main focus is on the impact on innovativeness of a search strategy
based on the exploitation of a firm's own technological base. We show that
search strategies based on the cumulative exploitation of a firm's own stock
of knowledge are positively related to the firms' rate of innovation. But
our results show also that this positive effect is moderated by the negative
effect arising from competition with other organizations trying to exploit
the same knowledge base of the focal firm. Finally, the results obtained
show a possible solution to this problem: a firm that has its knowledge set
crowded by too many competitors searching in its technological space may
join an R&D collaboration and thus reduce the intensity of competition
and, in this way, increase its rate of technological innovation.

## NOTES

1.   The numbers of firms were originally 391. We had to exclude 46 firms because of missing
     data.
2.   A better alternative would be that of using R&D spending data. The problem is that the
     time series for R&D data contains more missing values, thereby reducing the number of
     observations. Moreover, the high correlation existing between annual sales and R&D
     expenditures suggests that controlling for sales is a fairly good approximation to control-
     ling for R&D expenditures.
3.   In the case of regressions with fixed effects (Table 5.11), the coefficient of $IA_i$ is not stati-
     cally significant. However the sign is the expected one.

# BIBLIOGRAPHY

Afuah, A. (2000), '"How much do your competitors' capabilities matter in the face of technological change", *Strategic Management Journal*, **21**, 387–404.

Ahuja, G. (2000), "Collaboration networks, structural holes, and innovation: a longitudinal study", *Administrative Science Quarterly*, **45**, 425–55.

Borgatti, S.P., C. Jones and M.G. Everett (1998), "Network measures of social capital", *Connections*, **21** (2), 27–36.

Burt, R.S. (1992), *Structural Holes. The Social Structure of Competition*, Cambridge, MA: Harvard University Press.

Burt, R.S. (2001), "Structural holes versus network closure as social capital", in N. Lin, K. Cook and R.S. Burt (eds), *Social Capital: Theory and Research*, New York: Aldine de Gruyter.

Dutta, S. and A.M. Weiss (1997), "The relationship between a firm's level of technological innovativeness and its pattern of partnership agreements", *Management Science*, **43** (3), 343–56.

Edquist, C. (ed.) (1997), *Systems of Innovations: Technologies, Institutions and Organisations*, London: Pinter Publishers.

Granovetter, M. (1985), "Economic action and social structure: a theory of embeddedness", *American Journal of Sociology*, **91**, 481–510.

Gulati, R. (1999), "Network location and learning: the influence of network resources and firm capabilities on alliance formation', *Strategic Management Journal*, **20** (5), 397–420.

Hagedoorn, J. and J. Schakenraad (1994), "The effect of strategic technology alliances on company performance", *Strategic Management Journal*, **15** (4), 291–311.

Kale, P., H. Singh and H. Perlmutter (2000), "Learning and protection of proprietary assets in strategic alliances: building relational capital", *Strategic Management Journal*, **21**, 217–37.

Lam, A. (1997), "Embedded firms, embedded knowledge: problems of collaboration and knowledge transfer in global cooperative ventures", *Organization Studies*, **18** (6), 973–96.

Lundvall, B.-Å. (ed.) (1993), *National Innovation Systems: Towards a Theory of Innovation and Interactive Learning*, London: Pinter Publishers.

Mowery, D.C., J.E. Oxley and B.S. Silverman (1996), "Strategic alliances and inter-firm knowledge transfer", *Strategic Management Journal*, **17**, 77–91.

Nelson, R. and S. Winter (1982), *An Evolutionary Theory of Economic Change*, Cambridge, MA: Harvard University Press.

Newman, M.E.J. (2001), "The structure of scientific collaboration networks", *Proceedings of the National Academy of Science USA*, **98**, 404–9.

Podolny, J.M. and K.L. Page (1998), "Network forms of organisation", *Annual Review of Sociology*, **24**, 57–76.

Podolny, J.M. and T.E. Stuart (1995), "A role-based ecology of technological change", *American Journal of Sociology*, **100** (5), March, 1224–60.

Podolny, J.M., T.E. Stuart and M.T. Hannan (1996), "Networks, knowledge, and niches: competition in the worldwide semiconductor industry, 1984–1991", *American Journal of Sociology*, **102** (3), November, 659–89.

Powell, W. and P. Brantley (1992), 'Competitive cooperation in biotechnology: learning through networks?', in N. Nohria and R Eccles (eds), *Networks and Organizations*, Boston, MA: Harvard Business School Press.

Powell, W., K.W. Koput and L. Smith-Doerr (1996), "Interorganizational collaboration and the locus of innovation: networks of learning in biotechnology", *Administrative Science Quarterly*, **41**, 116–45.

Rosenkopf, L. and P. Almeida (2003), "Overcoming local search through alliances and mobility", *Management Science*, **49**, 751–66.

Rowley, T., D. Behrens and D. Krackhardt (2000), "Redundant governance structures: an analysis of structural and relational embeddedness in the steel and semiconductor industries", *Strategic Management Journal*, **21**, 369–86.

Shan, W., G. Walker and B. Kogut (1994), "Interfirm cooperation and startup innovation in the biotechnology industry", *Strategic Management Journal*, **15** (5), June, 387–94.

Stuart, T.E. (1998), "Network positions and propensities to collaborate: an investigation of strategic alliance formation in a high-technology industry", *Administrative Science Quarterly*, **43**, 668–98.

Stuart, T.E. (1999), "A structural perspective on organizational innovation", *Industrial and Corporate Change*, **8** (4), 745–75.

Stuart, T.E. (2000), "Interorganizational alliances and the performance of firms: a study of growth and innovative rates in a high-technology industry", *Strategic Management Journal*, **21**, 791–811.

Stuart, T.E. and J.M. Podolny (1996), "Local search and the evolution of technological capabilities", *Strategic Management Journal*, **17**, Summer, 21–38.

Tushman, M.L. and P. Anderson (1986), "Technological discontinuities and organizational environments", *Administrative Science Quarterly*, **31**, 439–65.

Uzzi, B. (1996), "The sources and consequences of embeddedness for the economic performance of organizations: the network effect", *American Sociological Review*, **61**, 674–98.

Walker, G., B. Kogut and W. Shan (1997), "Social capital, structural holes and the formation of an industry network", *Organization Science*, **8** (2), March–April, 109–25.

# 6. Partnership networks and knowledge networks in five sectors[1]

**Koichiro Okamura and Nicholas S. Vonortas**

## 1. INTRODUCTION

Industry analysis has been a field of rich study in economics. Two strands of literature can be distinguished here. One is rooted in the formal industrial organization tradition and has concentrated on the study of sectoral characteristics, including sectoral structure in terms of concentration, vertical integration, diversification; the dynamics of sectors in terms of technical progress, entry, firm growth, and so on; and strategic behavior (e.g. Caves, 1998; Scherer and Ross, 1990). This literature comes closest to the subject at hand in the theory of the firm, especially the development of the concepts of incomplete contracting which underlies a lot of the issues in partnership organization.[2] The analyses in this approach have, however, paid scant attention to knowledge and learning processes, institutional factors, the wide range of interactions among agents, and the transformation of sectors in terms of their boundaries, agents, and products.

The second strand of economic-based, industry analysis literature provides rich empirical evidence on the characteristics of sectors, on their technologies, production features, innovation, demand, and on the type and degree of change. In recent years, significant efforts have been undertaken internationally to provide a multidimensional, integrated and dynamic view of sectors, combining important elements from both analytical traditions described above in order to advance the concept of sectoral systems of innovation and production (Malerba, 2004). The basic analytical foundations underlying this work follow the traditions in evolutionary theory (Dosi, 1988; Nelson, 1995) and systems of innovation (Edquist, 1997). The important aspect of this work is its concern with all stages of industry evolution, from inception through maturity. The approach is quantitative and formal (with the development of history-friendly models of industry evolution), as well as qualitative and "appreciative," in that it focuses on several aspects such as learning, knowledge base, competencies, and relationships among agents. In general, the basic elements of a sectoral system could be identified as the following:

- Products.
- Agents (including both firms and other organizations such as universities, financial institutions, etc.).
- Knowledge and learning processes.
- Basic technologies, inputs, demand, and the related links and complementarities.
- Mechanisms of interactions both within and between firms and outside of firms (including market and non market interactions).
- Processes of competition and selection.
- Institutions (rules, norms, etc.).

This analytical approach enables rich conceptualizations of sector birth, death, and turbulence while linking these directly to different market structures and different patterns of innovation. An important role is played by the learning environment in terms of different technological regimes characterized by various degrees of technological opportunity, appropriability, cumulativeness, and properties of the knowledge base and learning processes (Malerba and Orsenigo, 1996; Gambardella and Malerba, 1999). During the past few years, this strand of literature has produced a focused attempt to create stylized arguments of industry evolution through "history-friendly models" (Malerba and Orsenigo, 2002; Malerba et al., 1999, 2001; Pyka and Saviotti, 2002; Kim and Lee, 2003). Such models hold great promise in developing firm understandings of industry evolution.

This work is also informed by an important strand of theoretical and empirical literature on industry evolution, initiated in the late 1960s by Mueller and Tilton (1969), and in Abernathy and Utterback (1975, 1978) (see Utterback, 1994, for a synthesis). Work in industry evolution has continued with numerous important contributions, as can be seen, for example, in Carlsson (1995), Gort and Klepper (1982), and Klepper (1996, 2002).

This popular, stylized argument of industry evolution suggests a strong expectation that exploration may be predominant in early (fluid) stages of industry/technology evolution, a mixture of exploration and exploitation in middle stages, and exploitation dominating the later stages of evolution of an industry. Such distribution sounds plausible given the following description of the features of exploration and exploitation by Nooteboom and Gilsing (2004, pp. 9–10):

> [I]n exploration, there is uncertainty about which technical standards will later yield a "dominant design," there is much volatility of prototyping, the emphasis in competition lies on technical feasibility and a "race to the market," there is

a great deal of trial and error, and knowledge is often highly tacit. In exploitation, technical development has consolidated in a dominant design, uncertainty in demand and supply has subsided, knowledge becomes more codified and diffused, new players and customers enter into the emerging market, competition shifts to efficient production and distribution, and the emphasis shifts to a new dominant design in organization.

With this background in mind, a natural question to ask is whether there are distinguishing features between sectors in terms of their innovation-related networking activity. For instance, given a set of sectors, one can consider:

- What has been the nature of the knowledge and partnership networks during a specific time period in the different sectors under investigation?
- Are there broad differences between the knowledge and partnership networks?
- Are there varying sectoral differences within each of these two types of networks?
- Do such networks establish effective channels of knowledge communication of different intensity across sectors?
- How do companies position strategically in these networks and how does positioning differ across sectors?

The study of innovation networks in different sectoral environments, however, has barely begun. In this chapter we present a preliminary analysis addressing such questions in five industrial sectors: pharmaceuticals, plastics, computers, electronics, and instruments. We analyze two types of networks in each sector: knowledge networks, based on patent citations; and partnership networks, based on technology partnerships. The principal objective of the analysis is to characterize virtual (knowledge) and real (partnership) networks in these sectors and the strategic positioning of firms and companies in them.

Our focus is on collaborative exchange in predefined industrial sectors. We classify the activity instead of the organization. That is to say, the examined knowledge and partnership networks are not the complete networks of the organizations that can be classified in the predefined sectors on the basis of their production. Rather, they are the inter-organizational networks constructed on the basis of the collaborative activities of these organizations that can be classified in these five sectors, irrespective of the organization's sectoral classification. For example, an electronics company can be part of the pharmaceuticals knowledge network if it owns a pharmaceuticals patent, and that same firm can be part of the pharmaceuticals partnership network if it has participated in a partnership classified in the pharmaceuticals area.

Our evaluation uses social network analysis tools such as graph density, average degree and distance, graph betweenness, number and size of components, graph diameter, degree distribution, clustering, small world concepts, technology crowding coefficients, and power centrality indexes. All of these tools previously have been utilized in the sociological, economic, and business literature to characterize networks and approximate organizational positioning in them.[3] What this study adds to the literature is the combination of the use of many such analytical tools in a cross-sectoral, cross-regional, two-network-type investigation.

The analysis is based on two extensive datasets constructed by two research teams at CESPRI (Bocconi University) and MERIT (University of Maastricht). The dataset underlying the knowledge network includes 1279 companies that applied for at least one patent classified in one of the five sectors in question during the time period 1996–99. The dataset underlying the partnership network includes 513 companies that participated in at least one publicly announced technology partnership classified in these five sectors during the same time period.

The investigation indicates that the social network methodology is a useful analytical approach for comprehending the social/competitive context within which companies operate. In particular, three sets of results are worth noting and require further attention:

1.  There is an apparent difference in the networking behavior in pharmaceuticals vis-à-vis networking behavior in computers, electronics, and instruments.
2.  There is an apparent difference between knowledge and partnership networks across all sectors in terms of their effectiveness as channels for knowledge communication.
3.  There is an apparent difference in the competitive positioning of European firms and firms from the United States and Japan in the knowledge networks across the examined industrial sectors.

## 2.  DATA DESCRIPTION

The knowledge network reflects the linkages between firms through patent citations for patents issued to them by the European Patent Office (EPO) during the period 1996–99. The patent citation data at the firm level have been constructed by CESPRI using its EP-CESPRI data set.[4] The partnership network reflects the linkages between firms through their participation in technology-based partnerships announced during the same time period (1996–99). By construction, the recorded partnerships are Euro-centric in the sense that they involve at least one European organization. The partnership data at the firm level have been constructed at MERIT using the CATI database.[5]

The two networks are constructed as shown in Figures 6.1 and 6.2. Regarding the knowledge network, we use patent citations to determine linkages between companies. The right-hand side of Figure 6.1 shows the basic observations. For example, a patent of company 1 cites a patent of company 3. The bottom left-hand side shows the actual data that the network records: companies 1 and 3 are linked once. The arrows shown in the citations are omitted in the analyzed network. A link is created between two firms (nodes) if there exists at least one citation between their patents classified in a sector, regardless of both the citation direction and the overall number of citations. Often, firms cite their own past patents (self-citation), resulting in self-loops in a network. Self-loops are discarded in the network analysis. In sum, the patent citation data are converted into an undirected, unweighted binary graph without self-loops.

The way we build our networks misses out on two potentially important pieces of information. First, the arrows in Figure 6.1 have been interpreted

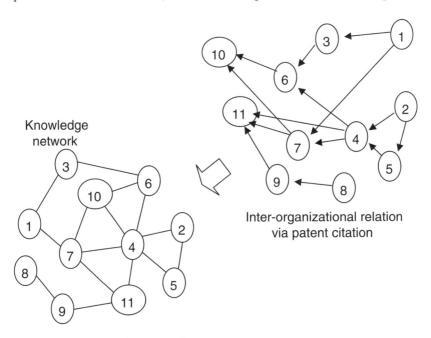

*Figure 6.1   Knowledge network*

Partnerships

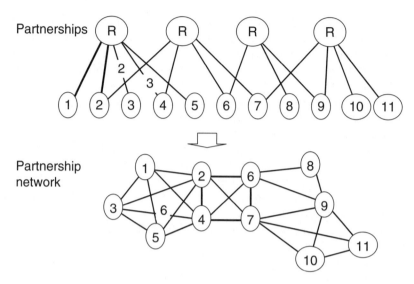

*Figure 6.2    Partnership network*

previously in the literature as indicators of the direction of knowledge flow (from the cited patent holder to the citing patent holder). We cannot say anything about the direction of knowledge flows in this chapter. Second, the number of citations has been interpreted previously as an indicator of the strength of knowledge flow. Discarded for analytical simplicity here, these pieces of information may have important implications regarding the extent of network concentration and the role of individual organizations in these networks.

Regarding the partnership network, we use partnership participation to determine linkages among companies. The upper part of Figure 6.2 shows the basic observations (with R indicating partnerships and numbers indicating companies). For example, company 4 participates in partnerships 1 and 2 and is thus linked to companies 1, 2, 3, 5, 6, 7. A link is created between two firms (nodes) if they participate in the same partnership, regardless of the number of shared memberships between these two companies. If multiple divisions or subsidiaries of a firm participate in the same partnership, self-loops occur. These are discarded in this analysis. Partnership data are converted into an undirected, unweighted binary graph without self-loops.[6]

Firms become part of a sectoral knowledge network if they have applied for at least one patent that can be classified in that sector during the examined time period. The network considers citations between patents registered in a particular industrial sector. Firms become part of the sectoral partnership network if they have participated in at least one partnership that can be classified in that sector during the examined time period. The network considers linkages between companies participating in partnerships registered in a particular industrial sector. The concordance between the original patent classification and the corresponding standard industrial classification (SIC), as well as concordance between the original partnership classification and the corresponding SIC, are shown in Table 6.1.

The knowledge and partnership networks are analyzed independently. That is, while there is a significant overlap between them in terms of participating firms, the underlying datasets were constructed independently and kept this way for the needs of this analysis.[7] Table 6.2 shows the number of firms that make up the knowledge and partnership networks of each of the five industrial sectors on the basis of the classification in Table 6.1. Clearly, knowledge networks are "thicker" across all sectors. Partnership networks are non-existent in plastics and quite "thin" (sparse) in computers and scientific instruments (affecting the reliability of the results reported in subsequent sections). Both the knowledge and partnership networks in pharmaceuticals are much more heavily populated than the networks in other sectors.

Tables 6.3–6.5 describe the data underlying the knowledge network. Table 6.3 shows the number of patents by industrial sector, indicating the dominant presence of pharmaceuticals (32 percent of all citing and cited patents). Table 6.4 shows the citation flow between sectors: again, pharmaceuticals are far ahead. As expected, the diagonal elements are larger: the majority of citations are intra-sector citations. We only use intra-sector

*Table 6.1   Industrial sector concordance*

| Sector | SIC code | Knowledge network | Partnership network |
|--------|----------|-------------------|---------------------|
| Pharmaceuticals | 2834 | Organic chemistry Drugs Biotechnology | Pharmaceuticals |
| Plastics | 2821 | Polymers | Polymers |
| Computers | 3571 3572 3575 | Information technology | Computers |
| Electronics | 3661 3663 | Telecommunications | Telecom |
|  | 3674 | Semiconductors | Microelectronics |
| Instruments | 3826 3827 | Medical technology Optics Control technology | Instrumentation |

*Table 6.2    Number of firms by industrial sector*

| Sector | Knowledge network | Partnership network |
|---|---|---|
| Pharmaceuticals | 638 | 252 |
| Plastics | 252 | 0 |
| Computers | 189 | 35 |
| Electronics | 266 | 140 |
| Instruments | 503 | 33 |
| Other | 107 | 93 |
| Total | 1279 | 513 |

*Note:* The numbers in each column do not sum up to the "total" because some firms are active in more than one industrial sector. The category "other" includes firms that registered at least one patent or had a partnership in sectors beyond the five studied here.

*Table 6.3    Number of patents by industrial sector*

| | Pharmaceuticals | Plastics | Computers | Electronics | Instruments | Other | Total |
|---|---|---|---|---|---|---|---|
| Number of citing patents | 17 583 | 4 288 | 1 655 | 5 941 | 5 515 | 19 663 | 54 645 |
| Number of cited patents | 16 107 | 4 394 | 1 678 | 5 564 | 5 131 | 17 547 | 50 421 |

*Table 6.4    Citation flow between industrial sectors*

| Citing\cited | Pharmaceutical | Plastics | Computers | Electronics | Instruments | Other | Total |
|---|---|---|---|---|---|---|---|
| Pharma | 17 388 | 347 | 4 | 5 | 208 | 1 020 | 18 972 |
| Plastics | 283 | 3 607 | 4 | 9 | 90 | 508 | 4 501 |
| Computers | 1 | 3 | 1 352 | 129 | 85 | 102 | 1 672 |
| Electronics | 4 | 18 | 173 | 5 402 | 197 | 260 | 6 054 |
| Instruments | 199 | 160 | 146 | 178 | 4 450 | 627 | 5 760 |
| Other | 1 448 | 780 | 129 | 254 | 632 | 17 498 | 20 741 |
| Total | 19 323 | 4 915 | 1 808 | 5 977 | 5 662 | 20 015 | 57 700 |

citations in order to make the analysis consistent with the definitions of industrial sectors in the chapter. The numbers of patents and citations by industry satisfying these criteria are shown in Table 6.5. For example, 11 628 patents have made 10 609 citations to 12 292 patents in the pharmaceuticals knowledge network.

Finally, Tables 6.6 and 6.7 describe the data underlying the partnership network. Table 6.6 shows that the vast majority of recorded partnerships

*Table 6.5   Number of citing patents, cited patents and citations*

|  | Pharmaceutical | Plastics | Computers | Electronics | Instruments |
|---|---|---|---|---|---|
| Number of citing patents | 11 628 | 2 403 | 1 261 | 4 841 | 3 331 |
| Number of cited patents | 12 292 | 2 497 | 1 273 | 4 940 | 3 463 |
| Number of citations | 10 609 | 2 272 | 1 185 | 4 609 | 3 179 |

*Table 6.6   Partnerships by number of participants*

| Number of participants | Pharmaceutical | Plastics | Computers | Electronics | Instruments | Other | Total |
|---|---|---|---|---|---|---|---|
| 2 | 229 | 0 | 20 | 84 | 15 | 94 | 434 |
| 3 | 5 | 0 | 1 | 4 | 1 | 9 | 19 |
| 4 | 1 | 0 | 1 | 7 | 0 | 2 | 10 |
| 5 | 0 | 0 | 0 | 2 | 1 | 0 | 3 |
| 6–10 | 1 | 0 | 0 | 2 | 0 | 1 | 4 |
| Total | 236 | 0 | 22 | 99 | 17 | 106 | 470 |

*Note:*   Row sums are not necessarily equal to the sum of the number of partnerships by sector because some partnerships belong to multiple industrial sectors.

in all sectors involve only two partners. Pharmaceuticals again appear with a dominant presence: this sector accounts for almost half of all recorded partnerships. Table 6.7 shows the distribution of firms by the number of partnership memberships. More than two-thirds of firms participate in only one partnership. Few firms participate in more than five partnerships. Unfortunately, these tables indicate that the partnership data are thinner (more sparse) than we would prefer, with the exception of pharmaceuticals. There is no partnership network in plastics.

The knowledge (patent) and partnership networks of the five sectors are visualized in Figures 6.3–6.11.

## 3.   SECTORAL NETWORK ANALYSIS

### Topological Characteristics of the Knowledge and Partnership Networks

System-level analysis requires assumptions about the nature of the inter-actions between nodes (firms), and the assessment of network properties

*Table 6.7     Firms by number of partnership memberships*

| Number of memberships | Pharma- ceuticals | Plastics | Computers | Electronics | Instruments | Other | Total |
|---|---|---|---|---|---|---|---|
| 1 | 175 | 0 | 29 | 114 | 28 | 107 | 365 |
| 2 | 39 | 0 | 3 | 9 | 5 | 19 | 62 |
| 3 | 12 | 0 | 1 | 7 | 0 | 9 | 36 |
| 4 | 6 | 0 | 1 | 3 | 0 | 4 | 12 |
| 5 | 3 | 0 | 1 | 0 | 0 | 2 | 9 |
| 6–10 | 12 | 0 | 0 | 5 | 0 | 5 | 17 |
| 11–20 | 5 | 0 | 0 | 2 | 0 | 0 | 9 |
| 21 or more | 0 | 0 | 0 | 0 | 0 | 0 | 3 |
| Total firms | 252 | 0 | 35 | 140 | 33 | 146 | 513 |
| Total memberships | 487 | 0 | 47 | 233 | 38 | 231 | 1013 |

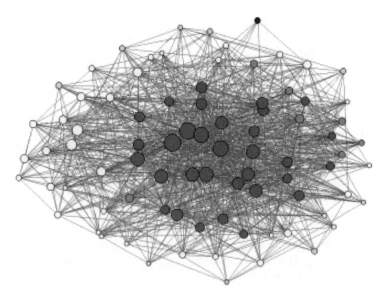

*Note:*   Node size represents the number of links with others: more links, larger nodes.

*Figure 6.3     Knowledge network: pharmaceuticals (degree centrality threshold: 20)*

*Note:* All nodes are displayed. Node size represents the number of links with others: more links, larger nodes.

*Figure 6.4    Partnership network: pharmaceuticals*

depends on these assumptions. Unfortunately, we lack detailed information about both the knowledge gained by a particular patent citation and the relationship between partners in individual partnerships. The default assumption for the knowledge network is that all citations are real and intentional channels of useful technical knowledge. The default assumption for partnerships is that all members of an agreement are connected directly to all other members of the same agreement. That is to say, an individual partnership is treated as a clique, and links are assumed to exist between all pairs of organizations that are part of the partnership.

In this section, we derive a number of indicators that previously have been applied widely in the network literature (Breschi and Cusmano, 2003; Newman, 2001; Wagner et al., 2004). The main topological features of the knowledge and partnership networks in the five examined sectors are shown in Tables 6.8–6.10.

There are various measures of social distance among organizations. One such measure is *connectedness*, referring to organizations belonging to the same component or being located in disconnected components. A component is a subset of the entire graph such that there is some path connecting any two nodes in it but no path connecting nodes inside the component

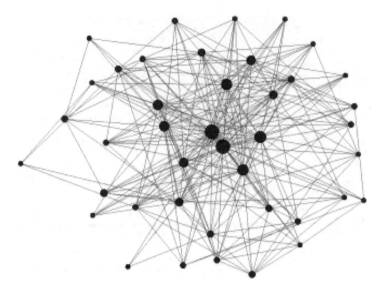

*Note:* The network is drawn in the same manner as Figure 6.3.

*Figure 6.5 Knowledge network: plastics (degree centrality threshold: 10)*

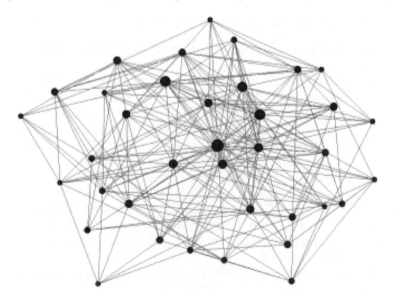

*Note:* The network is drawn in the same manner as Figure 6.3.

*Figure 6.6 Knowledge network: computers (degree centrality threshold: 10)*

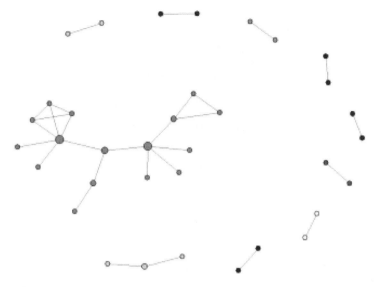

*Note:* The network is drawn in the same manner as Figure 6.4.

*Figure 6.7   Partnership network: computers*

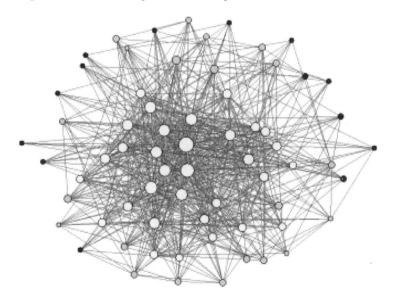

*Note:* The network is drawn in the same manner as Figure 6.3.

*Figure 6.8   Knowledge network: electronics (degree centrality threshold: 10)*

*Note:* The network is drawn in the same manner as Figure 6.4.

*Figure 6.9   Partnership network: electronics*

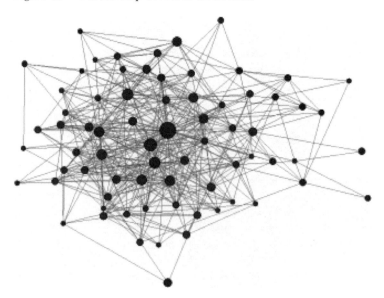

*Note:* The network is drawn in the same manner as Figure 6.3.

*Figure 6.10   Knowledge network: instruments (degree centrality threshold: 10)*

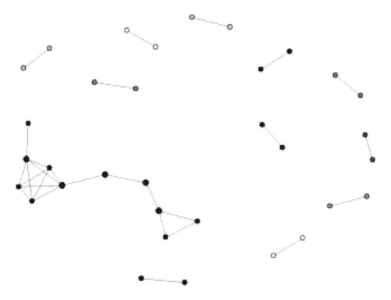

*Note:* The network is drawn in the same manner as Figure 6.4.

*Figure 6.11    Partnership network: instruments*

with those outside. Another measure is the *geodesic distance*, defined as the minimum number of steps (links/edges/degrees) that separate two distinct organizations in the network. Moreover, some organizations stand out in terms of the number of links they exhibit (*degree centrality*), whereas others may be particularly useful for serving as gateways between organizations or groups of organizations (*betweenness centrality*).

The above measures are aggregated to the network level. Several of them provide indications of the degree of closeness of the connections between organizations in the network, including graph density, average degree (path length) and distance. Close linkages suggest the facilitation of knowledge diffusion and local search, and the knowledge network is found to be highly connected (Table 6.8). There are very few components in each sector: only one in electronics, two in both pharmaceuticals and plastics, three in computers, and seven in instruments. Interestingly, in each sectoral knowledge network all, or almost all, nodes belong to the largest component, while the remaining components are made up of disconnected company dyads. That is to say, there are paths connecting the identified firms to each other in a given sector in terms of inter-linking patent citations.

Hence, the characteristics of the largest component of the five sectoral

*Table 6.8    Knowledge network characteristics*

|  | Pharmaceuticals | Plastics | Computers | Electronics | Instruments |
|---|---|---|---|---|---|
| Number of nodes | 606 | 222 | 161 | 240 | 447 |
| Number of links | 3477 | 752 | 520 | 1245 | 1338 |
| Graph density | 0.0190 | 0.0307 | 0.0404 | 0.0434 | 0.0134 |
| Average degree | 11.4752 | 6.7748 | 6.4596 | 10.3750 | 5.9866 |
| Average distance | 2.7843 | 2.6150 | 2.7711 | 2.4586 | 3.2986 |
| Graph diameter | 7 | 6 | 6 | 6 | 8 |
| Graph betweenness | 0.1341 | 0.3015 | 0.2716 | 0.3687 | 0.3861 |
| Number of components | 2 | 2 | 3 | 1 | 7 |
| Number of nodes in the largest components | 604 | 220 | 157 | 240 | 435 |

*Note:* The number of nodes (firms) is smaller than in Table 6.2 because some citations do not pass the intra-sector citation criterion, and thus, some firms are dropped off from the analysis.

knowledge networks (Table 6.9) are more or less identical to those of the whole network (Table 6.8). One notices here that the average distance between two nodes remains practically unchanged from what it was in the whole network. Moreover, the paths are short: on average, a company can find any other in less than three steps in four sectors, and in a bit more than three steps in the instruments sector. Looking at network density – the proportion of potential links that have actually been observed – one observes electronics and computers as being ahead of the other sectors, with pharmaceuticals and instruments following last. When average degree is also factored in – the number of other nodes to which a node is connected directly – the electronics knowledge network appears to be connected the most closely.[8]

Graph betweenness captures the overall degree of concentration of critical connections to some nodes in the network. Generally speaking, the more organizations have direct connections with one another, the smaller is the graph betweenness. A large value for graph betweenness suggests a network core, a group of highly connected firms playing the role of "hub" or "gatekeeper," which may control the connections, and thus knowledge flow, between organizations. We find that pharmaceuticals have the smallest graph betweenness, implying that firms in that knowledge network are well connected with each other. Instruments, on the other hand, has the largest value, meaning it is the least connected network, depending relatively more on gatekeepers. Graph diameter – the maximum distance

*Table 6.9    Knowledge network characteristics: largest component*

|                     | Pharmaceuticals | Plastics | Computers | Electronics | Instruments |
|---------------------|-----------------|----------|-----------|-------------|-------------|
| Number of nodes     | 604             | 220      | 157       | 240         | 435         |
| Number of links     | 3476            | 751      | 518       | 1245        | 1332        |
| Graph density       | 0.0191          | 0.0312   | 0.0423    | 0.0434      | 0.0141      |
| Average degree      | 11.5099         | 6.8273   | 6.5987    | 10.3750     | 6.1241      |
| Average distance    | 2.7843          | 2.6151   | 2.7714    | 2.4586      | 3.2987      |
| Graph diameter      | 7               | 6        | 6         | 6           | 8           |
| Graph betweenness   | 0.1345          | 0.3070   | 0.2855    | 0.3688      | 0.4076      |

*Table 6.10    Partnership network characteristics*

|                                          | Pharmaceuticals | Plastics | Computers | Electronics | Instruments |
|------------------------------------------|-----------------|----------|-----------|-------------|-------------|
| Number of nodes                          | 252             | 0        | 35        | 140         | 33          |
| Number of links                          | 285             | –        | 29        | 185         | 28          |
| Graph density                            | 0.0090          | –        | 0.0487    | 0.0190      | 0.0530      |
| Average degree                           | 2.2619          | –        | 1.6571    | 2.6429      | 1.6970      |
| Average distance                         | 4.1816          | –        | 2.7710    | 3.3527      | 2.4394      |
| Graph diameter                           | 10              | –        | 5         | 7           | 6           |
| Graph betweenness                        | 0.1722          | –        | 0.1126    | 0.1368      | 0.04599     |
| Number of components                     | 32              | –        | 10        | 26          | 12          |
| Number of nodes in the largest component | 172             | –        | 16        | 86          | 11          |

between the nodes – confirms this observation: the distance in pharmaceuticals, the largest network among these five, is (marginally) smaller than in instruments and only marginally larger than the other sectors.

Table 6.10 shows the characteristics of the four available sectoral partnership networks. Partnership networks are much smaller than knowledge networks. For instance, instruments have only 33 nodes and 28 links. Also, they are not so highly connected, as is indicated by the relatively large number of components and, compared to knowledge networks, much lower percentage of nodes in the largest component. Firms in the partnership networks have many fewer direct links to others (average degree) compared to firms in knowledge networks, reflecting at least partly their relatively small network size. The highest average distance is registered by pharmaceuticals. Moreover, firms operating in the pharmaceuticals sector register significantly higher average and maximum distance (graph diameter) in partnership networks compared to knowledge networks. Contrary to all other sectors, graph betweenness in pharmaceuticals is higher in the partnership network than in the knowledge network.

All in all, partnership networks are more fragmented than knowledge networks in all investigated sectors. This clearly agrees with the visual representation of these networks in Figures 6.3–6.11. This general characteristic aside, firms in pharmaceuticals appear much more interconnected in terms of the knowledge network than the partnership network.

These results must be interpreted carefully. The partnership data underlying our sectoral networks were collected on the principle that, in order to be included in the mix, a partnership ought to include at least one European organization. In other words, our partnership networks are those of identified European firms and do not cover all partnerships in the selected fields. In fact, our networks do not cover the majority of publicly announced partnerships, which tend to be defined by US–US and US–Japan collaboration during the examined time period.

A property that has attracted attention in various types of networks is the *degree distribution*. It indicates the distribution of the probability $P(k)$ that a randomly selected node has $k$ links (degrees). It is commonly found in the literature that, for a sufficiently large $k$, the degree distribution of many networks follows the power law $P(k) \sim k^{-\gamma}$ and the power exponent $\gamma$ takes a value between $2.1 < \gamma < 4$, irrespective of the network origin (Barabási and Albert, 1999). Networks following a power law are referred to as *scale-free networks* since they lack a "typical" degree that represents the network's characteristics adequately (Willinger et al., 2002).

The calculation of the degree distributions of our sectoral knowledge and partnership networks shows that the majority of nodes in both types of networks and across all sectors with reasonably large numbers of observations have a small number of links, while some nodes have many. Such degree distribution follows the power law. The exponent values for our knowledge and partnership networks are lower than the typical ones in the literature, ranging between 1.0 and 1.8. Again, we may be running up against small numbers, especially in partnership networks: caution in interpretation is required.

**Network Robustness**

The knowledge network is found to be highly connected. The degree distribution has shown that a small set of firms account for a proportionally large number of links compared to the rest. We also examined whether connectivity is widely spread in the network or if it is sustained by those firms featuring large numbers of links and functioning as "hubs." We followed Breschi and Cusmano (2003) to test for network robustness by removing a small fraction (up to 12 percent) of nodes and observing the changes in three indices: diameter, average distance, and the size of the largest component. The change of these three indices was observed twice: when removing nodes randomly and when removing the most important nodes in terms of their direct connections (highest degree).

The knowledge network is found to be robust to the random removal of nodes across all industrial sectors. All three indices remain stable. In contrast, the knowledge network is vulnerable to the removal of the most connected nodes: the knowledge network clearly starts disintegrating when a fraction of the most connected nodes are removed. The explanation lies in the heterogeneity of the connectivity distribution: the majority of firms in the knowledge network have only a few links, whereas relatively few firms are much more connected. The removal of the latter seriously hampers the ability of the former to communicate with each other. The message here is that the overall connectivity of the knowledge network is maintained by a few important organizations, whereas the majority of the rest play little role in this respect.

We have applied the same test to the largest component of the partnership network in pharmaceuticals and electronics. Other sectoral partnership networks are too sparse to test for robustness. The general result remains: the partnership networks in these two sectors are robust to random node removal but they are quite vulnerable to the removal of the most connected nodes. In fact, the partnership network in pharmaceuticals disintegrates more quickly than the knowledge network, resulting in smaller values in all three indices. The partnership network in pharmaceuticals thus is more dependent on some highly connected firms than its corresponding knowledge network.

**Network Structure and Efficiency in Knowledge Flow**

One of the ways to evaluate the effectiveness of networks is by appraising their efficiency as channels for knowledge flow between the participating organizations (nodes) in the network. This is very important to determine given that information communication has been regarded in the network literature as a core benefit of participation in self-organized networks (Gulati, 1998; Vonortas, Chapter 2 in this volume). Interesting considerations with policy relevance arise here. For example, the finding of the previous section regarding the critical role of some highly connected firms in determining the connectivity among participants in both the knowledge and partnership networks begs the question of the specific nature of that role. Is the role of these firms critical because they link relatively isolated sub-graphs with high "local" connectivity? Or is their role critical in the absence of such "local" connection phenomena?

It has been argued strongly that networks featuring "*small world*" characteristics are relatively efficient in transmitting and sharing information (Cowan and Jonard, 2003; Verspagen, 2004). "Small worlds," characterized by high local clustering and relatively short distances between the nodes in the network, are seen by Verspagen (2004) as a way of uniting two distinct perspectives of network topology: social capital, high values of which are assumed to be represented by high clustering (Coleman, 1990); and structural holes, referring to the opportunities for bridging local clusters (Burt, 1992). In essence, it is argued that networks are efficient in transmitting information if tight local clusters (high social capital) are combined with relatively extensive bridging across clusters.

A network features *clustering* if the probability of a tie between two nodes is much greater when these two actors have one or more other mutual acquaintances. The clustering coefficient is constructed as follows. If $k_i$ is the degree of node $i$ (number of other nodes directly linked to $i$), and if all these nodes are all connected to one another (they form a fully connected clique), then there will be $k_i(k_i - 1)/2$ links. If $K_i$ is the number of links connecting the selected $k_i$ nodes to each other, the clustering coefficient for node $i$ is $C_i = 2K_i/k_i(k_i - 1)$. Thus, clustering can be considered as the amount of social capital in a local environment. The clustering coefficient for the whole network is the average of $C_i$ over all nodes in the system, indicating the extent to which the nodes linked to any node $i$ are, on average, linked to each other. That is to say, clustering at the level of the network as a whole is defined as the average of clustering of all neighborhoods $i$.

High clustering values – all one's friends' friends are also one's own friends – imply that it is difficult to reach an unknown target node (to disseminate information) if this node is not already in one's circle of friends. In other words, high clustering goes hand in hand with long characteristic path length, and vice versa (Verspagen, 2004). *Characteristic path length* is defined as the median of average path length of all nodes in the network. *Average path length* of a node is defined as the average length of the (shortest) paths to all other nodes in the network. Smaller values mean shorter distances between nodes, implying that knowledge is more easily and quickly diffused among organizations in the network.

Watts and Strogatz (1998) and Watts (1999) use these two indices to define a *"small world" network* as one lying between the two extremes: a network resembling the "connected caveman world" characterized by high clustering (high local density) and long characteristic path length; and a network resembling a "Moore's graph" characterized by low clustering (low local density) and short characteristic path length. In the terminology of Watts and Strogatz (1998), the "connected caveman world" and "Moore's graph" correspond to a regular network and to a random network, respectively. Consider the following process: starting with the regular network, each link is rewired at random with probability $p$. A random network is the outcome of the rewiring process at $p = 1$, while $p = 0$ corresponds to the regular network. The "small world" network is defined at an interval of $p$ between its regular and random network values where the characteristic path length is as small as that of a random graph but clustering is much greater than that of a regular graph. Many networks, including biological, technological, and social networks, are known to lie somewhere between regular and random networks.

The observed (actual) network characteristics have been compared with the characteristics of the random version of the network for all sectors, and for both knowledge and partnership networks. The random network was constructed in each case using similar values for the number of nodes and average degree to those actually observed.[9] Our calculations indicate that all five sectoral knowledge networks could be argued to be "small worlds." Actual and random networks have similar characteristic path lengths, but actual networks have a much larger clustering coefficient. However, the same cannot be argued for the sectoral partnership networks. Even though the clustering coefficients are significantly larger than those of the corresponding random networks, their characteristic path length is much smaller, especially in pharmaceuticals.

However, the large characteristic path length of the partnership random network could be the result of our treatment of the partnership network: when evaluating the random networks, we assumed that they consist of only one component even though the actual partnership networks were found to be highly fragmented.

In order to check the robustness of these findings we have recalculated the characteristic path length and the clustering coefficients for the largest components of both the sectoral knowledge networks and the sectoral partnership networks. The results for the knowledge networks barely change at all: the largest components are small worlds. In contrast, the results for the partnership networks change dramatically. While the clustering coefficients of the actual networks (largest component) remain significantly larger than those of the corresponding random networks, the characteristic path lengths are much more aligned. The largest components of the partnership networks seem to move towards the small world case.[10]

In sum, the examined sectoral knowledge networks can be characterized as small worlds, facilitating knowledge flows among participating firms. The examined sectoral partnership networks cannot be characterized as such, even though their largest components come much closer to the small world phenomenon.

**Firms' Positions in the Knowledge Network**

We have so far studied the overall structures of knowledge and partnership networks. In this section we turn to the individual participating firm to study its relative position in the network. We focus on knowledge networks exclusively in this analysis and follow the approach of Podolny et al. (1996) and Breschi et al. (2004), who use the technological crowding coefficient and the power centrality index (Bonacich, 1987) to identify a firm's position.

For the needs of this analysis, we shift from the use of direct patent citations to so-called *niche overlap*, indicating the similarity between patents in terms of their citation patterns. Roughly speaking, this amounts to detecting relations among patenting organizations on the basis of (backward) citations to previous inventions. To the extent that two firms build on similar technological antecedents, their research profile and, consequently, their product profile are likely to be similar. Firm $i$'s niche overlap coefficient for another firm, $j$, is defined as the ratio of the citation overlap between firms $i$ and $j$ (number of similar citations) to the number of all citations firm $i$ makes. Thus, a firm's technological crowding coefficient is the sum of the niche overlap coefficients with all other firms in the network.

The *technological crowding coefficient* estimates the extent to which individual firms undertake R&D activities in crowded technological areas. A large value implies high similarity in technological competencies with others. Podolny et al. (1996) use the patent level citation information to compute the technological crowding coefficient. Following Breschi et al. (2004), we instead use the firm-level citation information to compute the coefficient. We believe that our technological crowding coefficient captures the intended similarity better.

The *power centrality index* captures the *status* of the individual firm in the network. It takes into consideration both the status of a firm in the local network and its status in the global network that also includes indirect connections. The power centrality index may be viewed as an extension of degree centrality. Degree centrality, the number of direct links with other nodes (neighbors), is often used to measure the centrality of individual firms. However, having more connections alone does not necessarily give an advantage to the firm: it also matters with whom the firm has connections. Putting it differently, at least a part of a firm's status depends on the status of those linked to it. Neighbors with higher status boost the firm's own status. It is also conceivable that having powerful neighbors may negatively impact the focal firm's status (e.g. decrease its bargaining power). However, a positive relationship is assumed for calculating the power centrality index in this study.

Figures 6.12–6.16 show the scatter plots of knowledge network participants in the five sectors, defined by the technological crowding coefficient on the horizontal axis and the power centrality index on the vertical axis. Two lines in each scatter plot indicate the average values of the technological crowding coefficient (vertical line) and the power centrality index (horizontal line). Podolny et al. (1996) have identified the different roles of firms located in each of the four partitions of the graph. Firms in the upper-left partition – not crowded, high status – are characterized as *brokers* of new technologies. These firms' R&D tends to concentrate in new and unexplored

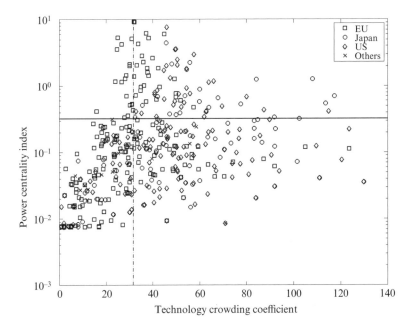

*Figure 6.12   Firms' knowledge network positioning: pharmaceuticals*

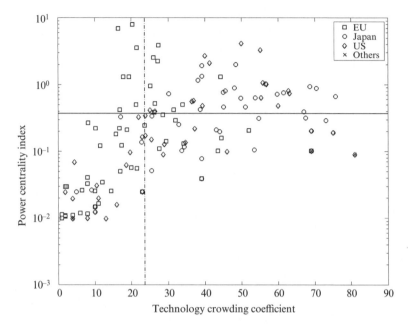

*Figure 6.13    Firms' knowledge network positioning: plastics*

technological fields. Firms in the upper-right partition – crowded, high status – are characterized as *leaders* in well-established technologies. They are engaged in R&D in relatively crowded fields but maintain high status in the network, indicating that they are more exploitation-oriented but no less R&D-intensive than are the brokers. Firms in the lower-right corner – crowded, low status – are *followers*. Their R&D efforts are concentrated in mature and crowded technological fields and do not contribute much to others. Finally, firms in the lower-left corner – not crowded, low status – are *isolates*. Their R&D is in technologies infrequently taken up by others. Isolation could be an indication of one of two things: either their technologies may be at the cutting edge, leading to future innovation opportunities but not yet taken up; or they may be on the verge of extinction (exiting the industry). This is where entrepreneurial activities are expected to be observed primarily, in that those firms that are successful may be able to gain the status of a technology broker (shift to the upper partition).

In pharmaceuticals (Figure 6.12), many EU firms are scattered all around but seem to reside with larger frequency on the left-hand side of the graph in the partitions of brokers and isolates. They actually fully dominate the broker partition. Several EU firms can also be found in the leader partition. The isolates partition also includes several US firms. Most Japanese

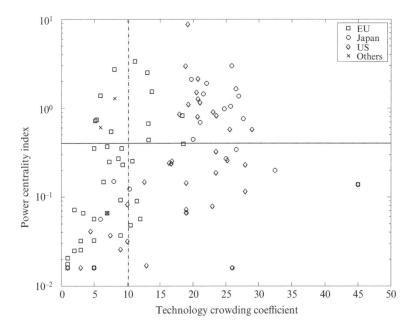

*Figure 6.14    Firms' knowledge network positioning: computers*

and US firms are found in the other two partitions. US firms include many leaders but also a sizeable number of followers. Plastics (Figure 6.13) demonstrate a similar general picture to pharmaceuticals. In computers (Figure 6.14) most EU firms are again found in the partitions of brokers and isolates. The majority of Japanese firms reside in the partition of leaders, while US firms are rather evenly distributed in the partitions of leaders and followers. In electronics (Figure 6.15), the partition of isolates is populated almost entirely by EU firms. EU firms are also found in the partition of leaders and followers. Almost all Japanese and US firms are found in the partitions of leaders and followers. Finally, in instruments (Figure 6.16), EU, Japanese and US firms are widely distributed across all areas except the brokers' partition, which is populated by EU firms. This industry has the heaviest concentration of isolates – which is not unexpected.

Looking across the five industrial sectors, one observes that innovative EU firms tend to reside primarily in the partitions of brokers or isolates. In contrast, innovative Japanese firms tend to reside in the partitions of leaders and followers. Innovative US firms tend to lie somewhere between EU and Japanese firms, but resemble more the Japanese firm distribution. Significant strategy and policy considerations arise from such classifications and are discussed briefly below.

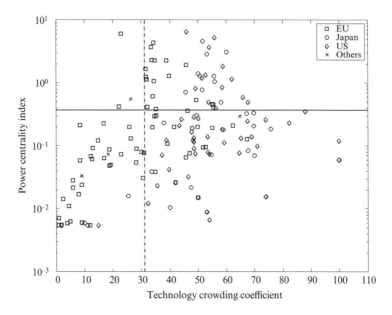

*Figure 6.15    Firms' knowledge network positioning: electronics*

## 4.    CONCLUSION

This chapter has examined a set of knowledge networks and technology partnership networks established in five industrial sectors – pharmaceuticals, plastics, computers, electronics, and instruments – during 1996–99.

   Our exploratory analysis points at three sets of results that require further attention:

1.   There is an apparent difference in the networking behavior in pharmaceuticals vis-à-vis networking behavior in computers, electronics and instruments.
2.   There is an apparent difference between knowledge and partnership networks across all sectors in terms of their effectiveness as channels for knowledge communication.
3.   There is an apparent difference in the competitive positioning of European firms and firms from the United States and Japan in the knowledge networks across the examined industrial sectors.

All five knowledge networks are found to be highly connected. That is to say, there are paths connecting the identified companies to each other in a

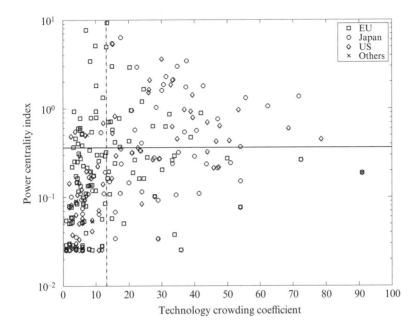

*Figure 6.16   Firms' knowledge network positioning: instruments*

given sector in terms of inter-linking patent citations. These paths tend to be short: on average, a company can find any other in less than three steps. There are, however, differences between sectors in terms of the nature of this connectivity. For instance, the knowledge network in pharmaceuticals appears to be the most broadly connected, whereas the knowledge network in instruments seems to depend more on gatekeepers and information "hubs" for its connectivity.

The sectoral partnership networks investigated here are much smaller than the knowledge networks. They are also more fragmented than knowledge networks in all five sectors. Among partnership networks, the pharmaceuticals network seems to be the least closely connected and to depend more than the other sectoral partnership networks on a few "hubs" for its connectivity.

The knowledge network is robust to the random removal of nodes across all industrial sectors, but quite vulnerable to the removal of the most connected nodes. The same is true for the partnership networks in pharmaceuticals and electronics. In fact, the partnership network in pharmaceuticals disintegrates more quickly than its knowledge network, indicating that it is more dependent on a few highly connected firms.

The apparent difference in networking behavior between pharmaceuticals and other sectors is an important finding that requires further attention in future investigations. Drug company networking behavior seems to be different in patenting and in strategic partnering. One should notice here that pharmaceuticals as an industry has different technology domain characteristics from computers, electronics, and instruments. In fact, the former has been characterized as a "simple technology" industry, whereas the latter fall into the "complex technology" industry set (Kash and Rycroft, 1999).

All five sectoral knowledge networks appear to be effective channels for knowledge flow between the participating organizations: they can all be characterized as "small worlds." In contrast, the examined sectoral partnership networks cannot, even though their largest components come much closer to the small world phenomenon. This difference between knowledge and partnership networks is a second, possibly important, result. It requires further investigation as well, given that the partnership data used in this exercise were relatively thin.

Finally, European firms tend to be positioned in less crowded partitions of the examined sectoral knowledge networks. They dominate the "technology broker" partitions of the sectoral graphs, where less crowded positions are combined with high status. They also appear in large numbers in the "technology isolate" partitions, where less crowded positions are combined with low status. In contrast, Japanese firms tend to reside mostly in the partitions of "technology leaders" and "technology followers," where more crowded positions are combined with high status and low status respectively. US firms tend to lie somewhere in between, their distribution among the four partitions resembling somewhat more that of the Japanese than the European firms.

This is the third important result of the chapter: it points out differences between European firms and their American and Japanese counterparts. The dominating presence of European firms in the "technology brokers" partition across all examined industries can have two explanations. It could imply a bright future for European firms: they are getting equipped with new, desirable technologies. Their early-stage research, however, may not be followed with equal success in commercializing the resulting technological advancements as Japanese and US firms dominate the technology leaders' partition, capturing the associated rents. Alternatively, it could be argued that EU firms tend to stick to unsuccessful technologies that die out sooner rather than later.

In contrast, Japanese firms seem to follow a "fast-second" approach, keeping close to the forefront of technology but not as brokers or isolates/ entrepreneurs. When they find promising technologies, Japanese firms concentrate their R&D effort on pushing the technology forward and reaping the benefits from commercialization. As for the American firms, their relatively more even spread in the graph indicates capabilities to follow diversified strategies. They maintain solid capabilities as technology leaders in all examined industries. They occupy a significant position as isolates in drugs, plastics, and instruments. Unexpectedly, however, they appear relatively weak as technology brokers. Significant numbers of US firms were also found in the followers' partition across all industrial sectors.

To conclude, we should add that, while characterizing the nature of the examined inter-organizational networks and the strategic positioning of companies in them has proven quite rewarding, the results ultimately beg the "so what" question. For a fuller picture, network analysis should be complemented with the more traditional investigative approaches in the economics and management/strategy fields dealing with the competitive behavior of individual companies and their market successes.

## NOTES

1.  This chapter draws extensively on the paper "European Partnership and Knowledge Networks" by the same authors published in *Technology Analysis and Strategic Management*, **18** (5), 535–60, December 2006. The research has been made possible by generous funding from the European Community (DG Research) through a multi-year grant supporting the collaborative research project "Network Indicators: Science, Technology and Innovation".
2.  See Vonortas (2004) for an extensive discussion.
3.  The literature on business networks is very extensive. See, for example, Ebers and Jarillo (1998), Gulati (1998), Gulati et al. (2000), Nohria and Eccles (1992), Oliver and Ebers (1998), Powell et al. (1996), Walker et al. (1997).
4.  This dataset currently includes all patent applications to the European Patent Office (EPO) from June 1, 1978 to December 2003. The dataset comprises a total of 1 136 587 patents, each with a full set of bibliographic variables. In addition, the dataset also contains, for each patent, all citations made to other EPO patent documents, including a total of 585 231 citing patents and 465 924 cited patents, corresponding to a total of 1 119 764 citations. The unique characteristic of the dataset that allows this kind of work is the transformation of the data from object-oriented to subject-oriented, that is the listing of all patents and citation under individual organizations.
5.  The MERIT Cooperative Agreements and Technology Indicators (CATI) database contains information on nearly 10 000 cooperative agreements in various sectors, ranging from high-technology sectors, such as computers and drugs, to less technology-intensive sectors, such as chemicals and heavy electrical equipment. Information about inter-firm partnerships is collected from various sources including newspaper and journal articles, books dealing with the subject, and, in particular, specialized journals, which report on business events.
6.  The number of shared partnership memberships has been previously interpreted in the literature as an indicator of the strength of the collaboration between two companies (a weight). Similar considerations apply to those mentioned earlier for the knowledge network.
7.  The two datasets have been combined by CESPRI at the level of the firm. The combined

dataset enables comparisons across knowledge and partnership networks for the same organizations. Although such comparisons are attempted in this chapter, they are kept to the industry level. Our objective is to discuss networks within predefined industrial sectors rather than to examine the complete networks of companies that can be classified in those sectors.

8. The most direct linkages are registered by pharmaceutical firms, indicating more citations per organization. The extent to which this reflects technology traits rather than differences in network behavior is unknown.
9. The results of these calculations are available from the authors on request.
10. We suspect that the result change may be because of the partnership data in hand. As emphasized in an earlier section, these networks are based on agreements involving at least one European company, thus leaving outside the examined population participants in US–US and US–Japanese agreements, which tend to be numerous.

# REFERENCES

Abernathy, William J. and James M. Utterback (1975) "A dynamic model of process and product innovation", *Omega, The International Journal of Management Science*, **3**, 639–56.

Abernathy, William J. and James M. Utterback (1978) "Patterns of industrial innovation", *Technology Review*, **80** (June/July), 40–47.

Barabási, A.-L. and R. Albert (1999) "Emergence of scaling in random networks", *Science*, 286, 509–12.

Bonacich, P. (1987) "Power and centrality: a family of measures", *American Journal of Sociology*, **92** (5), 1170–82.

Breschi, S. and L. Cusmano (2003) "Unveiling the texture of a European Research Area: emergence of oligarchic networks under EU Framework Programmes", *International Journal of Technology Management*, **15** (2), 255–71.

Breschi, S., L. Cassi and F. Malerba (2004) "A five-industry analysis of patent co-citation networks", Draft STI-NET Project Report to the European Commission, CESPRI, Luigi Bocconi University.

Burt, R.S. (1992) *Structural Holes: The Social Structure of Competition*, Cambridge, MA: Harvard University Press.

Carlsson, B. (ed.) (1995) *Technological Systems and Economic Performance: The Case of Factory Automation*, Boston, MA: Kluwer Academic Publishers.

Caves, Richard E. (1998) "Industrial organization and new findings on the turnover and mobility of firms", *Journal of Economic Literature*, **XXXVI**, 1947–82.

Coleman, J.S. (1990) *Foundations of Social Theory*, Cambridge, MA: Belknap Press.

Cowan, R. and N. Jonard (2003) "The dynamics of collective invention", *Journal of Economic Behavior and Organization*, **52** (4), 513–32.

Dosi, G. (1988) "Sources, procedures, and microeconomic effects of innovation", *Journal of Economic Literature*, **26**, 1120–71.

Ebers, M. and C.J. Jarillo (1998) "The construction, forms, and consequences of industry networks", *International Studies of Management and Organization*, **27** (4), 3–21.

Edquist, C. (ed.) (1997) *Systems of Innovation: Technologies, Institutions and Organizations*, London: Pinter.

Gambardella, A. and F. Malerba (eds) (1999) *Organization of Economic Innovation in Europe*, New York: Cambridge University Press.

Gort, M. and S. Klepper (1982) "Time paths in the diffusion of product innovations", *Economic Journal*, **92**, 630–53.

Gulati, R. (1998) "Partnerships and networks", *Strategic Management Journal*, **19**, 293–317.

Gulati, R., N. Nohria and A. Zaheer (2000) "Strategic networks", *Strategic Management Journal*, **21**, 203–15.

Kash, D.E. and R.W. Rycroft (1999) *The Complexity Challenge*, London: Pinter.

Kim, C.-W. and K. Lee (2003) "Innovation, technological regimes and organizational selection in industry evolution: a 'history friendly model' of the DRAM industry", *Industrial and Corporate Change*, **12** (6), 1195–221.

Klepper, S. (1996) "Entry, exit, growth, and innovation over the product life cycle", *American Economic Review*, **86**, 562–83.

Klepper, S. (2002) "Firm survival and the evolution of oligopoly", *RAND Journal of Economics*, **33** (1), 37–61.

Malerba, Franco (2004) "Sectoral systems of innovation: basic concepts", in F. Malerba (ed.), *Sectoral Systems of Innovation*, New York: Cambridge University Press.

Malerba, F, R.R. Nelson, L. Orsenigo and S. Winter (1999), "History friendly models of industry evolution: the case of the computer industry", *Industrial and Corporate Change*, **1**, 3–41.

Malerba, F., R.R. Nelson, L. Orsenigo and S. Winter (2001) "Competition and industrial policies in a 'history friendly' model of the evolution of the computer industry", *International Journal of Industrial Organization*, **19**, 635–64.

Malerba, F. and L. Orsenigo (1996) "Schumpeterian patterns of innovation are technology-specific", *Research Policy*, **25** (3), 451–78.

Malerba, F. and L. Orsenigo (2002) "Innovation and market structure in the dynamics of the pharmaceutical industry and biotechnology: towards a history-friendly model", *Industrial and Corporate Change*, **11** (4), 667–703.

Mueller, Denis C. and J.E. Tilton (1969) "Research and development costs as a barrier to entry", *Canadian Journal of Economics*, **2**, 570–9.

Nelson, R.R. (1995) "Recent theorizing about economic change", *Journal of Economic Literature*, **XXXIII**, 48–90.

Newman, M.E.J. (2001) "Clustering and preferential attachment in growing networks", available at http://arxiv.org/abs/cond-mat/0104209.

Nohria, N. and R. Eccles (eds) (1992) *Networks and Organizations*, Boston, MA: Harvard Business School Press.

Nooteboom, B. and V.A. Gilsing (2004) "Density and strength of ties in innovation networks: a competence and governance view", Working Paper, Rotterdam School of Management.

Oliver, A.L. and M. Ebers (1998) "Networking network studies: an analysis of conceptual configurations in the study of inter-organizational relations", *Organization Studies*, **19** (4), 549–83.

Podolny, J. M., T.E. Stuart and M.T. Hannan (1996) "Networks, knowledge, and niches: competition in the worldwide semiconductor industry, 1984–1991", *American Journal of Sociology*, **102** (3), 659–89.

Powell, W.W., K.W. Koput and L. Smith-Doerr (1996) "Inter-organizational collaboration and the locus of innovation: networks of learning in biotechnology", *Administrative Science Quarterly*, **41**, 116–45.

Pyka, A. and P. Saviotti (2002) "Networking in biotechnology industries – from translators to explorers", Working Paper, Economics Institute, University of Augsberg.

Scherer F.M. and D.R. Ross (1990) *Industrial Market Structure and Economic Performance*, Boston, MA: Houghton Mifflin.

Utterback, J. (1994) *Mastering the Dynamics of Innovation*, Boston, MA: Harvard Business School Press.

Verspagen, B. (2004) "Small worlds and technology networks: the case of European research collaboration", Technical Report, Centre for Innovation Studies, University of Eindhoven.

Vonortas, N.S. (2004) "Innovation networks in industry I", Working Paper, Center for International Science and Technology Policy, The George Washington University.

Wagner, C.S., R. Thompson, T. Tesch and R. Perez (2004) "Evaluation of networks of collaboration between participants in IST research and their evolution to collaborations in the European Research Area (ERA)", Interim Report TR-220-EC, Directorate-Generale Information Society, European Commission.

Walker, G., B. Kogut and W. Shan (1997) "Social capital, structural holes and the formation of an industry network", *Organization Science*, **8**, 109–25.

Watts, D.J. (1999) *Small Worlds: The Dynamics of Networks between Order and Randomness*, Princeton, NJ: Princeton University Press.

Watts, D.J. and S.H. Strogatz (1998) "Collective dynamics of 'small-world' networks", *Nature*, **393** (6684), 440–2.

Willinger, W., R. Govindan, S. Jamin, V. Paxson and S. Shenker (2002) "Scaling phenomena in the Internet: critically examining criticality", in N.R. Cozzarelli (ed.), *Proceedings of the National Academy of Science*, **99**, Washington, DC: National Academy of Science, pp. 2573–80.

# 7. What do you mean by "mobile"? Multi-applicant inventors in the European biotechnology industry

**Francesco Laforgia and Francesco Lissoni**

## 1. INTRODUCTION

Mobility of knowledge workers, such as R&D staff and other employees contributing to firms' innovation efforts, is often pinpointed as a major factor contributing to knowledge diffusion. Starting with Arrow's (1962) classic reference, the issue of mobility has been linked to diffusion via knowledge spillovers, a particular kind of externality that is of direct relevance for a number of phenomena, such as the correct estimation of innovation production functions (Griliches, 2000), the existence of market failures (Geroski, 1995), and the agglomeration of industries and innovative activities (Feldman, 1999). Knowledge spillovers are often referred to as "pure externalities", as opposed to "pecuniary externalities", which also contribute to agglomeration, but have much less impact on economic theory and policy.[1]

In most of the literature, mobility is interpreted as job mobility specified as, "when researchers leave a firm and take a job at another firm" (Jaffe and Trajtenberg, 1996). This kind of mobility generates a pure externality to the extent that the mobile researchers bring with themselves information, contacts and ideas that they generated or acquired while working in their previous firm. However, this is not the only mobility mechanism that can generate knowledge diffusion.

Mobility also can occur when employees of one company end up working for another firm as a consequence of mergers and acquisitions (M&A), in which case the absorbing company pays for the intellectual assets acquired as part of the absorbed company, including ideas embodied in individuals. In this case, "spillovers occur [only] when a researcher paid by one firm to generate new knowledge transfers to another firm [. . .] without compensating his/her former employer for the full inventory of ideas that travels with him/her" (Geroski, 1995, p. 78)." That is, in the absence of data on the economic details of the M&A operations, we cannot presume the existence, or quantify the relevance of, the externality. Nevertheless, M&As are so frequent in high-tech industries that any attempt to evaluate the importance of pure spillovers should compare the relative importance of different mobility mechanisms.

It may also be the case that an inventor found to be responsible for, say, two patent applications held by as many different firms may in fact be working for a third firm that performs contract research or consultancy; in which case we are at the opposite end of spillovers, and in the realm of markets for technologies (Arora et al., 2001). These can still generate externalities, but of a pecuniary kind. Recent work on academic inventors, that is university scientists responsible for patents owned by more than one business company, suggests that this may indeed be a relevant case (Balconi et al., 2004; Geuna and Nesta, 2003).

Following Almeida and Kogut (1999), many papers have tried to measure the extent of mobility of knowledge workers by relying on patent data, from which information is extracted on what we will call "multi-applicant" inventors, that is, inventors designated on patent applications filed by different companies. In most cases, multi-applicant inventorship has been taken as an indicator of job mobility. We argue that, in the absence of information on M&A activities and the nature of patent applicants, it is often hard to tell whether this is the case.

In this chapter, we follow in the tradition of making use of patent data to track multi-applicant inventors, but with the aim of setting straight a number of methodological issues. We also hope to find out the relative weight of job mobility, M&A-induced mobility, and markets for technologies.

We rely on the EP-CESPRI database on patenting activity at the European Patent Office (EPO). The surveyed time period is 1978–2003, from which we have extracted data on all the inventors with more than one patent application lodged in biotechnology-related fields, and with a European address. We focus on all inventors with two or more patent applications, and no less than two different applicants.

By making use of information on the identity and history of both the inventors and the applicants, we then propose a taxonomy of phenomena behind multi-applicant inventorship, among which job mobility turns out not to stand as the dominant factor.

The chapter is organized as follows. In section 2 we discuss the recent literature on inventor mobility and propose a taxonomy of multi-applicant inventorship. In section 3 we present the data and the methodology for the construction of the data set. In section 4 we present our results on the weight of the different typologies of multi-applicant inventorship, in terms of number of inventors. In the same section, by using the social network analysis technique, we show some of the characteristics of the network among applicants generated by the flows of inventors. Section 5 provides conclusions and directions for future research.

## 2. MULTI-APPLICANT INVENTORSHIP: A REVIEW OF PATENT-BASED STUDIES AND A TAXONOMY

Within the broad field of the economics of innovation, most of the attention devoted to knowledge workers' mobility has come from studies on geographical clusters and the spatial dimension of innovation diffusion.

In a pioneering contribution, Jaffe, Trajtenberg and Henderson (1993; from now on JTH) show that knowledge spillovers, which they measure with citation data, tend to be highly localized in space, even more than is readily apparent from only looking at industrial agglomeration patterns. Many authors who have built on JTH's findings have invoked both job mobility and social networks as explanations for JTH's results (for a survey: Breschi and Lissoni, 2001). Only a few studies, however, have addressed explicitly the issue of measuring inventors' mobility.

Agrawal et al. (2003) explore the impact on knowledge diffusion of inventors' mobility in space. They find that mobile inventors' patents tend to be cited by former co-inventors, which may be proof of the existence of social ties that both convey technological knowledge and are resistant to locational change. These results are consistent with those achieved by Rosenkopf and Almeida (2003), who find that job mobility contributes, along with alliances, to knowledge diffusion in the US semiconductor industry.

In the same vein, Song et al. (2001) focus on the patenting activities of engineers who moved from US to non-US firms, and investigate the extent to which mobility helps hiring firms to reach beyond their current technological and geographical boundaries. They find some evidence that learning-by-hiring is most useful when hired engineers are used for exploring new or distant knowledge rather than reinforcing existing expertise.[2]

Singh (2005) builds a social proximity graph of inventing teams for all US Patent Office patents from 1975 to 1995.[3] He finds that knowledge flows are more likely to occur if mediated by social proximity among inventors' teams, and that such social proximity explains geographic localization of knowledge spillovers. Teams are connected by inventors who move among those teams. Similar methodology and results can be found in Breschi and Lissoni (2003), based upon European Patent Office data.

None of these studies, however, investigates the different reasons why inventors move across firms or in space. The only exception is Stolpe (2002), who analyses the nature of R&D spillovers in the field of liquid crystal display technology.

> Research workers may move among different laboratories owned by one and [the] same firm, or they may become an employee of a new firm when their old employer is the target of a take-over. In a similar vein, inventors may meet and collaborate in temporary research joint ventures. (Stolpe, 2002, p. 1187)

However, Stolpe ends up encompassing all those forms of mobility in what he calls "changes of professional affiliation". In particular, he identifies such changes by simply counting the number of affiliations per inventor as found in patent documents. In a similar vein, Almeida and Kogut (1999, p. 913) define moves of inventors as "the number of times that a major patent holder changes firms, as revealed in an analysis of all semiconductor patents".

Trajtenberg et al. (2006) follows the same methodology. He analyses the patents of 1 565 780 inventors listed on US patent documents, of which 653 838 have at least two patents. In what may be the largest-scale attempt to measure inventors' mobility, he considers each multi-applicant inventor as a mobile inventor and finds that 216 581 (about 33%) of the inventors with at least two patents have changed applicant at least once.

However, counting any inventor's change of applicant as a "job move" across companies may be a highly misleading exercise.

Consider the case of an inventor, whose name appears on three patents filed at times $t-1$, $t$, and $t+1$ by companies A, B, and (again) A, respectively (Figure 7.1). As we show below, this is a frequent case: shall we interpret it as the result of two moves, one from A to B and one from B back to A? Or should we interpret it as the result of company A's decision, at time $t$, to perform some occasional contracts or cooperative research for/with company B, and trust it to the inventor of its past and future patents?

Information on *all* applicants served by one inventor may help in solving these doubts. The case of an inventor's name appearing on three patents filed by three different companies (say A, B, and C) is more likely to signal job mobility than the A–B–A pattern (Figure 7.2). This is because the A–B–A pattern is symmetrical: if the A–B sequence does not reflect mobility (but instead either the sale of an invention by A to B, or an independent inventor selling ideas first to A then to B), it is almost certain that the following B–A sequence will also be something different. On the contrary, the A–B and B–C sequences in the A–B–C pattern are independent events: if one is not an instance of mobility, it is still the case that the other may be.

An implication of this line of reasoning is that inventors who are

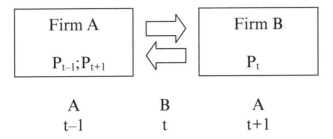

*Figure 7.1   Inventor's applicant sequence A–B–A*

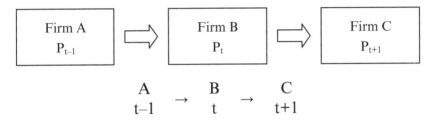

*Figure 7.2   Inventor's applicant sequence A–B–C*

observed to serve only two applicants (say A and B) can hardly be defined as mobile: is A merely a research contractor of B, or is it a company the inventor has left in order to move to B (and then to C)? Conservative estimates of inventors' mobility should consider only inventors with more than two patents, and at least three applicants.

Information on the nature of the applicants (business company vs university, or public research organization) may also be necessary. Consider the example in Figure 7.3, where an academic scientist works first in cooperation with company A (that takes a patent over the research results), then with company C (which also takes a patent), and also works on a federally funded project (whose results are patented by the scientist's university, B). This is not a case of mobility, but of a technology market transaction between A and B, and then A and C.

This is not an unlikely case. Describing the relationship between academic inventors and firms, Murray (2004) focuses on different typologies of academic inventors' affiliations, saying that an inventor can quit academia and move to the applicant firm, or enter the firm while retaining an academic affiliation, or keep a full-time academic position with no involvement with any firm but the sale of the invention. Actually, the relationship between academia and firms makes the analysis of mobility through patent data very complicated.

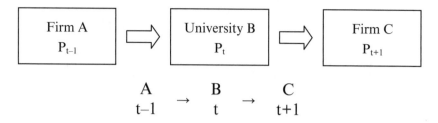

*Figure 7.3   Inventor's applicant sequence A–B–C, where B is a university*

Patterns similar to those generated by academic inventors also can be observed when only firms are involved. Arora et al. (2001, pp. 423–4) define markets for technologies as the

> transactions for the use, the diffusion and the creation of technology. This includes transactions involving full technology packages (patents and other intellectual property and know-how) and patent licensing. It also includes transactions involving knowledge that is not patentable or not patented (e.g. software or the many non-patented designs and innovations).

The rise of these markets marks the decline of the model of organizing innovation characterized by in-house R&D, in which R&D and the complementary assets required for innovation were integrated inside the firm. Therefore, trade in technologies has become very common and it is a result, among other reasons, of an increase in licensing revenues earned by firms and to an upsurge in patenting activities that reflect increased opportunities for technologies licensing (Kortum and Lerner, 1999).

Finally, information on property relationships between applicants may also be revealing. Consider the (frequent) case of an inventor whose name appears first on A's and then on B's patents. If it turns out that in between the two patents' application dates A has merged with or has been acquired by B (or B's holding company), we can conclude that the inventor has not moved at all, and has not generated any spillover. In fact, his or her intellectual assets have been bought along with the other assets of firm A.

It could also happen that when observing an inventor's apparent move from A to B, in reality, B is a spin-off of A, or there has been a research joint venture between A and B to develop one or more products in A's or B's pipelines. Only additional information about applicants can reveal what is actually being observed.

All these cases can be summarized in the "multi-applicant taxonomy" that we present in Table 7.1 and that can be applied to all multi-applicant inventors with more than two patents and at least two applicants.

The column labelled TYPE in Table 7.1 reports what we regard as

*Table 7.1   Multi-applicant inventorship: a taxonomy*

| TYPE | CATEGORY | PATTERNS | CASES |
|---|---|---|---|
| MOBILITY | 1 | A→B→C, No A→B→A | Inventor moves from one firm to another one, then to a third one. No loops are observed |
| | 2 | A→B→C where A and C are organizations, B is an individual*** (or vice versa) | One possible explanation regards the case of start-ups created by an inventor |
| M&A | 3 | A→B→C, where A is merged with B | A merger or acquisition occurred between inventor's applicant and another firm |
| MARKET FOR INVENTIONS | 4 | A→B→A, where A or B is a OS* | At least one inventor's affiliation is an university or a public research centre |
| | 5 | A→B→A, where A and B are both PT** or individual | It might be the case that B performs contract research for, among others, A, as well as taking lodging in its own name |
| OTHER | 6 | A→B→A and then A→ C→ D (or vice versa) | Patterns are a mix between mobility and other typologies. Further information is required |
| | 7 | A→B→B →B or A→A→A →B | It might be the case of an inventor who lodged a first patent for an academic institution and then moved to a firm. Also in this case further information is required |

*Notes:*

\* OS = open science organization: it includes universities and public research organizations.
\*\* PT = private technology organization, i.e. business companies (including private laboratories).
\*\*\* Individual = individual inventors (the inventor's and the applicant's name coincide).

the main types of multi-applicant inventorship, namely "job mobility", "mergers and acquisitions (M&A)", and "market for inventions". OTHER is a residual category for all patterns of multi-applicant inventorship that do not lend themselves to immediate interpretation. Therefore, the last category encompasses any residual cases; that is, cases one can classify only with information on patents and their applicants. For each typology of multi-applicant inventors, there is one or more corresponding sub-category (column CATEGORY), which refers to specific patterns of multi-applicant inventorship (reported in the column PATTERNS).

The last column of Table 7.1 (CASES) reports the most likely explanations for the observed patterns. To identify the distinct typologies of patterns of multi-applicant inventorship, we focus on the typologies of applicants and distinguish them into three types: open science organizations (OS), private technology organizations (PT) and individuals (I). We think of OS as all the institutions that correspond to an open science community setting, such as universities, public research centres or public foundations. All firms belong to the PT category. We refer to "Individual" patents as all the patents whose applicant is an individual.

Therefore, combined with the identity of the applicant, the taxonomy described in Table 7.1 allows us to identify seven distinct typologies of patterns of multi-applicant inventorship:

1.  A→B→C, where A, B, and C are all businesses (i.e. PT, private technology organizations). In this case we observe an inventor moving across three different applicants; that is, he or she does not "go back" to a previous applicant. It is the most likely pattern to signal job mobility.
2.  A→B→C, where A and C are private technology organizations, B is an individual (or vice versa). This pattern maintains the same characteristic of pattern 1, that is the inventor does not go back to the previous assignees. It might refer to cases of ventures started up by inventors.
3.  A→B→C, where A (and/or C) is merged with B. This category concerns all cases of mobility induced by M&A processes. To reconstruct the stories of M&A processes of all firms one needs to collect information about firms' organizational events.
4.  A→B→A, where A or B is an open science organization (OS), such as a university or a public lab. This pattern represents the activities of what have been called academic inventors. It is very likely that it does not deal with real mobility of individuals from one organization to another. Rather, it reflects the phenomenon of markets for inventions.

5. A→B→A, where A and B are both PTs or A is a PT and B is an individual (or vice versa). It is a likely case of B performing contract research and, occasionally, taking patents in its own name.
6. A→B→A and then A→C→D (or vice versa). This is a mixed pattern in which we observe in the first stage a pattern that can exclude mobility, and in the second stage a pattern similar to pattern 1. However, it is very challenging to assign such a typology to a specific category of multi-applicant inventorship. At this stage of our research we consider this as a "residual" case.
7. A→B→B→B or A→A→A→B. This category encompasses cases in which one observes an inventor lodging a first patent for an applicant and undertaking additional patenting activity for a distinct applicant. As we will see in the empirical results, this is a very critical case. In fact, this represents a very common case in which we observe an inventor's patenting activity characterized by a stable pattern of affiliation (the majority of patents are lodged for the same assignee) and only one patent lodged for a different assignee. At this stage of our research we consider this as a "residual" case.

To summarize the taxonomy, Categories 1 and 2 shape the typology of "job mobility": we believe that it is very likely that an inventor following such a pattern can be considered a true "mover" in that the inventor effectively has changed employers. Category 3 is what we call the "M&A effect". In this case, a change of assignee code is observed but actually no real move of the inventor occurred. Categories 4 and 5 represent the realm of what we have called "market for inventions". Categories 7 and 8 are residual categories. Nevertheless, they deserve deeper scrutiny and empirical understanding.

## 3.   DATA

In order to test the usefulness of our taxonomy, we rely on the EP-CESPRI database on patenting activity at the European Patent Office (EPO). The database contains all the patent applications filed at EPO from 1978 to 2003, complete with information on inventors. We have selected information on inventors who have lodged more than one patent application in biotechnology-related fields, from 1990 to 2003, and with addresses and applicants from one of the seven European countries with the highest number of biotech patents, namely Denmark, France, Germany, Italy, Netherlands, Switzerland, and the United Kingdom.

Biotechnology is a good field to test our taxonomy, since it is both patent-intensive and based on a cumulative pattern of knowledge advancement. Patent data, therefore, are a good indicator of both invention and innovation. It is also a field in which we may expect to find mobile inventors, markets for technologies, and remarkable M&A activity (Swann et al., 1998). Following the OECD classification (Devlin 2003; van Beuzekom and Arundel, 2006), we define as biotech patents all those classified by EPO under the following four-digit IPC (International Patent Classification) categories:

- C12M   Apparatus for enzymology or microbiology.
- C12N   Micro-organisms or enzymes. Compositions thereof. Propagating, preserving or maintaining micro-organisms. Mutation or genetic engineering. Culture media.
- C12P   Fermentation or enzyme-using processes to synthesize a desired chemical compound or composition or to separate optical isomers from a racemic mixture.
- C12Q   Measuring or testing processes involving enzymes or micro-organisms. Compositions or test papers thereof. Processes of preparing such compositions. Condition-responsive control in microbiological or enzymological processes.
- C12S   Processes using enzymes or micro-organisms to liberate, separate or purify a pre-existing compound or composition. Processes using enzymes or micro-organisms to treat textiles or to clean solid surfaces of materials.

Both inventors and companies in the EP-CESPRI database come with a unique code, which is the result of automated data-cleaning procedures (which correct for misspelling or use of societal forms in the names) and data user feedback (Lissoni et al., 2006). These codes were further refined through manual checks of all records.

In order to keep the manual checking effort within manageable proportions, we did not examine inventors' activity prior to 1990, nor did we examine their activity outside the selected IPC classes.[4] This implies an underestimation not only of these individuals' inventiveness, but possibly of multi-applicant inventorship.

We do not believe this limitation affects our results, as the consideration of the entire inventors' patent portfolios possibly would have helped us to track more cases of multi-applicant inventorship, but there is no reason to believe that we would have ended up with more cases of one phenomenon as opposed to another (e.g. job mobility vs markets for technologies).

The final dataset contains 13 246 inventors, who have lodged 8233 patents, and a total of 1643 applicants (see Table 7.2).

*Table 7.2*   *Inventors in European biotech, after 1990; by number of*
            *patents*

| No. of patents per inventor | No. of inventors | % |
|---|---|---|
| 1 patent | 9 123 | 68.87 |
| 2 | 2 137 | 16.13 |
| 3 | 836 | 6.31 |
| 4 | 402 | 3.03 |
| 5 | 207 | 1.56 |
| 6 or more | 541 | 4.08 |
| Total | 13 246 | 100 |

*Source:*   Elaboration from EP-CESPRI data.

The distribution of patents per inventor is highly skewed: almost 70 per cent of inventors (9123) lodged just one patent, and are not pertinent to our analysis. Of the remaining 4123 inventors, we are interested in those who have changed applicants at least once (1508). These individuals make up more than one third (36.58%) of all inventors with more than one patent (Table 7.3). It is worth noting that this figure is very close to that found by Trajtenberg et al. (2006) in an altogether different setting, namely USPTO patents in all technological classes, from 1975 to 1999.

We can look also at the differences between mono- and multi-applicant inventors in terms of patent counts (from now on we consider only mono-applicant inventors with at least two patents). On average, multi-applicant inventors lodge 0.5 more patents than do mono-applicants (Table 7.4). This confirms the importance of multi-applicant inventors, at least in terms of productivity (Trajtenberg et al., 2006).

In order to classify multi-applicant inventors according to the seven categories of the taxonomy presented in section 2, we further focused our analysis on those multi-applicant inventors with at least three patents over time, yielding a total of 945 individuals.

In order to exploit Category 7 of the taxonomy we needed additional information on M&A activities, and in general on the changes of property and/or name of all the patent applicants involved for all firms holding at least one patent signed by the 945 multi-applicant inventors with at least three patents. We retrieved this information manually from a variety of sources. First, we retrieved company histories from all the websites of the patent applicants in our database, when available. In many cases we found detailed information on the chronological sequences of key M&As, plus all reorganizational processes in which the firms have been involved. Second,

*Table 7.3    Inventors in European biotech, after 1990; by number of applicants*

| No. of applicants, per inventor | No. of inventors | % |
|---|---|---|
| 1 | 2615 | 63.42 |
| 2 | 1212 | 29.40 |
| 3 | 203 | 4.92 |
| 4 | 62 | 1.50 |
| 5 | 22 | 0.53 |
| 6 | 6 | 0.15 |
| 7 | 2 | 0.05 |
| 8 | 1 | 0.02 |
| *No. of multi-applicant inventors* | *1508* | *36.58* |
| Total | 4123 | 100 |

*Source:*    Elaboration from EP-CESPRI data.

*Table 7.4    Summary patent statisics, per type of inventor (European biotech, after 1990)*

| | Mono-applicant inventors | Multi-applicant inventors |
|---|---|---|
| Mean no. of patents | 3.04 | 4.68 |
| Median no. of patents | 2.00 | 3.00 |
| Standard deviations | 2.56 | 4.58 |

*Source:*    Elaboration from EP-CESPRI data.

the same websites contain the firms' annual reports, which helped us to decipher the missing information about events of dismissing or acquiring parts of firms' assets. Finally, additional information was obtained by searching the Internet for papers and press releases on the pertinent companies.

## 4.    RESULTS

Table 7.5 presents the results of our taxonomic exercise, that is of the assignment of all multi-applicant inventors with at least three patents to one of the categories described in Table 7.1. We first notice that the

*Table 7.5  Multi-applicant inventorship in European biotech, after 1990[a]*

| TYPE | CATEGORY | PATTERNS | Number of inventors | Total (%) |
|---|---|---|---|---|
| JOB MOBILITY | 1 | A→B→C, No A→B→A | 174 | 186 |
| | 2 | A→B→C, where A and C are organizations, B is individual*** (or vice versa) | 12 | (19.68) |
| M&A | 3 | A→B→C, where A is merged with B | 105 | 105 |
| | | | | (11.11) |
| MARKET FOR | 4 | A→B→A, where A or B is an OS* | 63 | 246 |
| INVENTIONS | 5 | A→B→A, where A and B are both PT** or individual | 183 | (26.03) |
| OTHERS | 7 | A→B→A and then A→C→D (or vice versa) | 39 | 408 |
| | 8 | A→B→B →B or A→A→A →B | 369 | (43.17) |
| TOTAL | | | 945 | 945 |
| | | | | (100) |

*Notes:*

[a] Only inventors with at least three patents and two applicants are considered.

\* OS = open science organization: it includes universities and public research organizations.

\** PT = private technology organization, i.e. business companies (including private laboratories).

\*** Individual = individual inventors (the inventor's and the applicant's name coincide).

*Source:*   Elaboration from EP-CESPRI data.

inventors who can be considered truly mobile, that is those who have changed employers, represent less than one fifth of the total sample.

By using the information that we collected on firms' M&A processes, we find that a consistent number of biotech inventors (around 11%) seem to have changed applicant because of an M&A operation.

The proportion of inventors whose multi-applicant status may not reflect true mobility, and who are more likely to have contributed to the market for technologies, is around 26 per cent. Within this category, the more consistent sub-category is that concerning the multi-affiliation of inventors to the typology of PT applicant. It is likely that inventors belonging to this category are involved in a network of firm relationships resulting from a variety of research and technology transactions, including licensing in and out, firms' collaborations to jointly develop one or more products in firms' pipelines, markets for patents, and so on.

Moreover, 63 cases of markets for inventions involve one or more open science organizations, namely universities or public research centres. As already said, this reflects a special case of markets for inventions. It might refer not only to academic scientists who sell the IPRs of their research results to some private firm, but also to scientists who temporarily collaborate with business companies for one or more R&D projects, without leaving their academic position.

The residual category covers many inventors (408 inventors out of 945), which is too high a percentage to allow us to consider our taxonomy entirely satisfactory. However, until a deeper scrutiny is made with regard to what such categories really refer to, it might be unfair to assign the residuals to one of the specific categories, either movers or non-movers, at least according to our restrictive criteria.

What emerges from this exercise is that, as we expected, the core of what can be defined as inventor mobility is very small. Indeed, it is the least populated set among the four we describe, in terms of number of inventors. If we calculate the weight of such a category on the whole sample of inventors with at least two patents (those who in theory might show movement), they do not represent a very common case (12.33%). This leads us to suspect that inventors' mobility has so far been grossly overestimated by the existing literature relying on patent data.

In section 2 we suggested that different kinds of multi-applicant inventorship provide different kinds of knowledge transfer. In a related paper, we explore this claim by looking at the citation rates and the identity of citing companies for patents coming from multi-applicant inventors. In the present chapter, we show only how applicants are connected to each other by multi-applicant inventors, according to the type of phenomena described in Tables 7.4 and 7.5.

In particular, we focus on two of the four categories of multi-applicant inventors' taxonomy, namely "mobility" and "M&A", whose resulting networks are described in Figures 7.4 and 7.5, respectively. In both figures, nodes represent patent applicants, with a distinction between private technology organizations (that is, business companies: grey nodes) and open science organizations (black nodes).[5] Node size reflects the applicant's number of biotechnology patents.[6]

The uni-directional arrows represent the flows of mobile inventors from one node (the organization who loses one or more inventor) to another (the organization that receives the inventors from the losing organization). The thickness of the arrows reflects the number of inventors exchanged between nodes. The resulting networks are strikingly different.

The network created by job mobility is wide (it involves 280 applicants, and 346 inventors' moves), highly connected (all nodes belong to one giant component), and with a very short average geodesic distance, very much along the lines of "small world" networks spotted in science by Newman (2001). Notice that although the network is more dense around the primary patent holders, there is not a core of applicants associated with the exchange of the majority of mobile inventors. As a consequence, we may expect knowledge exchanges induced by job mobility to be as sparse and far reaching as they are often depicted in the literature.

We also notice that although most inventor exchanges occur between PT organizations (177 moves), the number of moves in which at least one OS organization is involved is far from negligible (122 moves).

The picture emerging from multi-applicant inventorship explained by M&As is quite different (Figure 7.5). First, although the number of inventors involved is less than half the number involved in job mobility (186 vs 105 in Figure 7.4), the applicants involved also are much fewer (only 66 against 280). As a result, the network in Figure 7.5 is built around a relatively small number of nodes that, with a few exceptions, exchange inventors with just one other node. These exchanges are often more sizeable than those resulting from job mobility (comparing the thickness of lines with those of Figure 7.4).

While inventors' job mobility has the potential to give rise to a widespread knowledge diffusion mechanism, the same does not happen with M&As. As an example, let's consider the thickest area in Figure 7.5, which involves firms such as Aventis, Hoechst, and Behringwerke, among others. Many "moves" have been identified from (26) and to (11) Aventis. The information on the selected firms' reorganizational processes (mainly M&As) allows us to reconstruct the firm-level events. In 1996 Chiron Corporation acquired 49 per cent of Behringwerke AG, a subsidiary of Hoechst, creating a new company: Chiron Behring GmbH & Co. In 1998 Chiron Corporation

*Notes:*
Black nodes = open science (OS) organizations; grey nodes = private technology (PT) organizations.
    The size of the nodes reflects the size of the organzation's patent portfolio; the size of the ties reflects the number of inventors exchanged.

*Figure 7.4    Job mobility network flow of inventors*

acquired Sclavo. In 1998 Chiron Corporation completed the acquisition of Behringwerke when it acquired the residual Hoechst AG's interest in Chiron Behring Gmbh & Co. In 1999 Rhône-Poulenc SA merged with Hoechst Marion Roussel, which itself was formed from the merger of Hoechst AG with Roussel Uclaf and Marion Merrell Dow. The merger led to the crea-tion of Aventis. This is just a part of the story highlighting the complexity of the exchange of inventors among such firms.

    If we consider another case, that of the firms Novo Nordisk and Novozymes, we find that a slightly different typology of reorganizational process occurred that explains the "apparent" flow of inventors. In 1989 Novo Nordisk was created through a merger between two Danish

*Notes:*
Black nodes = open science (OS) organizations; grey nodes = private technology (PT) organizations.
  The size of the nodes reflects the size of the organzation's patent portfolio; the size of the ties reflects the number of inventors exchanged.

*Figure 7.5     "Market for technologies" network flow of inventors*

companies – Novo Industri A/S and Nordisk Gentofte A/S. In 2000 Novo Nordisk split into three separate companies operating under the umbrella of the Novo Group: Novo Nordisk A/S, Novozymes A/S and Novo A/S. This would explain why we have identified 30 moves from Novo Nordisk to Novozymes.

In both our examples, we have a large number of apparently mobile inventors, who in reality hardly moved and certainly did not contribute to knowledge diffusion beyond the boundaries of the bilateral negotiations involving the firms for which they worked. Counting them as truly mobile inventors, such as those described by Figure 7.4, may lead to grossly over-estimated mobility and knowledge diffusion figures.

## 5. CONCLUSIONS

The aim of this chapter was two-fold. The first aim was a methodological one: we meant to contribute to the empirical literature on inventors'
mobility. We have argued that not all the phenomena behind what we
called "multi-applicant" inventorship may be equated to genuine "job"
mobility. By applying our taxonomy to EPO patent data in biotechnology, we have found that both the existence of markets for inventions and
M&A activity contribute to a multi-faceted phenomenon that the existing
literature has most often put under one label only, that of mobility. We
also found that mobility of inventors is far from being the dominant force
behind multi-applicant inventorship.

The second aim of the chapter was to provide a hint of the reason why
it is important to separate the various phenomena behind multi-applicant
inventorship, namely that these phenomena bear different consequences
in terms of knowledge diffusion. In this respect, we showed that the firms'
networks generated by job mobility are very different from those created
by M&As. The former are widespread but not very dense: they involve
a high number of nodes (firms), but a relatively limited number of ties
(movements of inventors between any two firms), each one of limited
intensity (few inventors move between any two firms). The latter, on the
contrary, are smaller and denser: they involve fewer firms, but movements
of inventors between such firms tend to be large.

Based on this evidence, one may hypothesize that knowledge diffusion
processes induced by job mobility may be further reaching than those
induced by M&As, in the sense of touching on more firms. In future
research, we will build on our methodology to test this hypothesis, by
looking at the citation rate impacts of both mono- and multi-applicant
inventors, and of different categories of multi-applicant inventors. By
doing so, we will contribute not just to the literature on inventors' mobility and its effect on knowledge diffusion, but also to the fast-growing
literature that exploits data on inventors and patent citations to assess the
effects of M&As on knowledge transfer (Holger and Vitt, 2000; Ahuja and
Katila, 2001; on the effectiveness of patent citations as a proxy for knowledge transfer through M&A, see Duguet and MacGarvie, 2005).

## NOTES

1. Pecuniary (or "rent") externalities allow co-localized firms to access traded inputs and
   labour at a lower price than rivals located elsewhere; as such, they pass through market
   interactions. Pure externalities (of which free access to knowledge is an example), on the

contrary, materialize through non-market interactions and, in principle, are accessible to all members of the local community (Scitovsky, 1954).

2. This result is consistent with other works dealing with the linkage between technological benefits from alliances and mobility and technological distance between firms: going far beyond geographical boundaries could avoid technological path dependence and increase technological diversity.

3. The graph is defined to have an edge between any two teams with a common inventor. Teams with socially linked inventors have nodes belonging to the same connected component of this graph. The strength of their social link, or the social distance between the teams, is given by the number of intermediate nodes on the minimum path between the two.

4. If we had considered all the patents (from all technological classes) signed by the inventors in our sample (that is inventors with at least one biotech patent), from 1990 to 2003, we would have had 18 413 patents, as opposed to 8233 patents now in our dataset. By limiting the data collection to only the "multi-applicant inventors" in our sample, the total patents in all technological classes would have been 2098, as opposed to 1507 patents by such multi-applicant inventors now in our database. Therefore, "multi-applicant inventors" with at least a patent in biotechnology appear to be more specialized in this technological fields than the average inventor.

5. Figure 7.4 does not include the (few) cases of individual inventors moving to or from an organization. We also neglected nodes and ties involving Italian companies, which again are too few to change the overall network pattern.

6. By "biotechnology patents" we exclusively mean the patents we consider in our dataset.

# REFERENCES

Agrawal, A., Iain M. Cockburn and J. McHale (2003), "Gone but not forgotten: labour flows, knowledge spillovers and enduring social capital", NBER Working Paper, no. 9950.

Ahuja, G. and R. Katila (2001), "Technological acquisitions and the innovation performance of acquiring firms: a longitudinal study", *Strategic Management Journal*, **22**, 197–220.

Almeida, P. and B. Kogut (1999), "Localisation of knowledge and mobility of engineers in regional networks", *Management Science*, **45** (7), 905–17.

Arora, A., A. Fosfuri and A. Gambardella (2001), "Markets for technology and their implications for corporate strategy", *Industrial and Corporate Change*, **1** (1), 419–451.

Arrow, K.J. (1962), "Economic welfare and the allocation of resources for invention", in R.R. Nelson (ed.), *The Rate and Direction of Inventive Activity: Economic and Social Factors*, NBER Special Conference Series, Vol. 13, Princeton, NJ: Princeton University Press.

Balconi, M., S. Breschi and F. Lissoni (2004), "Networks of inventors and the role of academia: an exploration of Italian patent data", *Research Policy*, **33**, 127–45.

Breschi, S. and F. Lissoni (2001), "Knowledge spillovers and local innovation systems: a critical survey", *Industrial and Corporate Change*, **10** (4), 975–1005.

Breschi, S. and F. Lissoni (2003), "Mobility and social networks: localised knowledge spillovers revisited", CESPRI Working Paper, no. 142.

Devlin, A. (2003), "An overview of biotechnology statistics in selected countries", STI Working Paper 2003/13, OECD, Paris.

Duguet, E. and M. MacGarvie (2005), "How well do patent citations measure flows of technology? Evidence from French innovation surveys", *Economics of Innovation and New Technology*, **14** (5), 375–93.

Feldman, M.P. (1999), "The new economics of innovation, spillovers and agglomeration: a review of empirical studies", *Economics of Innovation and New Technology*, **8**, 5–25.

Geroski, P.A. (1995), "Do spillovers undermine the incentive to innovate?", in Dowrick, S. (ed.), *Economic Approaches to Innovation*, Aldershot, UK and Brookfield, USA: Edward Elgar, pp. 76–97.

Geuna, A. and L. Nesta (2003), "University patenting and its effects on academic research", SPRU Electronic Working Paper Series, no. 99.

Griliches, Z., (2000), *R&D, Education and Productivity*, Cambridge, MA: MIT Press.

Holger, E. and J. Vitt (2000), "The influence of corporate acquisitions on the behaviour of key inventors", *R&D Management*, **30** (2), 105–20.

Jaffe, Adam B. and M. Trajtenberg (1996), "Flows of knowledge from universities and federal labs: modelling the flows of patent citations over time and across institutional and geographic boundaries", NBER Working Paper, no. 5712.

Jaffe, Adam B. M. Trajtenberg and R. Henderson (1993), "Geographic localization of knowledge spillovers as evidenced by patent citations", *Quarterly Journal of Economics*, **108**, 577–98.

Kortum, S. and J. Lerner (1999), "What is behind the recent surge in patenting", *Research Policy*, **28**, 1–22.

Lissoni, F., B. Sanditov and G. Tarasconi (2006), "The Keins database on academic inventors: methodology and contents", CESPRI Working Paper 181, available at: http://www.cespri.unibocconi.it/workingpapers

Murray, F. (2004), "The role of academic inventors in entrepreneurial firms: sharing the laboratory life", *Research Policy*, **33**, 643–59.

Newman, M.E.J. (2001), "The structure of scientific collaboration networks", *Proceedings of the National Academy of Science USA*, **98**, 404–9.

Rosenkopf, L. and P. Almeida (2003), "Overcoming local search through alliances and mobility", *Management Science*, **49** (6), 751–66.

Scitovsky, T. (1954), "Two concepts of external economies", *Journal of Political Economy*, **62**, 143–51.

Singh, J.H. (2005), "Collaborative networks as determinants of knowledge diffusion patterns", *Management Science*, **51** (5), 756–70.

Song, J., P. Almeida and G. Wu (2001), "Mobility of engineers and the cross-border knowledge building: the technological catching up case of Korean and Taiwanese semiconductor firms", in H. Chesbrough and R. Burgelman (eds), *Research in Technology and Innovation Management*, New York: JAI Press.

Stolpe, M. (2002), "Determinants of knowledge diffusion as evidenced in patent data: the case of liquid crystal display technology", *Research Policy*, **31**, 1181–98.

Swann, G.M.P., M. Prevezer and D. Stout (eds) (1998), *The Dynamics of Industrial Clustering: International Comparisons in Computing and Biotechnology*, Oxford: Oxford University Press.

Trajtenberg, M., G. Shiff and R. Melamed (2006), "The 'Names Game': harnessing inventors' patent date for economic research", NBER Working Paper, no. 12479.

Van Beuzekom, B. and A. Arundel (2006), *OECD Biotechnology Statistics – 2006*, Paris: Organisation for Economic Co-operation and Development.

# 8. Science as a communications network: an illustration of nanoscale science research

## Caroline S. Wagner and Susan A. Mohrman

## 1. INTRODUCTION

Science shares many features with organic, complex adaptive systems. Indeed, it is practical for evaluation purposes to characterize scientific discovery as a network of communications (Hesse, 1974). This is the natural extension of considering science as a system (Von Bertalanffy, 1972), and specifically as a system of communications, as Nicolas Luhmann and others have done (Luhmann, 1986). Those who conduct scientific research organize in response to opportunity, generally created by the possibility of advancement married to funding (Whitley, 1984). Some scientific research is corporately organized, but the majority of research projects self-organize – researchers identify beneficial collaborations and voluntarily form into teams.

These self-organizing networks of scientists – often working on projects across geographic or disciplinary boundaries – are the most notable feature of science in the late 2000s. As the scientific knowledge base has grown, it is becoming increasingly difficult for any one researcher to know all the things needed to innovate (Gibbons et al., 1994). The collaborative teams that conduct cooperative research constitute an invisible college of practitioners who collaborate not because they are told to but because they want to, who work together not because they share a laboratory or even a discipline but because they can offer each other complementary insight, knowledge, or skills (Wagner, 2008).

Scientific research networks are the artifacts that emerge from these connections among scientists. Networks organize the physical and intellectual churn of researchers around the world as they travel to access the subject of research or to share research results. Networks have an underlying structure that furnishes the communications with form as research teams form, dissolve, and reform. Through weak links, small worlds, and preferential attachments, networks help to bring together scientists from different disciplines and diverse backgrounds and send them out again with new knowledge to share. In the twenty-first-century melting pot of science, national citizenship or allegiance plays a minor role. Scientific curiosity and ambition are the principal forces at work in the collaborative model (Whitley, 1984).

Network analysis as tool to track, monitor and evaluate these communications has not been well developed. To advance this tool, we based research on the premise that network measures have promise for improving tracking and monitoring of government spending on basic scientific research and evaluating its contribution to the knowledge system. The research protocol was applied to six laboratories contracted within the US Department of Energy (DOE) which have established research centers – called the Nanoscale Science Research Centers (NSRCs) – dedicated to nanoscale science. The NSRCs operate in a highly interdisciplinary and flexible organizational structure. We analyzed the networks in which the labs and the centers operate (locally and globally), and their links to the centers of excellence to which they connect around the globe.

Within this context of understanding science as a communications system using a networked structure, this chapter presents the results of this network analysis of the Department of Energy national laboratories in their role of promoting research and development in nanoscale science – uncovering and exploring properties of matter at their smallest known sizes (sub-atomic level) and within different environments (such as zero degrees kelvin).[1] Network analysis was applied to uncover the structure of social relationships within a research community based on the assumption that these relationships transmit and diffuse information; we assume that the transmission of information is both influenced and constrained by the structure of the network itself.

Network analysis offers a method to analyze the underlying structure of the relationships that create and diffuse knowledge. The tools can be applied to social groups as well as to groups of journals, institutions, countries, and even to clustering of concepts. The analysis is based on expectations of what is known about the structure and evolution of these networks (Newman et al., 2008). These structures can be visualized for pattern recognition and analysis (De Nooy et al., 2005). The network structure can also be analyzed statistically to reveal aspects of the dynamics of information flows. Importantly for analyzing knowledge creation, the structural aspects of networks represent opportunities for and constraints on the flow of information. In the case presented here, a link between two institutions is considered to flow in both directions, where knowledge can be exchanged between the two parties, rather than simply being passed from one to the other. We expected to find increased density in the network as more and more institutions formed collaborations around the resources offered by the DOE. Along with this, we expected to see the measure of centrality for the labs go down as more connections are made between the institutions within the network. We expected to find that the number of clusters grows overall, but that the clustering coefficient would stay the same: because this is a basic research network, we did not expect to see exclusive teams form that seek to be separated from others within the network.

To improve the ability to apply network analysis to reveal the dynamics of scientific research, we began by examining the place of the DOE laboratories viewed as nodes within actual research networks; then we examined the structure of the network as a whole, as well as the organization of connections within subsections of the network (clustering and density) to test whether the structure influenced the resulting connections. The analysis was conducted by examining a time series to show both the antecedents to the formation of the new centers as well as the years when the NSRCs were announced and began operations. In the earlier years covered in the study (1990–2000), the parent laboratory is the point of reference for the network analysis, either because the NSRCs were not yet created or because the smaller centers cannot be seen in the network at a particular level of aggregation. Whenever possible, emphasis is given to the NSRCs as they emerge from within the operations of the parent laboratories.

## 2. METHODOLOGIES AND DATA

Network analysis tools are implemented to examine the dynamics of the knowledge system growing around specific DOE labs beginning in 1990. The networks are analyzed from data pulled from actual project participation and records of co-authorship of journal articles and conference papers drawn from databases. Project participation data were provided by the DOE research centers; journal records were drawn from the Institute for Scientific Information (ISI) Web of Science.

Within each of the data sets, analyses were conducted to determine the network structure of the underlying knowledge system – be it social or knowledge-based. Measures were chosen to examine the extent of cohesion among collaborators, the possibility for knowledge sharing and diffusion, and to examine the relative power and position of particular nodes. (Measures of cohesion drawn from the data differ slightly for the various datasets; this is noted where appropriate.) The network measures most relevant to understanding knowledge creation in the DOE labs are the ones dealing with: (1) numbers of nodes and links; (2) distance across the network; (3) cohesion of the network; and (4) short-cuts in the network.

1.  Measures of the number of nodes and links are fairly straightforward as they involve counting. Then a measure is taken of the extent to which nodes are redundantly connected into clusters and into components. The numbers of nodes, links, clusters, and components give a baseline of participation in the networks as they existed when the NSRCs began operations. This becomes a point of comparison that can be used against other knowledge networks and against future states of the networks.
2.  Distance across the network gives us insight into the extent to which knowledge and information can flow among members. Distance measures include the average path length, the shortest path length, and the diameter of the network, again, described in more detail later.
3.  Cohesion of the network reveals two things: first is the extent of connectivity within the network itself and therefore possibilities for complementarity in the research community; second, it reveals the role of specific, important nodes within the network as go-betweens or gatekeepers of knowledge, access, and influence.
4.  Short-cuts in the network, also known as "small world" measures, show the extent to which unexpected connections can appear within the network. It has been suggested that small worlds create the dynamics where new ideas and unexpected information can enter and be passed through the network.

## 3.   DYNAMICS OF THE NANOSCALE SCIENCE RESEARCH SYSTEM

The Department of Energy laboratories have a long history of conducting research in atomic physics and the basic properties of chemicals and materials. Their experience in related sciences gave their scientists a head-start as equipment was developed that enabled significant advances in understanding nanoscale properties of materials. The DOE scientists already operated within a global network of collaboration. The network that began to grow around the DOE labs influences their work, and the creation of the NSRCs, in turn, can be expected to influence the global network. While this collaboration often cannot be observed directly without a great deal of effort, indicators of collaborations that were productive can be found in project lists, co-authorships, and patent listing connections can be visualized into network structures that provide a snapshot of the connections that underlay the research. This section describes the dynamics of the global system of science and technology research and development drawn from network analysis, with a view towards understanding the positions of the labs within the network.

Drawn out to its fullest dimensions, the relevant research network includes thousands of institutions conducting some aspect of nanoscale science in physics, biology, chemistry, materials, and interdisciplinary sciences. Given its sheer size, analyzing the entire network is not practicable nor is it necessary if the goal is to understand the dynamics of the system – the system can be understood at the subsystem level because of the scale-free structure of the network.[2] For the purposes of understanding the impact of the DOE NSRCs on the network, we have examined the core of the network in the related fields, and within that data set, we have viewed the citation strength of the institute in question. In addition, we analyzed the positions of the DOE labs within the core network over time with the expectation of seeing them become more influential to the overall system.

The core of the network is drawn from those journals that were determined, through factor analysis, to be the core journals for scientists publishing papers on nanoscale science and technology. For each of three years – 2002, 2004, and 2006 – all the articles appearing in the relevant journals were drawn into a data set and analyzed using Ucinet software (Borgatti et al., 2002). The networks that emerged from this analysis constituted a single component (one where all nodes can be reached from all other nodes by some number of pathlengths). The component was analyzed at the country-to-country level of collaborations, and then at the institutional level and compared over time. The role and position of the DOE labs within the network was of central interest to the analysis.

Over the three years examined, the country-to-country collaborations are active but do not change significantly. We expected to find that the network becomes more cohesive over time – that the nodes at the periphery become more tied into the network and that more links grow among countries. However, at the country-to-country level, the networks show only an insignificant amount of growth in cohesion. This may be because each nation grew their internal program, reducing the need to reach out to other countries for collaboration.

Each of the years examined show about 55 countries in the core network. It is noteworthy that, even with a weighted dataset, the central part of the network is inhabited by the United States, the United Kingdom, the larger European nations, Russia, Japan, and China. These nations are central to the network not simply because of their size; they are central because of the collaborations they maintain with others. Network theory suggests that the larger the number of sources available for any given information, the easier it is for someone in the network to obtain that information. It follows that centrality is an important position to hold in knowledge networks since the ability to gain access to information is greatly enhanced by being in the center. A central position provides an advantage to the research centers in these countries in terms of access and power. The number of ties or links among the nations overall numbered more than 600 per year within the core group; this means that each nation has an *average* of 12 ties. However, in network terms, average has very little meaning. The nodes at the edges of the network have one, two or three ties to others, while the nodes in the center of the network have more than 20 ties to other countries. Further analysis is needed to understand the influence of the more central nodes on knowledge sharing and power, but we assume that centrality is a key measure for the role of the NSRCs and their position in the knowledge system.

To gain further insight into the role of the DOE labs in the overall network, the same network data were examined at the level of the institutions involved in collaborative research. At the level of individual labs, it is possible to see the role of institutions within the broader network and to gain insight into their impact on the knowledge system. This analysis can then be aggregated back to the level of nations to shed light on the role of individual nations, their scientific strength, and the impact of political support on the advancement of science. The DOE labs are shown to be central to the nanoscale science network even before the establishment of the NSRCs. We expected to see that the addition of the collaborative centers, equipped with the very latest research instruments, would further enhance the attraction of US research centers as an attractive location for research and/or collaboration. To the extent this is the case, the position in the knowledge system is a benefit to any nation that has an attractive node in the network. The laboratory level analysis is described in the following section.

## 4. ROLES AND POSITIONS OF THE DOE NANOSCALE SCIENCE LABS

In the knowledge system of research and development in the nanoscale sciences, links (or a finding of a *lack* of links) among key institutions are examined to reveal the structural possibilities for exchange and diffusion of information, or the lack of access to key centers. In order to draw out these connections, the first level of analysis is presented for the parent lab, since the NSRCs are expected to operate within larger research laboratories. Prior to the establishment of the NSRCs, the larger parent laboratories were participating actively in nanoscale science and technology research – a line of research that can be traced back to the late 1980s when the nanoscale sciences first emerged as a new line of research (Mohrman and Wagner, 2006).

In an earlier study, for example, we found that the DOE laboratories were central to the nanoscale research community as collaborators and user centers long before the National Nanotechnology Initiative considered dedicating research centers at these locations (Mohrman and Wagner, 2006). The DOE laboratories conducted atomic level physics, materials research, condensed matter physics, and chemical research prior to the development of the equipment, theory, and experimentation that led to the spectacular rise in current research. This history of related research put the laboratories into a position where they were prepared to take advantage of new findings about the properties of materials at the nanoscale even before they hosted dedicated centers. We expected to see that the position of the labs would be enhanced at the local, national, and international levels because of the new emphasis on collaborative research. Accordingly, we expected to find an increase in the number and quality of connections around those laboratories as the NSRCs were established. This was examined in several ways: the number of collaborators within a network, the extent of actual and possible connections, the change in the connectivity of the network over time, and the role of the individual labs within the network.

For the dataset drawn from co-authored publications in relevant journals (which we called the "global data"), the number of components increased in number over the six years studied. In other words, the number of integral units of co-authoring institutions increased.[3] Table 8.1 shows the network statistics for the global institutional datasets. The number of institutions in the networks increased, as did the number of links among all the institutions within the networks, with the number of links increasing faster than the number of institutions, suggesting increasing connections among those institutions within the networks. The overall increase in nodes and links provides more potential sources of information to any individual member.

Within the global data, the position of nodes is an indicator of the attractiveness of the node for other research centers. It is also an indicator of the role that any institute plays in creating and diffusing knowledge based on its position and access – nodes at the periphery may be scanning for information, but can be assumed to have little to share. Nodes in the center of the network can be assumed to be diffusing information, but may be assumed to be fully optimized in their ability to innovate. The expectation is that the more useful an institution is as an actual or

*Table 8.1  Measures of the nanoscale science research collaboration at the global level*

|                                            | 2002  | 2004  | 2006   |
|--------------------------------------------|-------|-------|--------|
| Number of nodes                            | 1 882 | 2 177 | 2 736  |
| Number of components >2                    | 59    | 56    | 67     |
| Ties                                       | 6 970 | 9 988 | 11 624 |
| Centrality (Freeman)                       | 7.3   | 6.7   | 8.5    |
| Overall weighted clustering coefficient    | 0.3   | 0.22  | 0.35   |

potential partner, the more it will attract collaborators in a virtuous cycle called "preferential attachment." To analyze this, at the global level, two measures are instructive:

1.  The centrality of the network as a whole – a highly centralized network has a distinct core which controls the access of the peripheral members and acts as a powerful force on the sharing of information.
2.  The ego betweenness of key nodes – this shows the position of nodes as a measure of that institution's ability to broker or mediate access and information for others.

Table 8.1 shows the centrality measure for the global network. This core global network is not highly centralized, meaning there are many nodes that have a large number of connections relative to the network as a whole. This suggests that much of the system is still fluid, with collaborations changing relatively rapidly. This fluidity is to be expected in a network that is creating knowledge through basic research. The clustering coefficient shown in the table is also low: again, a basic research network can be expected to have low clustering because teams will not have a vested interest in protecting and hoarding information. (In contrast, an innovation network that is close to the market may be expected to have a high clustering coefficient since practitioners have a need to share a deep common knowledge as well as to hoard information from contagion across the network.)

Table 8.2 shows the centrality of specific nodes in the network. The table demonstrates the fluidity of the network, since only two institutions hold a central place in the network in each of the three years. The two highly central institutions are also large organizations with many researchers; these institutions can be expected to have more pull in the network in terms of attracting contributing collaborators. The two highly central institutes that remain in place are the French Centre National Recherche Scientifique

*Table 8.2    Collaborating institutions with high degree centrality (2002, 2004, 2006)*

| Institutions with high group centrality (alphabetical) | Year that they appear in the top 10 list of most central institutions | | |
|---|---|---|---|
| | 2002 | 2004 | 2006 |
| Argonne National Lab (USA) | | | √ |
| Centre National Recherche Scientifique (CNRS) (France) | √ | √ | √ |
| Consejo Superior de Investigaciones Científicas (CSIC) (Spain) | √ | √ | |
| Institute of Chemistry – Chinese Academy of Sciences | | √ | |
| Instituto Nacionale per la Fisica della Materia (INFM) (Italy) | √ | | √ |
| Lund University (Sweden) | | √ | |
| Max Planck Institute (Germany) | | √ | |
| Nanjing University (China) | | | √ |
| National Cheng Kung University | | | √ |
| National Institute of Advanced Industrial Science & Technology (AIST) (Japan) | √ | √ | √ |
| National Institute of Standards & Technology (USA) | | √ | |
| National Research Council of Italy (CNR) | | √ | |
| Oak Ridge National Laboratory (USA) | √ | | |
| Osaka University (Japan) | √ | | |
| Penn State University (USA) | √ | | |
| Tohoku University (Japan) | √ | | |
| Tokyo Institute of Technology | | √ | √ |
| Univ California–Berkeley (USA) | √ | | |
| University of Cambridge (UK) | | | √ |
| University of Illinois (USA) | √ | | |
| University of Paris (France) | | √ | |
| University of Tokyo (Japan) | | | √ |

*Source:*    ISI, Thomson.

(CNRS) and Japan's National Institute of Advanced Industrial Science and Technology (AIST). Each of three DOE labs appears once in the list: Argonne National Lab appears as a central node in 2006, Oak Ridge in 2004, and University of California–Berkeley (which hosts the Lawrence Berkeley National Lab) in 2002.

## 5.  EGO BETWEENNESS OF KEY INSTITUTIONS

The strength of the relationships for each individual node also can be measured as a component of the network as a whole. This is called ego betweenness – it shows the position of individual nodes as they relate to their own links; in network theory, it shows the relative power of individual nodes. Box 8.1 shows the top 25 institutions for 2006 that had a high ego betweenness measure. Among the most "between" institutions in the network in 2006 are two of the DOE labs, Argonne National Lab and Oak Ridge National Lab: their inclusion here represents the activities related to the NSRCs as well as activities in other parts of the labs, so that measure in itself it does not show the impact of the formation of the NSRCs. These two labs are also among the research institutions with the highest ego-betweenness measures in 2002 and 2004. No other DOE laboratories were among the top highly centralized or ego-between institutions.

Each of the NSRCs also began their operations with a pump-priming program called "Jump Start." Jump Start took advantage of some existing research activities already underway in the labs; these activities were transferred to the NSRCs. The new staff at the NSRCs also took the Jump Start opportunity to invite specific collaborators to initiate projects in a newly-created NSRC. Figure 8.1 shows the network of collaborations created around the labs as a result of investments in the Jump Start programs. The figure shows the strength of the parent labs, and the beginning of the NSRCs as they join the network of collaborators. Figure 8.1 reveals the strength of Argonne National Lab and Oak Ridge National Lab in creating collaborations. These two labs are in an excellent position to gain access to cutting-edge knowledge, to identify and open doors for new entrants into relevant research, and to diffuse knowledge to other research centers, as the measure and the visual show.

## 6.  CONCLUSION

Using network analysis, the DOE contract research laboratories can be shown to be key players in the nanoscale sciences even before the announcement of the creation of new interdisciplinary research centers under the National Nanotechnology Initiative in the United States. The NSRCs were designed to enable interdisciplinary research teams to self-organize around the demands of the science in teams defined by the researchers themselves. The concept underlying this design principle is that truly new discoveries – those that revolutionize the path of scientific progress and potentially contribute to innovation – are nearly impossible to predict

---

## BOX 8.1     TOP 25 INSTITUTIONS WITH HIGHEST EGO-BETWEENNESS MEASURES (2006)

University of Cambridge
National Institute of Advanced Industrial Science and Technology
University of Tokyo
Tokyo Institute of Technology
National Institute of Material Sciences
CNR Italy
ETH (Sw)
Nanjing University
Institute of Chemistry, Chinese Academy of Sciences
CNRS France
Japan Science and Technology Corporation
Nagoya University
Institute of Physics, Chinese Academy of Sciences
Kyoto University
Hahn Meitner Institute Berlin GmbH
Peking University
Eindhoven University of Technology
Tsing Hua University
Argonne National Laboratory
MIT
University of California, Berkeley
Oak Ridge National Laboratory
Osaka University
University of California, Santa Barbara
Hokkaido University

---

and thus cannot be defined or constructed in advance (Mohrman and Wagner, 2006). Increasingly, the study of research dynamics shows that transformative change results from the combination of insights from very different fields, a point made by several people interviewed for this project such as Bob Hwang, a physicist who heads the Center for Functional Nanomaterials at the US Department of Energy's Brookhaven National Laboratory. He explained his view:

> Our present definition of nanoscience comes from the fact that materials scientists, physicists, and others have recognized that something fundamentally

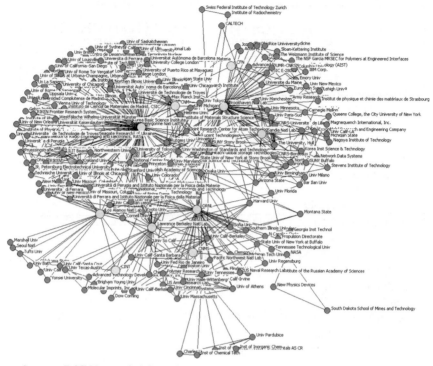

*Source:*   DOE Nanoscale Science Centers.

*Figure 8.1   Networks of collaborations around the DOE labs and the NSRCs in the initial Jump Start program*

different happens to materials at the nanoscale – different from what you see at other levels. We [scientists] discovered this phenomenon – so in that sense it grew out of the traditional work in science, but in another sense it is new: new departments in universities are forming all the time because of that particular discovery. The concepts underlying nanoscience are so encompassing that they stretch over all the present disciplines. . . . The real success in science comes when one takes a multidisciplinary approach, because this [discovery] would not have happened otherwise.[4]

During the years 2002–06, the NSRCs emerged from within their parent laboratories, drawing strength from the robust networks built by these DOE laboratories over more than 15 years of NSE research and collaborations with other institutions from around the world. As the NSRCs formed their own networks, in some cases they appear to draw off collaborators from the parent lab's networks, actually reducing the strength of the parent network in the global system while not building up the small centers into highly attractive nodes – at least not in a visible way in 2007. This does not satisfy the expectation we had at the start of the research when we expected to see the labs becoming more attractive as a result of having the new centers. We expect this diminished position to be only a temporary phenomenon as both research institutions stabilize and grow their positions in the global system.

Nevertheless, this suggests that the capability of the NSRCs to act as an attraction for the parent lab is not operating in the way we expected. The NSRCs are less internationally connected than their parent labs, but again, this may be poised to change as the centers mature. The networks revealed by analysis of collaboration networks appear to be basic research networks – revealed by the lack of clustering and the large number of connections to many nodes – this means they are well structured to draw from and diffuse knowledge across the United States, and to a lesser extent to other places in the world.

The finding is that the creation of a spin-off research center may actually have a short-term negative effect on the positions of both the parent and the spin-off institution in the short term while social networks catch up with the prior positions held by the parent labs. This may mean that, for the time that the spin-offs are being created, and while the parent labs are regaining their position, the research centers actually lose power and influence in the network as a result of the reorganization. While this may be a short-term loss – and may be viewed as acceptable to those organizing the new institutions – it may also mean a loss of ability to contribute to regional or national innovation for a significant period of time, perhaps as much as two years, as new connections are made.

The research shows that network analysis can be a highly effective way to view the organization of knowledge-creating research teams. Network analysis allows the creation of indicators of dynamic change that were unavailable to research assessment in the past. It allows the analyst to draw conclusions about the roles of research centers to create, diffuse and absorb knowledge, and to theorize on the importance of connection to the type of research being conducted. The analysis presented here suggests that at least two of the DOE labs are in an excellent position within the global network to trade knowledge. They are highly central to the network, they have many connections to other highly connected and highly cited centers, and they maintain state-of-the-art equipment with which to conduct research. Additional research will reveal the extent to which the labs are able to turn this into an informational advantage.

## ACKNOWLEDGMENTS

The authors wish to thank the US Department of Energy for funding the research presented in this chapter.

Funding for this research was subcontracted to Advanced Systems Technology and Management, Inc. (AdSTM) by the US Department of Energy/Office of Science through Contract No. DE-AC02-04ER30321. This is a continuation of Research Contract No. 84882: *The Organizational and Managerial Factors that Contribute to the Stream of Value from the Basic Research Funding of the Office of Science*. We acknowledge the generous encouragement and support from William Valdez and Christine Chalk of the Office of Science, from Patricia Dehmer and Altaf Carim of the Office of Basic Energy Sciences, and from the more than 120 directors, leaders and scientists associated with the Nanoscale Science Research Centers that we are studying. We are also thankful for the data management support and other resources from the Center for Effective Organizations at the Marshall School of Business, University of Southern California, and would especially like to thank Nora Osganian and Alice Yee Mark for their substantial contributions to this research. We also thank Christopher Ordowich at SRI International and Rich DeJordy at Boston College for assistance.

## NOTES

1. Nanoscale science focuses on understanding and controlling matter at dimensions of roughly 1 to 100 nanometers, where unique phenomena enable novel applications. A nanometer is one-billionth of a meter; a sheet of paper is about 100 000 nanometers thick. Encompassing nanoscale science, engineering and technology, nanotechnology involves imaging, measuring, modeling, and manipulating matter at this length scale. Research at these scales has been revolutionized by the development of scanning force microscopy in the late 1980s (NNI website accessed September 2005).
2. A scale-free network has a power law form that can be studied at any sublevel. In a power law form, the structure of a subsystem will have the same statistical fingerprint as the network as a whole.
3. If institute A collaborated with institute B, and B with C, the three institutes would be connected into a single component. The number of members of a single component is not limited; the only limitation is the existence of a collaborative link. One would expect to find a single component within a research network where most institutes are connected to one another. Satellites of other smaller components might exist outside of the core group, although the members of satellite components may come and go within the core group over time. We did not examine this phenomenon.
4. Telephone interview with Susan A. Mohrman, Brookhaven National Laboratory, November 18, 2005.

# REFERENCES

Borgatti, S.P., M.G. Everett and L.C. Freeman (2002), *Ucinet for Windows: Software for Social Network Analysis*, Cambridge, MA: Harvard, Analytic Technologies.

De Nooy, W., A. Mrvar and V. Batagelj (2005), *Exploratory Social Network Analysis with Pajek*, Cambridge: Cambridge University Press.

Gibbons, M., H. Nowotny, C. Limoges, M. Trow, S. Schwartzman and P. Scott (1994), *The New Production of Knowledge: The Dynamics of Science and Research in Contemporary Societies*, London: Sage Publications.

Hesse, M., (1974), *The Structure of Scientific Inference*, London: Macmillan.

Luhmann, N. (1986), "The autopoiesis of social systems", in F. Geyer and J. van der Zouwen (eds), *Sociocybernetic Paradoxes*, London: Sage Publications.

Mohrman, S.A. and C.S. Wagner (2006), *The Dynamics of Knowledge Creation: A Baseline for the Assessment of the Role of the Department of Energy's Nanoscale Science Research Centers*, Los Angeles: Center for Effective Organizations, University of Southern California.

Newman, M.E.J., A.L. Barabasi and D.J. Watts (2008), *The Structure and Dynamics of Networks*, Princeton, NJ: Princeton University Press.

Von Bertalanffy, L. (1972), *General Systems Theory: Foundations, Developments, and Applications*, New York: Braziller.

Wagner, C.S., (2008), *The New Invisible College: Science for Development*, Washington, DC: Brookings Institution Press.

Whitley, R. (1984), *The Intellectual and Social Organization of the Sciences*, Oxford: Oxford University Press.

PART III

Public policies for networking in ICT

# 9. European policy favouring networks in ICT

## Stefano Breschi, Lorenzo Cassi, Franco Malerba and Nicholas S. Vonortas

## 1. INTRODUCTION

This chapter advocates the use of social network analysis to evaluate aspects of public programmes supporting research and development. For the specific empirical analysis, the chapter draws on a recent study that appraised the partnership and knowledge networks created locally and globally in relation to the Information Society Research and Technological Development (IST-RTD) programmes of the Sixth Research Framework Programme (FP6) of the European Community. It is found that the examined IST-RTD programmes play an important role in generating and diffusing knowledge by managing to attract key industry actors and by creating and increasing network connectivity. We argue that public policy should try to facilitate the development of more European organizations that can be characterized as Global Network Hubs and to draw larger numbers of the most technologically dynamic small and medium-sized enterprises (SMEs) into these programmes.

The typical appraisals of RTD expenditures have tended to concentrate in the past on the additionality of public funding in terms of either the resources added into the system (input additionality) and/or the extra private and social returns created (output/outcome additionality). Such appraisals have, however, tended to miss the sustainable effects beyond the infusion of resources and/or the extraction of outputs that such investments create, such as improving the competencies, capabilities, organizational structures and strategies of firms (behavioural additionality). This chapter focuses on the latter.

In today's globally competitive and fast changing environment, most innovations involve the collaboration of several different organizations. The collaborative networks leading to new technologies, products and services are very complex, involving not only diverse kinds of formal contracts, but also informal exchanges of knowledge. In a technological development that involves a greater array of products and processes, systems and components, no single firm can deploy all of the required core capabilities and complementary assets at reasonable cost. In this context, a network serves as a locus for innovation because, for any member, it provides timely access to external knowledge and resources while also valorizing internal expertise and expanding learning abilities. A large part of the behavioural additionality of RTD investments is, thus, realized through the partnership and knowledge networks that such investments create.

We have utilized social network analysis to assess several aspects of behavioural additionality in specific IST-RTD programmes. We have investigated whether the projects selected for funding by the first two calls for proposals of FP6 in the IST Thematic Areas 1, 2 and 3 ("Applied IST Research Addressing Major Societal and Economic Challenges", "Communication, Computing and Software Technologies", "Components and Micro Systems") during the period 2002–04 have been effective in supporting network hubs that nurture global knowledge leadership and European cohesion. Hubs were defined in this study as organizations with many linkages and the ability to connect disparate parts of the network. In RTD networks, such organizations operate as knowledge depositories and sources of information and ideas. A large-scale empirical analysis using several extensive data sets has been carried out to place the IST-RTD networks within the context of broader global networks of collaborative knowledge relationships that have developed independently of Community funding.

In order to address questions of knowledge network effectiveness, we have used a novel methodology which studies relationships. The research team developed and applied a quantitative methodological framework for high-quality, comparative assessment of inter-organizational networks established by IST-RTD programmes with global networks developing independently of Community funding. In addition, more qualitative information obtained through a series of expert/practitioner interviews was utilized to calibrate some of the results and obtain stakeholder suggestions for the future. The analysis purported to demonstrate the applicability of social network concepts and analytical tools in appraising the relative global positioning of IST-RTD networks and their effectiveness in creating leading knowledge hubs in selected technological domains.

The rest of the chapter is structured as follows. Section 2 provides the context of the study. It first summarizes key features of the Framework Programme and of its IST priority and then illustrates the rationale for a network approach to evaluating IST-RTD programmes. Section 3 provides a description of the adopted methodology and data. Section 4 reports the main findings related to the role of IST-RTD funding in creating and sustaining knowledge hubs, the relative importance of these hubs in the global

IST network, the role of the new funding instruments (Integrated Projects and Networks of Excellence) in supporting and extending the network, and the inclusiveness of core national research organizations. Finally, section 5 summarizes the results and offers policy recommendations.

## 2. STUDY CONTEXT

### The Framework Programme as a Networking Environment

The Framework Programme (FP) for RTD is the main policy instrument of the European Community for research and development. The current Treaty of the European Union identifies two core strategic objectives for the FP: (1) strengthening the scientific and technological bases of industry to encourage its international competitiveness, and (2) supporting other policies of the European Union. The FP has undergone significant changes during the past decade and a half, reflecting developments in the socio-economic context of the region and the Community's realization of the Programmes' importance. FP3 (1990–94) had the development of the internal market in the background, FP4 (1994–98) had the Maastricht Treaty and the White Paper on Growth Competitiveness and Employment, FP5 (1998–2002) had the rising interest in socio-economic values, and FP6 (2002–06) has had the European Research Area (ERA) in the background. One feature has not changed in this process: successive FPs have tried to achieve their objectives by promoting collaborative research, a procedure put in place in the early 1980s when the FP was being established on the foundations of the industry roundtable organized in the early 1980s by Commissioner Davignon to assist the competitiveness of the European electronics industry.

Aiming at facilitating the ERA, the FP6 has had an even stronger focus on research integration than any of its predecessors. The programme has introduced new funding instruments that combined with more traditional instruments to provide a multitude of opportunities for collaboration. The salient features of the FP instruments are as follows:[1]

- *Integrated Projects* (IPs) are large projects with holistic work-plans that connect a range of research, development and deployment activities. Overall workflow is fairly well laid out from the beginning. The coordinating organization has a key role and mediates participation. IPs are likely to involve a wide range of organizations from the research and business communities. In some cases, work tends to be modular.

- *Networks of Excellence* (NoEs) are large projects with much more internal flexibility to pursue "portfolio" exploration from a range of alternatives. They are primarily intended to combine and cross-fertilize existing strands of research around a common core issue. They are more likely to involve publicly supported research organizations and to have less centralized or hierarchical structures than IPs.
- *Specific Targeted Research Projects* (STRePs) reflect smaller consortia and more narrowly focused research that is innovative within a predetermined work-plan. They are self-contained and the closest instrument to the typical collaborative research that has been traditionally supported by the FPs.
- *Coordinated Actions* (CAs) and *Specific Support Actions* (SSAs) provide other forms of support or coordination to ongoing research efforts and areas of policy application in other instruments.

The European Union has supported research and technological development (RTD) work through six Framework Programmes for RTD implemented since the early 1980s. The Framework Programme (FP) is agreed on by the member states of the European Union and is implemented over the span of five years (changing in FP7). It functions as an umbrella under which many more specific programmes fund research across a variety of fields such as information and communications technologies, energy, biotechnology, health, advanced materials, and manufacturing. The supported RTD must have European added value and the projects are almost exclusively undertaken by consortia of at least three partners representing a minimum of three member states of the European Union or affiliated countries.

Information Society Technologies (IST) has been a core priority of the Framework Programmes since the very start. This investment has been encapsulated in a host of well-known earlier programmes such as ESPRIT I-IV, RACE I-II, ACTS, DELTA, DRIVE, TAP I-II, and AIM. Such programmes and their derivatives were placed under the overall IST Thematic Priority in the Fifth Framework Programme (1998–2002) that has continued in the Sixth (2002–06), now also including media applications of all kinds. IST has maintained a leading position in successive FPs as it is a core piece of the policy objective of the Community to establish a leading global knowledge economy (so-called Lisbon strategy). The IST Thematic Priority has thus commanded a large share of the FP throughout the years, amounting to almost a quarter of overall funding in FP6. The Community has high expectations for the contribution of its IST investment to competitiveness, economic growth and employment as it is emphasized in the renewed Lisbon Strategy and the Plan i2010.[2]

## Modern Evaluation Concepts and Networks

Public support for RTD has traditionally been justified in the economics literature on the basis of market failures. The market failure rationale is based on the difference between the benefits to society (social returns) and the benefits to the individual/organization undertaking the RTD investment (private returns). The greater this difference is, the larger the spillovers from the private party to the rest of society, and the less the willingness of the private party/sector to invest at the socially optimal level.

More recently, analysts have also promoted the rationale of system failures for government intervention. Supporting arguments reflect issues of path dependence, technological lock-in, investment timing (technology life-cycles, trajectories), institutional constraints (general infrastructure), coordination failures (e.g. standards), and the efficiency of mechanisms facilitating knowledge flows. Above and beyond accounting for inputs and outputs/outcomes, the systems approach concentrates on the dynamics of RTD and innovation; that is, the processes involved in generating innovation outcomes. A primary interest here is in an organization's or a nation's capacity to innovate and in the mechanisms that allow it to take full advantage of its capabilities.

Such considerations have underlined the concept of *additionality*, which has proved useful as an organizing device when considering public support for RTD:

- *Input additionality*: Has public expenditure created additional funds to be spent, and on what?
- *Output/outcome additionality*: Has public expenditure generated additional private and social returns?
- *Behavioural additionality*: Has public expenditure created sustainable effects beyond the infusion of resources and outputs such as improving the competences, capabilities, organization and strategies of firms?

It is the third aspect of additionality where the network approach can make its greatest contribution. By studying relationships, exchanges, network location and status, network structure and evolution through time, and so forth, this approach provides a new prism to examine important aspects of the longer-lasting, more sustainable contributions of public policy in affecting organizational and national/regional capabilities to innovate. The results reported in this chapter primarily relate to the third concept of (behavioural) additionality.

Two earlier studies made significant progress in mapping the IST research networks in Europe and in examining the topological features of such networks.[3] They found that the network of European IST-RTD research collaborations has:

- A "scale-free architecture" at the thematic level, meaning a pattern of (preferential) attachment that underlines the extensive influence of relatively few "hub" organizations and the relatively minor influence of a much larger number of peripheral organizations.
- "Small world" connectivity, meaning efficient communications between local clusters that facilitate the dissemination of knowledge.
- Closer, stronger, denser linkages among organizations with the introduction of Integrated Projects and Networks of Excellence in FP6, with large firms and research institutes taking on even more central network positions than in earlier Framework Programmes.
- Participants that are also likely to be part of other European networks such as COST (focusing on science) or EUREKA (focusing on technology application).

Our work complemented the earlier studies and significantly expanded the scope of using the network methodology for evaluation purposes by both examining at greater length the IST-RTD networks and by comparing them to the global networks. The analysis has addressed important phenomena such as the role of IST-RTD funding in creating and sustaining knowledge hubs, the relative stature of these hubs in the global IST network, the role of the new funding instruments (Integrated Projects and Networks of Excellence) in supporting and extending the network, and the inclusiveness of core national research organizations.

## 3.  METHODOLOGY

### Network Data

We use large-scale quantitative data on the participation of European organizations in various knowledge-related collaboration activities. More specifically, the study examined three types of network relations, as shown in Table 9.1.

The IST-RTD Network provides the core network. On the basis of available information, we built two networks for IST-RTD projects: the IST Applications Network, which includes projects in Thematic Area 1, and the IST Development Network, which includes projects in Thematic

*Table 9.1   Three types of network relations*

| Type of network | Description | Source |
|---|---|---|
| IST-RTD Network | European network formed by organizations participating in FP6 IST TA1 and TA2/3 projects (partnership network) | Internal EC database (not publicly available) |
| Global Network | Global network formed by companies involved in privately funded alliances (partnership network) | INNET dataset (George Washington University) |
| Knowledge Network | Knowledge network arising from cross-organizational patent citations | EP-CESPRI dataset (European Patent Office) |

Areas 2 and 3. The IST-RTD Network is complemented by two broader networks within which knowledge and resources are exchanged and transferred: the Global (partnership) Network and the Knowledge (patent) Network. This way, the IST-RTD network is placed in the broader context of networks of knowledge relations spontaneously emerging from the initiatives of individual organizations.

Examining the global network of strategic alliances allows one to assess the extent to which European organizations involved in the IST-RTD Network are also involved in the broader global network of RTD collaborations in the relevant technological domains. More importantly, it permits one to evaluate whether and to what extent IST-RTD projects have achieved the objective of nurturing global knowledge leaders, on the one hand, and supporting the creation of additional knowledge linkages over and above those autonomously forged by private companies, on the other. To this purpose, we have used the INNET database, which reports information on worldwide strategic alliances. For this study we have selected only those strategic alliances whose technological content is related to the domains pertaining to IST-RTD projects in the examined thematic areas.

The network formed by collaborative RTD projects can be studied as an affiliation network (or bipartite graph); that is, a network in which the actors (organizations) are joined together by common membership to groups (collaborative RTD projects). Affiliation networks can be represented as a graph consisting of two kinds of vertices, one representing the actors and the other the groups. In order to analyse the patterns of relations among actors, however, affiliation networks are often represented simply as unipartite (or one-mode) graphs of actors joined by undirected edges (clique assumption). In this study, we refer to the analysis of the unipartite graph of organizations involved in RTD consortia.

On the other hand, an important channel of knowledge transfer is represented by the disembodied flow of scientific and technological information (knowledge spillovers). Although capturing these types of knowledge flows in their totality is difficult, an approximation frequently used in the economic literature involves patent citations to prior art. The fact that patent A cites patent B as prior art is perceived as an indication of some kind of knowledge flow from the organization responsible for patent B to the organization responsible for patent A. Moreover, the fact that organization B's patents are frequently cited by patents of other organizations suggests that organization B represents an important repository of knowledge and ideas for other organizations; that is, it is a knowledge leader.

Based on patent citation data, the analysis of the knowledge network in this study aimed therefore to assess to what extent European organizations involved in IST-RTD projects are effective knowledge leaders. To this purpose, we have used the EP-CESPRI dataset, which provides information on patent applications to the European Patent Office. For this study we have collected all patent documents whose technological classification is related to the domains pertaining to IST-RTD projects in the examined Thematic Areas.

**Analytical Methodology**

Analysis was conducted at the level of individual organizations. Three basic types of organizations were considered: private companies (IND), higher education institutions (HE), and public research organizations (REC). The main analytical tool is graph theory and its applications, also known as social network analysis. This section briefly illustrates the key terminology and the main concepts of social network analysis adopted in this study.

A network may be defined as a set of actors (or nodes) linked by some kind of relational tie. A network thus defined may be visually depicted as a sociogram in which nodes are represented as points in two-dimensional space, and relationships among pairs of actors are represented by lines (edges) linking the corresponding points. In this study, nodes are organizations, while relational ties are of three different types:

- Organizations *a* and *b* are linked by an edge if they have been partners in at least one IST-RTD project (IST Applications Network and IST Development Network).
- Organizations *a* and *b* are linked by an edge if they have been partners in at least one strategic alliance (Global Network).

- Organizations *a* and *b* are linked by an edge if organization *a*'s patents cited (or have been cited by) organization *b*'s patents (Knowledge Network).

To keep the analysis as simple as possible, we used only undirected and binary valued networks. This means that we disregard both the direction and the intensity of the ties linking pairs of organizations. To do otherwise would require much more data than are currently available (e.g. on the intensity of collaboration between organizations *a* and *b* in a network versus organizations *a* and *c*). The following sociogram (Figure 9.1) illustrates a hypothetical network, where nodes represent organizations and edges may be thought of as capturing any of the relational ties just described.

A core concern of the study was to examine the position occupied by different types of organizations in the various types of networks and, more specifically, to understand how the position of European organizations involved in the network represented by IST-RTD funded projects maps onto their position within the broader set of knowledge relations.

Although there are different ways to characterize the position of a node in a network, a very important dimension of it relates to the notion of a *Network Hub*. Informally, a hub may be defined as a node with a large number of connections or, alternatively, as a node that is highly influential by playing the role of network *connector*; that is, one connecting nodes that would otherwise remain unconnected. Hubs have therefore an extremely important role in partnership and knowledge networks as they contribute towards the effective and fast diffusion of knowledge even to the most peripheral nodes of the network.

More formally, the notion of a network hub may be captured by two indicators: degree centrality and betweenness centrality. Degree centrality is simply defined as the number of lines incident with a node. In the context of this study, degree centrality is defined as the number of other organizations with which the focal organization has a relational tie.[4] Betweenness centrality, on the other hand, is a measure of

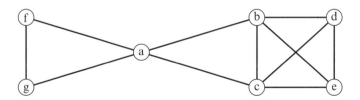

*Figure 9.1   A sociogram illustrating a hypothetical network*

the influence a node has over the spread of information and knowledge through the network. The basic idea is that a node, which lies on the information path linking two other nodes, is able to exercise a control over the flow of knowledge within the network. Formally, it is defined as the fraction of shortest paths (i.e. the minimum number of lines connecting two nodes) between node pairs that pass through the node of interest.[5]

Degree centrality and betweenness centrality have been calculated for all organizations and a synthetic index has been composed from the joint rankings of organizations in terms of these two indicators. *Hubs* have been defined as the top 2 per cent of the organizations on the basis of the joint ranking.[6] (see Box 9.1)

This procedure has been separately applied for each type of relational tie. It defines three types of hubs, each corresponding to one of the three kinds of networks considered herein (the most important hubs are listed in the Appendix Tables 9A.1 and 9A.2):

- IST-RTD Hubs (33 hubs for the IST Applications Network and 23 hubs for the IST Development Network).
- Global Hubs (300 hubs for the Global Network).
- Knowledge Hubs (374 hubs for the Knowledge Network).

The notion of hubs applies to single networks. Once one considers multiple networks in which an organization is embedded at the same time – for example the IST-RTD Network and the Global IST Network – the relevant concept is that of *Gatekeeper*, defined as an organization that plays the role of hub in more than one network.

## 4. FINDINGS

### Various Types of Organizations Play the Role of Hubs in IST-RTD Networks

One objective of FP6 is to encourage networking among different types of organizations, including industry, higher education institutions and research centres. Given the absence of quantitative targets, one can consider that the objective has been achieved if the shares of these different types of organizations are somewhat balanced in terms of their participation and in terms of the role they play in the network. To address this issue we have identified the top organizations playing the role of hubs in the IST Applications and IST Development Networks.

---

## BOX 9.1 THE ROLE OF HUBS IN KEEPING CONNECTED NETWORKS

*"If you go for the biggest nodes and take a couple of them out, you can break the system into clusters that don't communicate with each other"*. (Albert-Laszlo Barabasi)

The idea developed by Barabasi in several studies and summed up in his previous quote could also be easily applied in the context of this study. It is enough to focus on the size of the greatest subpart of a network: the so-called *giant component* (i.e. the greatest set of actors directly or indirectly connected). As one starts deleting the top ranked organizations in terms of centrality as well as their links, the size of the giant component as a percentage of the nodes included in it drops dramatically. In the case of the Global Network, deleting the top 2 per cent of hubs reduces the giant component to one third of its initial size.

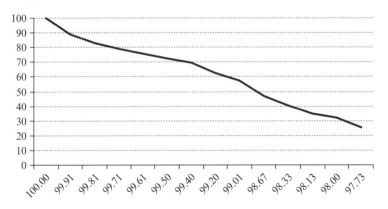

*Note:* The size of the Global Network giant component is set equal to 100.

---

Table 9.2 reports the distribution of hubs by organizational type for the IST Applications Network and the IST Development Network[7] and compares the distribution with the participation rates in the IST-RTD projects. In both networks, one finds a rather even distribution of hubs among firms, higher education institutions and public research organizations. Universities play a disproportionate role as hubs compared to their participation rates in the IST Applications Network. Public research

*Table 9.2    Hubs in IST-RTD networks*

|  | IST applications network | | IST development network | |
|---|---|---|---|---|
|  | Participants (%) | Hubs (%) | Participants (%) | Hubs (%) |
| Higher Education | 25.5 | 39.2 | 32.7 | 29.0 |
| Industry | 35.1 | 37.3 | 39.0 | 34.4 |
| Research centre | 14.4 | 23.5 | 10.9 | 36.6 |
| Others | 25.0 | 0 | 17.4 | 0 |
| Total (%) | 100 | 100 | 100 | 100 |
| Total (abs value) | 1660 | 33 | 1112 | 23 |

organizations are far more represented as hubs compared to their weight in terms of participation in the IST Development Network.[8]

Importantly, the different funding instruments affect the type of hubs in the network. If the linkages formed by NoEs are excluded, the role of industrial organizations as hubs increases: they now account for 55 per cent of all hubs in the IST Applications Network and around 45 per cent of all hubs in the IST Development Network. This reflects the fact that NoEs host a larger proportion of participants from higher education institutions and public research organizations. Moreover, it reflects the propensity of different organizations to take a leading role in projects, which differs across instruments: industrial actors tend to assume coordinating roles relatively more frequently in projects funded by instruments such as IPs and STRePs, while leaving that task primarily to higher educative and public research centres in NoEs.

**Important Global Hubs Actively Engage in the IST-RTD Networks**

An important concern is the extent to which IST projects have been able to attract the major actors in the global network of RTD collaborations in information and communication technologies (ICT) and, therefore, have managed to activate direct and indirect links with the major global network players. Figure 9.2 shows the geographical distribution of hubs in the global network. Few of them are European. Even discounting the US dominance, few European organizations are able to occupy core positions in the global ICT alliance networks.

At the same time, there are also strong indications that IST projects are able to attract global hubs. Figure 9.3 shows that more than half of the top 25 global hubs participate in the examined IST-RTD projects. This share rises to around 70 per cent if companies are weighted by their

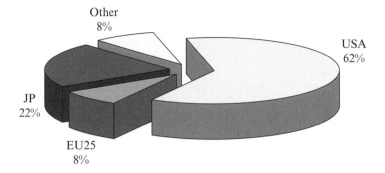

*Figure 9.2    Distribution of top 100 global hubs by area*

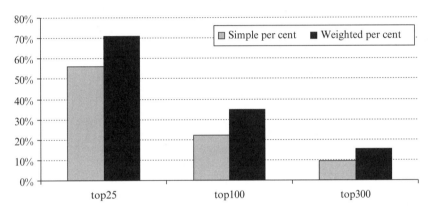

*Figure 9.3    Percentage of global hubs participating in IST projects*

ranking, meaning that the relatively most influential companies in the global network also participate in the IST-RTD projects. A comparison with the top 100 and 300 global hubs shows that the share participating in IST-RTD projects is lower than for the top 25 shown here, but the weighted share (according to the ranking of hubs) is always higher.

More important, some of the global players attracted to the IST Thematic Priority serve the dual role of the global hub and the hub in the IST-RTD network. These organizations are labelled here Gatekeepers as they are able to effectively put in contact organizations involved in IST-RTD with the broader global network of RTD collaboration. Their position in both networks puts them at the crossroads of information and knowledge flowing within IST-RTD projects and information and knowledge flowing within the much broader global network of strategic alliances.

This is illustrated by Figures 9.4 and 9.5, which report a subset of the IST

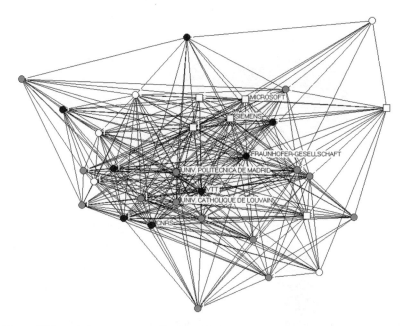

*Note:* White = industry; grey = university; black = public research centre; ○ = IST-RTD hub, □ = Gatekeeper (IST-RTD *and* global hub).

*Figure 9.4   IST applications hubs*

Applications and the IST Development Networks respectively. The partition contains only organizations (nodes) that are hubs in these two networks and the ties among them. IST-RTD hubs have been assigned different shading and shapes according to the organizational type and to their also being global hubs. The organizations' names are reported only for the first seven organizations according to the ranking based on centrality indexes.

The graphs show that a few industrial actors play the dual role of IST-RTD hub and global hub at the same time (Gatekeeper). This occurs both in both the IST Applications Network and the IST Development Network.

**Effectiveness in Connecting IST-RTD Organizations and Global Hubs**

We start by examining the fraction of all linkages between pairs of actors accounted for by the three major funding instruments of Framework Programmes: Integrated Projects (IPs), Networks of Excellence (NoEs) and Specific Targeted Research Projects (STRePs). The results are reported in Figures 9.6 and 9.7 for the IST Applications Network and the IST Development Network respectively. IPs and NoEs account for the bulk of

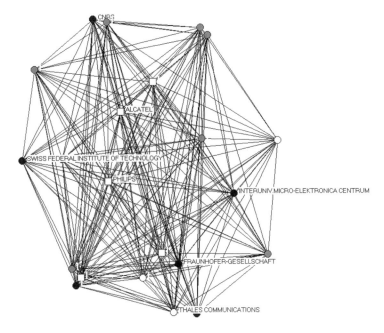

*Note:* White = industry; grey = university; black = public research centre; ○ = IST-RTD hub, □ = Gatekeeper (IST-RTD *and* global hub).

*Figure 9.5 IST development hubs*

linkages and STRePs account for the bulk of projects. STRePs, in particular, account for half of all projects but for just 10 per cent of the links.

In order to examine the effectiveness of the various funding instruments in linking IST project participants to global hubs, we have focused on the linkages among the various types of hubs, and among them and other non-hub organizations. More specifically, the following groups of actors have been considered: IST-RTD hub, global hub, gatekeeper, and other IST-RTD organizations. In terms of instruments, we consider IPs, NoEs, and STRePs.

Results are reported in Figures 9.8 and 9.9 for the IST Applications and the IST Development Networks respectively. The figures report the relative importance of an instrument in linking *groups of actors pairwise*. The relative importance is defined in terms of the ratio of the percentage share of links between two *specific* groups of actors depending *exclusively* on an instrument and the percentage share of links among *any* organizations that depend on that instrument. A ratio higher than one means that the instrument in question is relatively important in bridging the two specific

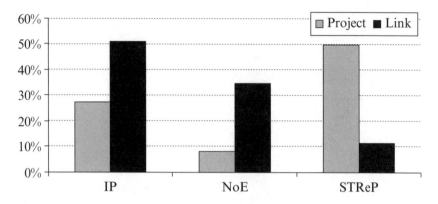

*Figure 9.6    IST applications network (percentage of projects and links*
*depending on three instruments)*

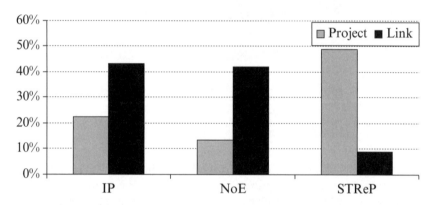

*Figure 9.7    IST development network (percentage of projects and links*
*depending on three instruments)*

groups. For example, in the IST Applications Network, IPs play a relatively important role in bridging IST-RTD hubs and organizations that
are global hubs (but are not hubs in the IST Applications Network) since
the share of links between these groups of organizations depending exclusively on IPs is significantly higher than the average share of links depending exclusively on IPs. In the figure, only instruments playing a relatively
important role in bridging two groups of actors are reported.

The results are striking and provide strong support to the idea that
IPs are highly effective instruments for connecting IST-RTD hubs and
global hubs, and for connecting global hubs (gatekeepers or not) to other
organizations. On the other hand, NoEs seem to be relatively less effective

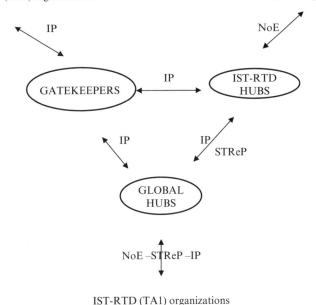

*Figure 9.8 Relative importance of IPs, NoEs and STRePs in bridging IST applications network organizations*

in this specific role; they are more relevant in linking IST-RTD hubs to other organizations. STRePs are effective in linking global hubs to other organizations in both examined networks.

Another way to test the importance of IPs in connecting populations is by taking a subset of the IST-RTD networks containing only hubs (both IST-RTD and global hubs) and investigating how many linkages among them would be severed without the IPs. This is shown in Figure 9.10.

The graphs illustrate that the elimination of the linkages attributable to IP projects has a major impact on overall connectivity, especially in relation to the IST applications network. Several hubs become isolates, while degree centrality is substantially reduced for others. In sum, IPs can be considered as an effective instrument directly connecting global hubs to IST-RTD hubs and, largely through them, to many other IST organizations.

For companies, NoEs seem less effective than IPs in connecting global hubs and IST-RTD hubs. One reason is that NoEs are more effective in connecting higher education organizations to each other and to public research organizations than to other kinds of organizations.

The apparent effectiveness of IPs for putting together heterogeneous

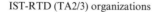

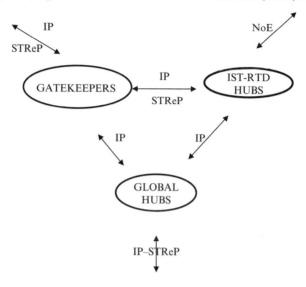

*Figure 9.9    Relative importance of IPs, NoEs and STRePs in bridging IST development organizations*

actors with different and complementary competences could be considered a strength of this instrument in terms of promoting the ERA objectives. IPs would seem to create the scale and ambition necessary to develop technology platforms, thus propelling some European hubs to positions of global stature. Because they are large and ambitious, IPs also tend to attract global hubs, which provides connectivity to the best and brightest in the world.

Our interviews with European experts in the IST field highlighted the fact that IPs are considered the turf of larger organizations, which are more diversified, have more diffuse research capabilities and broader market reach. Their ability to include the smaller, gazelle-type companies, and in what capacity, was questioned. The role of the prime contractor was reportedly critical in IPs. Experience in coordinating large projects becomes paramount for success and, it was argued, should be one of the criteria in picking IP projects. This, in turn, gives these organizations significant bargaining power.

Universities and research centres play an important role in IP networks by focusing on more long-term and fundamental parts of the research. The promotion of more intensive knowledge transfer between university

IST Applications Network

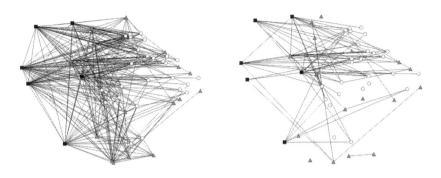

IST Development Network

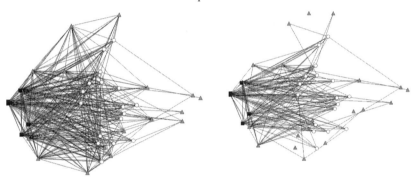

*Note:*   ○ = IST-RTD hubs only; □ = gatekeepers; △ = global hubs only.

*Figure 9.10    Linkages among hubs in the IST-RTD networks with IPs
(left panel) and without IPs (right panel)*

and industry was considered by the experts an area where the FP could contribute significantly. This means greater mobility of people, increased opportunities where the two meet, more funding for the maintenance of the research infrastructure, and improvement of channels for technology take-up and exploitation.

As for the other funding instruments, STReP projects were considered highly effective in achieving their technical goals by the interviewed experts because they are narrowly focused and are easier to coordinate. As previously mentioned, NoEs are dominated by higher education and research organizations and they tend to be very large and diffuse. Industry has been hesitant to participate because NoEs are perceived to have difficulty with research quality control, they do not necessarily involve all excellent partners, and they are often too big (creating problems for coordination and knowledge diffusion and sharing).

### Hubs' Effectiveness at Producing and Diffusing Knowledge

The first part of section 4 identified hub organizations in the IST partnership networks, including both the FP-IST context (IST-RTD hubs) and the global IST context (global hubs). In both these networks, organizations align in order to get access to the knowledge assets of partners, diversify risk and complement resources regarding important RTD projects, and more generally network with others considered important in specific fields. The implication is that an organization will not be asked to participate if it does not have something useful to offer in terms of intellectual capital, especially in the case of prime contractors in FP networks and core organizations in partnership networks.

One may expect a high degree of correlation between partnership hubs and knowledge hubs in their respective contexts. The interviews with experts from industry and from public research centres made clear that a prerequisite for assuming a core position in a partnership network like those analysed herein is the "respect" an organization commands among its peers, suppliers and buyers for its capabilities. Larger organizations with widespread resources and capabilities, especially intellectual capital, that span several fields are prime candidates.

This prompted us to consider the inventive record of each partnership hub and its role in diffusing and exchanging the accumulated knowledge as reasonable proxies to evaluate its effectiveness. We have adopted the following definition: "An effective knowledge hub operates as a knowledge depository and/or is a recognized source of information and ideas." Effectiveness, in this sense, reflects the contribution of an organization in enriching the knowledge network with new knowledge, on one hand, and in facilitating the dissemination of knowledge among network members, on the other.

We have used the EP-CESPRI patent database to measure inventive activity and to derive indicators of knowledge diffusion and human capital mobility. For that purpose we have used all patent applications to the European Patent Office in the ICT-related fields. In this sense, the coverage of the patent database is global.

Three indicators have been used to capture the effectiveness of organizations in producing new knowledge:

- *Number of patents:* number of patent applications filed from 1996 to 2002 in the relevant technological fields.

- *Number of citations received* (weighted by the number of patents): number of citations received by patents of an organization divided by the total number of patents of that organization. It is a measure of quality of the patent portfolio of an organization.
- *Number of highly cited patents*: number of frequently cited patents. It is a measure of importance of the patent portfolio of an organization.

As argued earlier, an important channel of knowledge transfer is represented by the disembodied flow of scientific and technical information; that is, knowledge spillovers. Information contained in patent citation patterns can be used to assess the effectiveness of an organization in disseminating knowledge. Specifically, patent citations have been used to build up the knowledge network in which nodes are patenting organizations and ties are patent citation relationships among them. On the basis of this network, we have calculated for each organization, two indicators:

- *Degree centrality* in the knowledge network: number of direct connections of an organization (nodes). Nodes with the highest degree are the most active in the sense that they have the most ties to other actors in the network graph.
- *Betweenness centrality* in the knowledge network: an actor is central if it lies between many pairs of other actors not directly connected between them. A node with high betweenness centrality has great influence over knowledge flows in the network.

Results show that IST-RTD hubs[9] are more inventive and more central than other IST-RTD participants, thus being quite effective in both the generation of new knowledge and the diffusion of existing knowledge (Figure 9.11, top panel). More interestingly, IST-RTD hubs are also more effective in the generation and diffusion of knowledge and inventiveness than global hubs (Figure 9.11, bottom panel).

Further investigation also reveals the following:

- The global hubs that participate in IST-RTD are more effective in every respect than those global hubs that do not participate. The FP attracts global hubs that are relatively more effective in terms of both producing and diffusing information.
- Global hubs that are also IST-RTD hubs (i.e. gatekeeper organizations) are relatively more effective than those global hubs that just participate in IST-RTD but play no major role in it.

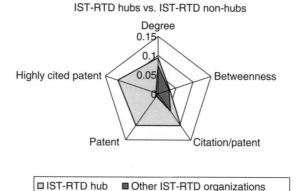

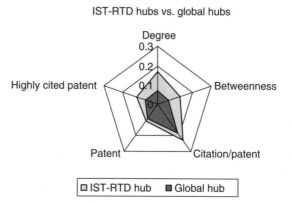

*Figure 9.11    Effectiveness in producing and diffusing knowledge*

● Gatekeepers compare favourably to organizations that are only IST-RTD hubs.

The analysis so far has considered all kinds of organizations that serve as hubs: industry, universities and public research centres. However, given that not all types of organizations emphasize patenting equally, one would worry about bias in measures of effectiveness based on inventive activity to the extent that different groupings – say, IST-RTD hubs and other IST-RTD participants – host significantly different proportions of non-patenting organizations.

We have checked the sensitivity of the results reported above when considering only firms. They turn out to be quite robust.

The importance of hubs is related to the scale-free nature of the examined networks (see the second part of section 2). Scale-free nature implies that a relatively small number of hubs – that is, organizations that are most highly sought after – offer important benefits to partners in terms of knowledge assets and network resources. Hubs are viewed by others as high-status partners either because they are perceived as depositories of knowledge and/or because they are situated in privileged sections of the network facilitating flows of information and ideas. Larger organizations with widespread resources and capabilities, especially intellectual capital, that span several fields are prime candidates.

According to the interviewed experts from industry and from leading research centres engaged in the IST field, this reflects a set of key hub characteristics. One is research excellence and the sustenance of strong areas of in-house expertise. Another is strong technological capability, including the maintenance of multi-talented teams and expertise across several areas. A third is organizational, related to the ability to manage effectively sets of alliances involving different partners. Then there is global reach – or European reach if we are referring to a European network – in terms of alliances, markets and organization. Last but not least, are market exploitation capabilities in terms of holding strong market positions that make partnering desirable to others.

## 5. CONCLUSIONS, POLICY RECOMMENDATIONS

Every emergent social network has a "scale-free" architecture, indicating a wide discrepancy in the criticality of different nodes (organizations, individuals) for the network. Few nodes appear to be placed in more critical positions in the network than the large majority of other nodes. More central network positioning (locally or globally) generates visibility and reputation, facilitates timely access to resources and information and, thereby, also ensures higher leverage and control. This, in turn, raises the status of these nodes and makes them especially desirable as partners. Such nodes possess atypical bargaining power in the network: they become brokers and shapers of events.

The European Research Framework Programmes create emergent social networks through the voluntary participation of organizations and individuals in the funding competitions. By extension, the Framework Programmes create networks that are subject to scale-free architectures. The implication for policy is straightforward: core organizations may provide the critical policy lever in the effort to approximate optimal solutions. Such organizations could play a pivotal role in steering the network toward desired socio-economic situations. For the Framework

Programme, these translate into strengthening the scientific and technological bases of industry to encourage its international competitiveness, and supporting other policies of the European Union.

In this study we have applied social network analysis to a set of specific programmes of FP6 in a two-year time window. We used social network analysis with the help of large datasets to assess the nature and relative network positioning of core European organizations identified as "knowledge hubs". Hubs were defined to be organizations with a large number of connections and/or organizations that are highly influential by playing the role of connector of parts of the network that would otherwise remain unconnected. We were concerned with questions such as: How are hubs positioned in the networks created through IST-RTD funding and how does it compare to their positioning within the broader global networks in IST? What may be the role of the new funding instruments of FP6 – Integrated Projects (IPs) and Networks of Excellence (NoEs) – in facilitating the effectiveness of such knowledge hubs? To what extent are IST-RTD collaboration networks inclusive of national research networks and key large and small IST enterprises around Europe?

Perhaps the most important outcome of the study is the confirmation that social network analysis is an empirical tool amenable to application in appraising the effectiveness of publicly funded RTD programmes, and especially suited to answer questions of "behavioural additionality" that have hitherto been addressed only qualitatively. While still far from standardized, we feel that it provides an avenue for analysis with very significant potential to get at difficult issues.

Regarding the specific example of IST-RTD programmes appraised herein, network analysis showed the following:

- *Attracting key actors to the European IST Knowledge Network*
  IST-RTD projects are able to attract global hubs whether these hubs are based in Europe or not. The examined IST-RTD thematic area programmes tend to include a good share of the top knowledge hubs of most of the EU15 member states. Probably because of the timing, the programmes include fewer such organizations from new member states. There is a rather even distribution of hubs among firms, higher education institutions and public research organizations in the examined IST-RTD programmes. The role of firms as hubs in IST-RTD networks increases significantly when Networks of Excellence (NoEs) are excluded.
- *Creating and strengthening the connectivity among actors*
  IST-RTD programmes create linkage additionality. IST-RTD projects add new and complementary links to existing linkages.

IST-RTD programmes incorporate key organizations that are both IST-RTD hubs and global hubs. Mostly private sector companies, these organizations play a critical role as *gatekeepers*, effectively putting in contact organizations involved in IST-RTD with the broader global network of collaborations in information and communication technologies. Gatekeeper organizations are at the crossroads of information and knowledge flowing both within IST-RTD projects and within strategic alliances around the world. Integrated projects (IPs) play a critical role in connecting IST-RTD participants to the rest of the world. Integrated projects are responsible for a very large fraction of ties in the IST Applications Network and the IST Development Network. Moreover, IP linkages account for a major part of overall connectivity among hubs. IPs are found to be an effective instrument in terms of connecting global hubs to IST-RTD hubs and, through them, connecting many other IST-RTD participants to the broader global IST network. For companies, NoEs seem less effective than IPs in that particular role.

- *Generating and diffusing new knowledge effectively*
Hubs are effective in producing and diffusing knowledge. Gatekeeper organizations – simultaneously global hubs and IST-RTD hubs – are the most effective in terms of both enriching the network with new knowledge and facilitating the dissemination of knowledge among network members. In turn, IST-RTD hubs are more effective than other IST-RTD participants in terms of both producing and disseminating new knowledge.

Let us close with a final observation. This and earlier studies have argued that the network emerging from IST-RTD projects has the characteristics of being at the same time a *small world* and a *scale-free* network. On the one hand, the property of small world refers to the fact that the average distance among all organizations in the IST-RTD network is relatively low and, at the same time, each organization is embedded in a tightly connected cluster of other organizations. This structure is believed to be optimal both for the creation (high cliquishness) and the dissemination (low distance) of knowledge, especially when complex and difficult-to-absorb knowledge is at stake. On the other hand, the IST-RTD network also has the property of being a scale-free network, implying that it contains relatively few highly interconnected hubs while the vast majority of nodes are weakly connected. The IST-RTD network hubs are not only highly connected to other organizations, but are also highly interconnected to each other.

The emergence of a small-world topology in the IST-RTD network may be interpreted as the (unintended) consequence of the rules governing the participation in IST-RTD projects as well as of the initial conditions of the industry, which have favoured the formation and consolidation of a few 'supernodes'. In particular, high transaction costs in framework programmes combined with the typical relative scarcity of resources in smaller firms have been major factors making such players refrain from taking a coordinating role in IST projects. The most feasible way for getting access to IST funding for these companies is often through joining projects led by larger and more reputed organizations in the industry. The goal of achieving long-run cohesion and diffusion of knowledge in this field seems, then, to have been achieved indirectly by focusing on funding a restricted set of network participants and relying upon their coordination capabilities to attract more and more peripheral organizations. The network that has emerged from IST-RTD projects can thus be depicted to have a two-layer structure, where a very large number of small organizations (non-hubs) float around and are highly dependent on a small group of core and highly interconnected organizations (hubs).

This structure provides an important input in efforts to streamline funding instruments in order to increase the effectiveness of the IST-RTD network. The instruments used so far have been successful at creating a network structure that is effective in producing and disseminating knowledge at the RTD level by strengthening links among hubs while also favouring the formation of links between hub organizations and non-hub organizations, therefore pulling into the network more peripheral actors. However, a few potential risks should be also noted. In particular, as long as participation and funding of IST-RTD projects remain conditioned on the access to a few anchor companies and institutions, it is unlikely that organizations that join the network late will ever become hubs. Moreover, to the extent that the research priorities and network organization are defined by core participants, the risk of lock-ins and the resistance to re-orienting the network towards more productive research areas increase accordingly. The policy implication would be that, beside instruments aimed at further increasing linkages among hubs (e.g. IPs) and among hubs and non-hubs organizations (e.g. NoEs), emphasis should be placed towards more flexible and manageable instruments that allow smaller organizations to take a leading and coordinating role in IST projects. If one of the objectives of EU IST policies is to nurture the development of new European hubs, policies and instruments better tailored to the needs and constraints of non-hub organizations should also be promoted.

# NOTES

1. Summary descriptions are based on "ERAnets: evaluation of networks of collaboration between participants in IST research and their evolution to collaborations in the European Research Area (ERA)", Final Report by RAND Europe, DG Information Society and Media, March 2005, pp. 7–8.
2. Communication from the Commission "i2010 – a European Information Society for growth and employment", SEC(2005)717. Communication to the Spring European Council "Working together for growth and jobs: a new start for the Lisbon strategy", COM(2005) 24, 2/2/05.
3. J. Stefan Institute study: "Data mining and decision support for business competitiveness: a European virtual enterprise" (Cordis Project reference: IST-1999-11495). RAND study: "ERAnets: evaluation of networks of collaboration between participants in IST research and their evolution to collaborations in the European Research Area (ERA)", March 2005 (Tender OJ 2004/S 177-151255).
4. With reference to the hypothetical sociogram depicted in Figure 9.1, nodes *a*, *b* and *c* present the highest values of degree centrality, being connected to four other organizations.
5. With reference to the hypothetical sociogram depicted in Figure 9.1, it is intuitive that node *a* has a high influence as a network connector. For example, the shortest path between organizations *d* and *g* has length 3 and organization *a* lies on it. If one takes all possible pairs of organizations (excluding *a*) and counts the number of shortest paths connecting them, it turns out that organization *a* lies on 8 out of 15 of them. The betweenness centrality of organization *a* is therefore equal to 8/15 = 0.53. It is therefore highly influential in mediating knowledge flows taking place among the nodes in the network. By contrast, organization *b* lies only on three shortest paths (connecting node *d* with *a*, *f* and *g*) and is thus characterized by a lower value of betweenness centrality (0.20).
6. The 2 per cent cut-off is obviously arbitrary. We also considered different values (both higher and lower than 2 per cent) to check for robustness. The main results go through.
7. The percentage values for each type of organization have been weighted according to the ranking in the overall list of hubs. The rationale for using weighted percentages is that organizations ranking high in the list of hubs are likely to be relatively more influential than organizations ranking low. The weights have been defined in the following way: $w_i = (\max r + 1 - r_i)/\Sigma r_i$, where $r_i$ is the ranking of organization *i* and max *r* is the maximum value of the ranking. Please note that the weights sum to 1.
8. Firms participating in IST projects have been consolidated according to the ultimate parent company. For example, Nokia Italy has been considered as part of the Nokia group. The research labs of large public research organizations (e.g. Fraunhofer Gesellschaft) have been also consolidated. As a robustness check, we have recalculated the list of hubs by considering each subsidiary or research lab as an independent unit. Results are not significantly sensitive to the consolidation of companies and research laboratories.
9. In this section, IST Applications and IST Development hubs are examined jointly.

# BIBLIOGRAPHY

Albert, R., H. Jeong and A.-L. Barabasi (2000), "Error and attack tolerance of complex networks", *Nature*, **406**, 378–82.
Breschi, S. and L. Cusmano (2004), "Unveiling the texture of a European Research Area: emergence of oligarchic networks under EU Framework Programmes", *International Journal of Technology Management. Special Issue on Technology Alliances,* **27** (8), 747–772.

Caloghirou, Y., N.S. Vonortas and S. Ioannides (eds) (2004), *European Collaboration in Research and Development: Business Strategy and Public Policy*, Cheltenham, UK and Northampton, MA, USA: Edward Elgar.

CESPRI (2006a), "Evaluation of progress towards a European Research Area for information society technologies", Final Report, European Commission – DG Information Society and Media, December.

CESPRI (2006b), "Evaluation of progress towards a European Research Area for information society technologies", Technical Report, European Commission – DG Information Society and Media, December.

Edquist, C. (2004), "Systems of innovation: perspectives and challenges", in J. Fagerberg, D.C. Mowery and R.R. Nelson (eds), *Oxford Handbook of Innovation*, Oxford: Oxford University Press.

European Commission (2005a), "i2010 – a European information society for growth and employment", SEC(2005)717.

European Commission (2005b), "Working together for growth and jobs: a new start for the Lisbon strategy", COM(2005) 24.

J. Stefan Institute (1999), "Data mining and decision support for business competitiveness: A European virtual enterprise", European Commission – DG Information Society and Media.

Jaffe, A.B. and M. Trajtenberg (eds) (2002), *Patents, Citations, and Innovations*, Cambridge, MA: MIT Press.

Peterson, J. and M. Sharp (1998), *Technology Policy in the European Union*, London: Macmillan.

Powell, W.W., K.W. Koput and L. Smith-Doerr (1996), "Interorganizational collaboration and the locus of innovation: networks of learning in biotechnology", *Administrative Science Quarterly*, **41**, 116–45.

RAND Europe (2005), "ERAnets: evaluation of networks of collaboration between participants in IST research and their evolution to collaborations in the European Research Area (ERA)", Final Report, European Commission – DG Information Society and Media, March.

Wasserman, S. and K. Faust (1994), *Social Network Analysis*, New York: Cambridge University Press.

# APPENDIX

*Table 9A.1    IST applications network hubs*

| Rank | Organization | Organization type |
|---|---|---|
| 1 | FRAUNHOFER-GESELLSCHAFT | REC |
| 2 | **SIEMENS AG** | IND |
| 3 | UNIVERSITÉ CATHOLIQUE DE LOUVAIN | HE |
| 4 | UNIVERSIDAD POLITÉCNICA DE MADRID | HE |
| 5 | VTT TECHNICAL RESEARCH CENTRE OF FINLAND | REC |
| 6 | CENTRE NATIONAL DE LA RECHERCHE SCIENTIFIQUE | REC |
| 7 | **MICROSOFT** | IND |
| 8 | SWISS FEDERAL INSTITUTE OF TECHNOLOGY | HE |
| 9 | FIAT | IND |
| 10 | **HEWLETT-PACKARD** | IND |
| 11 | ECOLE POLYTECHNIQUE FÉDÉRALE DE LAUSANNE | HE |
| 12 | **NOKIA** | IND |
| 13 | CENTRE FOR RESEARCH AND TECHNOLOGY HELLAS | REC |
| 14 | UNIVERSITY OF SOUTHAMPTON | HE |
| 15 | ARISTOTLE UNIVERSITY OF THESSALONIKI | HE |
| 16 | **IBM** | IND |
| 17 | UNIVERSITAT POLITECNICA DE CATALUNYA | HE |
| 18 | SCHLUMBERGER | IND |
| 19 | KUNGL TEKNISKA HÖGSKOLAN (ROYAL INSTITUTE OF TECHNOLOGY) | HE |
| 20 | THALES COMMUNICATIONS | IND |
| 21 | INSTITUTE OF COMMUNICATION AND COMPUTER SYSTEMS | REC |
| 22 | **MOTOROLA** | IND |
| 23 | UNIVERSITÄT DUISBURG-ESSEN | HE |
| 24 | VODAFONE | IND |
| 25 | DAIMLERCHRYSLER AG | IND |
| 26 | THE UNIVERSITY OF SURREY | HE |
| 27 | UNIVERSITÀ DEGLI STUDI DI SIENA | HE |
| 28 | VIENNA UNIVERSITY OF TECHNOLOGY | HE |
| 29 | UNIVERSITÀ DEGLI STUDI DI ROMA "LA SAPIENZA" | HE |
| 30 | INSTITUT NATIONAL DE RECHERCHE EN INFORMATIQUE ET EN AUTOMATIQUE | REC |

*Table 9A.1*   (continued)

| Rank | Organization | Organization type |
|------|--------------|-------------------|
| 31 | DEUTSCHES FORSCHUNGSZENTRUM FÜR KÜNSTLICHE INTELLIGENZ GMBH (GERMAN RESEARCH CENTER FOR ARTIFICIAL INTELLIGENCE) | REC |
| 32 | TECHNICAL UNIVERSITY OF CRETE | HE |
| 33 | FOUNDATION FOR RESEARCH AND TECHNOLOGY – HELLAS | REC |

*Notes:*   REC = public research organizations; IND = industry; HE = higher education.
Organizations in bold characters are also hubs in the global network (i.e. gatekeepers).

*Table 9A.2    IST development network hubs*

| Rank | Organization | Organization type |
|------|-------------|-------------------|
| 1 | FRAUNHOFER-GESELLSCHAFT | REC |
| 2 | INTERUNIVERSITAIR MICRO-ELEKTRONICA CENTRUM VZW | REC |
| 3 | CENTRE NATIONAL DE LA RECHERCHE SCIENTIFIQUE | REC |
| 4 | THALES COMMUNICATIONS | IND |
| 5 | SWISS FEDERAL INSTITUTE OF TECHNOLOGY | HE |
| 6 | **PHILIPS** | IND |
| 7 | **ALCATEL** | IND |
| 8 | **TELEFONICA INVESTIGACION Y DESARROLLO SOCIEDAD ANONIMA UNIPERSONAL** | IND |
| 9 | UNIVERSITAT POLITECNICA DE CATALUNYA | HE |
| 10 | BUDAPEST UNIVERSITY OF TECHNOLOGY AND ECONOMICS | HE |
| 11 | VTT TECHNICAL RESEARCH CENTRE OF FINLAND | REC |
| 12 | INSTITUT NATIONAL DE RECHERCHE EN INFORMATIQUE ET EN AUTOMATIQUE | REC |
| 13 | FRANCE TELECOM | IND |
| 14 | INSTITUTE OF COMMUNICATION AND COMPUTER SYSTEMS | REC |
| 15 | UNIVERSIDAD POLITECNICA DE MADRID | HE |
| 16 | **SIEMENS AG** | IND |
| 17 | ECOLE POLYTECHNIQUE FEDERALE DE LAUSANNE | HE |
| 18 | UNIVERSITE CATHOLIQUE DE LOUVAIN | HE |
| 19 | THE UNIVERSITY OF SURREY | HE |
| 20 | **MOTOROLA** | IND |
| 21 | CHALMERS UNIVERSITY OF TECHNOLOGY | HE |
| 22 | KUNGL TEKNISKA HÖGSKOLAN (ROYAL INSTITUTE OF TECHNOLOGY) | HE |
| 23 | STMICROELECTRONICS | IND |

*Notes:*    REC = public research organizations; IND = industry; HE = higher education.
Organizations in bold characters are also hubs in the global network (i.e. gatekeepers).

# 10. Evaluating the links between research and deployment networks of innovation in information society in Europe

**Lorenzo Cassi, Nicoletta Corrocher, Franco Malerba and Nicholas S. Vonortas**

## 1. INTRODUCTION

This chapter assesses the effectiveness of network collaboration and knowledge transfers within the Information Society and Technology programme for Research and Technology Development (IST-RTD) within the Sixth Framework Programme (FP6) and suggests ways to strengthen the links between IST-RTD, innovation and deployment at the EU and regional levels. It draws on the report "Networks of Innovation in Information Society: Development and Deployment in Europe", European Commission, DG Information Society and Media, 2006. It also builds on earlier studies[1] of IST-RTD networks to examine the extent to which networks are serving the purposes of regional reach and exchange. In particular, the study complements those earlier ones by going one step further to examine the link between research, innovation and IST technology deployment activities at the EU, national and regional levels. While research networks were the central focus of the earlier studies, the *effects* of networks on market application and deployment of new IST technologies become the central focus of the present evaluation study.

The study combines quantitative network indicators and field interviews. Its limitations should be also emphasized. Given the concentration of network indicators only on formal (observed) linkages and the limited number of interviews conducted, the study only evaluates a small part of the overall European picture of knowledge flows across networks and regions. Therefore, rather than aiming at generalization, the study purports to identify trends and issues, and to put forward observations regarding the efficacy of European IST-RTD and regional development programmes. The rest of the chapter is organized as follows. Section 2 presents a brief literature review on the role of networks in bridging research and knowledge dissemination, especially at the regional level. Section 3 reports the methodology adopted, illustrating the rationale behind the choice of the technological domain, the data and the criteria used to select a relevant subset of regions to focus on, and the organizations to be interviewed. Furthermore, it describes the main characteristics of research and deployment networks and also defines some key actors in our approach, namely network hubs. Section 4 analyses the complementarity and overlaps between the two types of networks. Section 5 summarizes the interview material from the different regions, concentrating on the effects of IST networks on the deployment of information and communication technologies (ICT), the role of national and regional networks in technology deployment, and two key industrial players in deployment including multinational corporations and small and medium-size enterprises (SMEs). Finally, section 6 sums up the lessons learned and discusses policy implications.

## 2.   CONCEPTUAL FRAMEWORK

Science, technology and innovation networks are regarded as the emerging organizational mode in environments of complex technologies and rapid technological advance. Success in knowledge-intensive industries depends on organizational learning and commercialization of technologies across different networks. Networks serve as a locus for innovation, because they provide more timely access to external knowledge and resources, represent a test for internal expertise and learning abilities, and give better monitoring and control over fast-moving developments (Powell et al., 1996).

Science, technology and innovation networks have also gained momentum in the policy agenda of the member states of the European Union. They have been perceived as an integral part of the efforts of the EU to develop the European Research Area (ERA) by integrating the systems of member states into a coherent whole (European Commission, 2000). The creation of the ERA is viewed as a critical step towards the development of a broad infrastructure for scientific and technological development; that is, a set of interconnected elements that support research and diffusion in Europe, and facilitate the circulation of information and knowledge, the development of transnational organizational forms, the definition of common standards, and the promotion of shared values.

To this end, the main policy tool has been the Framework Programme (Peterson and Sharp, 1998). Several studies have started to investigate the effectiveness of the FP in building such an infrastructure (e.g. Caloghirou et al. 2004; Breschi and Cusmano, 2004; Roediger-Schluga and Barber, 2006). Breschi and Cusmano (2004) and Roediger-Schluga and Barber (2006) focus on R&D networks promoted under the first five FPs and show that the FP funding schemes support the construction of complex networks with structural properties that facilitate dissemination. Moreover, it is shown that there is a significant overlap of participants for consecutive FP and recurring patterns of collaboration amongst the same organizations: "This core may constitute the backbone of the present European Research Area" (Roediger-Schluga and Barber, 2006, p. 36). In an assessment of information society technologies (IST) in FP6, Breschi et al. (2007) find that the examined IST research programmes played an important role in generating and diffusing knowledge, as they managed to attract key industry players and boosted network connectivity.

Existing studies concentrate on the effectiveness of research networks at the European level. A key issue that has been much less analysed refers to how these research networks impact on regional systems and how they interact with research and diffusion activities carried out at the regional level.[2] As Storper (1997) has emphasized, however, one of the most relevant issues in a knowledge-based economy is the tension between globalization and "territorialization", the latter referring to the development of knowledge-intensive regional clusters. Similarly, Bathelt et al. (2004) have indicated the need for complementarities between close and distant interaction in order to foster an effective process of knowledge creation and dissemination and, consequently, for policies able to balance developing of "global pipelines" (e.g. international collaboration) with efforts in generating and promoting local social capital. The main aim of this chapter is to investigate the major complementarities between the ICT research network built through the Framework Programmes and the diffusion networks built through both dedicated EU funded programmes and other national and regional programmes in ICTs that focus more on technology exploitation and development.

## 3.   RESEARCH AND DEPLOYMENT NETWORKS

### Methodology

We focus on the innovation and deployment projects within the technological domains of "Applied IST Research Addressing Major Societal and Economic Challenges"; that is, the first IST Thematic Area of FP6. This thematic area is very appropriate to analyse the links between innovation and deployment since it connects well to IST deployment programmes, especially eTen and eContent. eTen is designed to help the deployment of telecommunication networks based services (e-services) with a trans-European dimension. It focuses strongly on public services, particularly in areas where Europe has a competitive advantage. eContent is a market-oriented programme, which aims to support the production, use and distribution of European digital content and to promote linguistic and cultural diversity in the global networks. We identify organizations participating in FP6, eTen and eContent projects and use them as the initial sample of analysis, as Table 10.1 displays.

On the basis of information available, we build two partnership networks: research and deployment. In order to do that, we assume that if two organizations participate in the same project they are directly linked.[3] Following the economic literature, our analysis assumes that each of these partnership links represent a channel of collaboration, knowledge exchange and information spillovers. Data concerning organizations and projects are elaborated using network analysis software tools. In particular, for each network, we examine their structural properties and their interactions and overlaps, as well as the specific role played by the organizations acting as hubs and/or gatekeepers.

In order to gain additional insights into knowledge networks within the ERA, we have investigated research and deployment activities within specific regions (NUTS 2 level). The regions were chosen to represent a spectrum of capabilities and capacities, by considering:

- geographic clusters of IST projects;
- networking within the region;
- occurrence of other European instruments to support regional growth;
- strength of science, technology and economic (STE) capability.

*Table 10.1   Data*

|  | IST research projects | IST deployment projects |
| --- | --- | --- |
| Description | European network formed by organizations participating in *FP6 IST – TA1* projects | European network formed by organizations participating in *eTen* and *eContent* projects |
| Data source | Internal EC database (not publicly available) | Internal EC database (not publicly available) |
| Period | First 4 calls of FP6 2002–05 | eTen: 2000–05 eContent: 2002–05 |

*Table 10.2   Selected regions*

| | | |
|---|---|---|
| East Wales (UK) | Rhône-Alpes (France) | Bremen (Germany) |
| North Jutland (Denmark) | Lansi Suomi (Finland) | Norte (Portugal) |
| Attiki (Greece) | Emilia Romagna (Italy) | Malopolskie (Poland) |

Correlations among these factors show different levels of development in different regions. For the current evaluation analysis, we have selected a subset of regions (Table 2) representing the spectrum of STE capabilities that could characterize European regions, and the different location: three are from Central Europe – Rhône-Alpes, Bremen and East Wales; two from Northern Europe – North Jutland[4] and Lansi Suomi; three from Southern Europe –Attiki, Emilia Romagna and Norte; and one from a new accession country – Malopolskie in Poland.

By investigating networks and organizations within these regions, we identify different patterns of network collaboration and knowledge transfers between RTD and innovation and deployment activities. Network analysis and in-depth interviews are conducted to seek answers and insights into a range of evaluation questions that guided the project. We examine research and deployment networks (FP6, eTen and eContent) by looking at the position and role of regional organizations. We first identify networks in the selected thematic area at the regional level supported by EU structural funds (e.g. ERDF, LEADER+, and INTERREG). In addition, we identify other networks in the selected thematic area supported by member state and regional funds. This allows us to explore the relationships among different networks: FP6, eTen and eContent, regional networks supported by structural funds, and other networks supported by state and regional funds.

In-depth field interviews have been conducted with a set of carefully selected organizations in order to support the empirical network analysis. The questions have been aimed at projects that were carried out in different regions in order to understand the linkages between innovation and deployment processes at the regional level. We selected two subsets of interviewees per region. The first subset comes from *the results of our network analysis*, which allows us to identify a group of large and small effective IST producers participating in FP6 and/or eTen and eContent projects. The second subset stems from *the investigation of the projects at the regional level*, which allows us to identify organizations that do not participate in IST research projects, but have strong IST deployment records in the examined thematic area. Emphasis is placed on interviews with key actors at the regional level, such as: representatives of companies

*Table 10.3   Interviewed organizations*

| Type of organization | Number (per cent) |
|---|---|
| Industry (IND) | 22 (35.4) |
| Research centre (REC) | 18 (29.0) |
| University (HE) | 13 (21.0) |
| Other organization (OTH) | 9 (14.6) |
| Total | 62 (100) |

*Table 10.4   Research and deployment projects and organizations*

| | IST research projects | IST deployment projects |
|---|---|---|
| Participants | 4198 | 2008 |
| Projects | 249 | 287 |
| Participants per project | 17 | 7 |
| Organizations | 2417 | 1634 |
| Projects per organization | 1.7 | 1.2 |

identified in the networks; representatives of public research centres and/ or universities; representatives of government and quasi-government organizations that facilitate IST deployment in the selected thematic area and the selected member state(s) and region(s). Table 10.3 illustrates the characteristics of the 62 interviewed organizations – on average 7 per region.

**Research and Deployment Network Characteristics**

The basic characteristics of the research and deployment data concerning projects and organizations are displayed in Table 10.4.

Table 10.5 reports the main topology features of the research and deployment networks.

The differences between the structural properties of the two networks depend mainly on the size (number of participants) of each network. Indeed, the number of participants in research projects is more than twice as large as the number of participants in deployment projects.

Both networks are highly connected. Most participants are in the largest components, meaning that most of them are connected in some way to each other.[5] However, in spite of the high connectivity of both networks, the research network supports a significantly higher exchange of information compared to the deployment network. In the first network almost

*Table 10.5 Network characteristics*

|  | IST research network | IST deployment network |
|---|---|---|
| Number of nodes (organizations) | 2417 | 1634 |
| Number of edges (links) | 61686 | 7422 |
| Network density | 0.02 | 0.006 |
| Size largest component (giant component) | 2373 (98.18%) | 1153 (70.56%) |
| Size largest bi-component (giant bi-component) | 2340 (96.81%) | 733 (44.86%) |
| Average degree | 51.04 | 9.08 |
| Average distance* | 2.5 | 5.08 |
| Max distance* | 5 | 11 |
| Clustering coefficient* | 0.0377 | 0.1292 |

*Note:* * These indexes refer to the giant component.

all participants are connected to each other (as Table 10.5 shows, 98.18% of organizations are in the largest component). Deployment networks are less connected: the largest component contains only 71 per cent of organizations.

More striking differences between the research and the deployment networks emerge, if the giant bi-component is considered. The condition that a set of nodes have to satisfy in order be classified as a bi-component requires that all its nodes are reachable from any other node at least via *two* (and not only one) different paths.[6] This feature implies that organizations belonging to a bi-component have a higher probability of receiving the information spreading around the network than an organization belonging to a component.[7] The bi-component of the research network has almost the same size as the component (2340 instead of 2373), while the bi-component of the deployment network is dramatically smaller: 733 organizations instead of 1154. This means that only 63 per cent of the organizations belonging to the giant component have also *another* path connecting to the others. Therefore, in the deployment network the number of organizations connected to each other is proportionally smaller than in the research network and, even for those who are connected, the connection is weaker. These differences in the connectivity of the two networks reflect both the institutional features and objectives of the two programmes, and probably the fact that the deployment network deals with more focused activities regarding marketable products.

Information flows more easily in research networks than in deployment networks. The average distance in the research network is lower than the one in the deployment network: any node can reach any other node in the network in 2.5 steps on average. In the deployment network, the average number of steps needed to get from one node to another one is over 5 (this only applies to the nodes in the largest component).

On the other hand, deployment activities are locally more cohesive and dense.[8] This is suggested by the value of the clustering coefficient for the deployment network, which is greater than the same coefficient of the research network.

Despite these differences, however, both networks are well structured to be effective and useful as knowledge systems. Their structural properties – that is, low average distance and high clustering coefficient[9] – point out that both networks have *small world* properties.

If the IST research and deployment networks are considered together (Table 10.6) (i.e. all the organizations participating in FP6 *and* the organizations participating in eTen and eContent as members of the same network) the giant component[10] (which includes 3499 organizations, 92.7%), is characterized by an average distance of 3. This is a quite relevant result. It means that the overall network is well connected, as each organization is on average three links away from any other. So each organization has rather easy access to innovation and diffusion within the network.

However, the research network and the deployment network overlap very little. Only 277 organizations[11] participate in both networks. The two networks overlap even less in terms of links: the research and the deployment networks have only 131 links in common.[12]

*Table 10.6    Global IST research and deployment network: structural properties*

|  | IST network |
| --- | --- |
| Number of nodes (organizations) | 3774 |
| Number of edges (links) | 68977 |
| Network density | 0.0097 |
| Giant component | 3499 (92.7%) |
| Giant bi-component | 3150 (83.5%) |
| Average degree | 36.55 |
| Average distance* | 3 |
| Max distance* | 9 |
| Clustering coefficient* | 0.0138 |

*Note:*    * These indexes refers to the giant component.

**The Role of Network Hubs**

Important actors within the networks are the so-called *network hubs*. A hub may be defined as a node with a large number of connections that is highly influential by playing the role of *network connector*, that is, one that connects nodes that would otherwise remain unconnected. More formally, the notion of network hub can be captured by two indicators: (1) degree centrality and (2) betweenness centrality. Degree centrality and betweenness centrality have been calculated for all organizations, and a synthetic index has been created that ranks organizations according to their performance in terms of both these indicators. Hubs have been defined as the top 2 per cent of the organizations on the basis of this ranking.[13] We chose this percentage, as the top 2 per cent of organizations manage 30 per cent of total links. This procedure has been applied to each network, resulting in the definition of two types of hubs: IST research hubs (48 organizations from FP6) and IST deployment hubs (32 organizations from eTen and eContent).

Hubs have an extremely important role in networks, as they facilitate more than other network participants the rapid and effective dissemination of knowledge even to the most peripheral sections of the network. The analysis of the *hubs* in the different networks – research and deployment – shows highly functional structures. As expected, *research networks* are dominated by higher education and research institutions, while *deployment networks* are dominated by industry (Figure 10.1).

There are important differences between the two networks. Higher education institutions and research organizations play a greater role in the research network, while private companies and other organizations have a more relevant role in deployment networks (as expected). It is interesting to notice however that higher education institutions are also active in the deployment network. Five "other organizations" that appear as hubs in the deployment network include three city councils, one regional government, and one municipal company. These institutions promote economic growth, strengthening the networks at the local levels.

Differences in the role of hubs at the local versus the national levels emerge when evaluating research and deployment hubs. Figures 10.2 and 10.3 consider the links of each hub, distinguishing between links with organizations located in the same country and links with organizations located in the same region (NUTS 2) of the hub. We have excluded from this picture organizations located in more than one place (i.e. multinational companies or national research centres) and have considered only the EU15 countries. We have thus obtained 28 research hubs and 26 deployment hubs.

Deployment hubs are more locally linked than research hubs. Note that

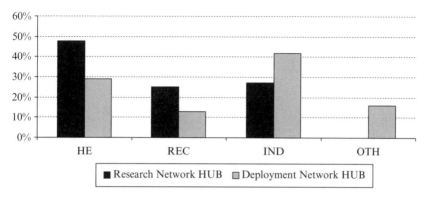

*Figure 10.1   Network hubs (% of total)*

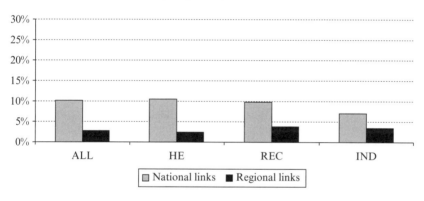

*Note:*   *Regional links are a subset of national links, so that it does not make sense to sum them.

*Figure 10.2   National and regional links of research hubs (% of total)**

national links in research are more than twice the number of national links in deployment, and regional links in research are more than three times the number of regional links in deployment.

There are also striking differences between the links of different types of hub organizations. First, in the research network private companies are less geographically limited, while the opposite is true for the deployment network. Second, in the deployment network, the "other organizations" are those with the most localized links. In particular, the number of regional links is more than twice as much as the average number. These actors indeed play a key role in deployment at the regional level. Academic hubs, on the contrary, do not show any differences in the two networks as far as the localization of their links is concerned.

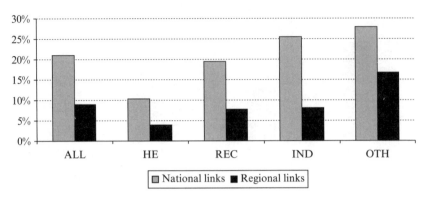

*Figure 10.3   National and regional links of deployment hubs (% of total)\**

**Research and Deployment Networks at the Regional Level**

The research and deployment networks have been examined for each of our nine regions (Table 10.7). In general, each regional network in the nine regions has a higher density than the density of the overall network, suggesting that being co-localized makes it more likely to be connected. Attiki and Emilia-Romagna – regions with low capability in science, technology and economy measured in terms of a set of indicators of R&D development, human capital, and industrial structure[14] – have the highest number of organizations participating in IST research and diffusion networks. The latter signals the important role of the European programmes in terms of inclusion and cohesion, and is an illustrative example of the effectiveness of the FP6 in strengthening the connection between research and diffusion.

Fielding a large number of organizations, however, does not necessarily imply that the region has a stronger connection to external hubs, as Table 10.8 shows. In fact, it is the presence of hubs in a region (this is the case of Attiki and Rhône-Alpes for research and of Emilia Romagna for diffusion) that increases the connectivity of the region to other external hubs. Therefore, in general, regions should increase the number of hubs in order to strengthen the regional innovation network and the deployment of research results.

In summary, as far as the European networks are concerned, we can conclude that:

*Table 10.7   Regional networks: structural properties*

| Region | STE strength | IST network organiza-tions | Research network | | Diffusion network | |
|---|---|---|---|---|---|---|
| | | | Organiza-tions | Density | Organiza-tions | Density |
| UK – East Wales | High | 2 | 1 | – | 1 | – |
| FR – Rhône-Alpes | High | 20 | 12 | 0.15 | 9 | 0.11 |
| DE – Bremen | High | 16 | 10 | 0.53 | 9 | 0.27 |
| DK – North Jutland | High | 3 | 3 | 0.66 | 0 | – |
| FI – Lansi Suomi | High | 11 | 10 | 0.53 | 1 | – |
| PT – Norte | Very Low | 22 | 13 | 0.35 | 9 | 0.11 |
| GR – Attiki | Low | 116 | 56 | 0.14 | 84 | 0.039 |
| IT – Emilia Romagna | Low | 54 | 25 | 0.14 | 38 | 0.11 |

*Table 10.8   Regional networks: hubs and external connections*

| Region | Research network | | | Diffusion network | | |
|---|---|---|---|---|---|---|
| | Organiza-tions | Hubs | Connection to external hubs | Organiza-tions | Hubs | Connection to external hubs |
| UK – East Wales | 1 | 0 | 0 | 1 | 0 | 0 |
| FR – Rhône-Alpes | 12 | 2 | 0.11 | 9 | 0 | 0 |
| DE – Bremen | 10 | 0 | 0.06 | 9 | 0 | 0.021 |
| DK- N. Jutland | 3 | 0 | 0.09 | 0 | – | – |
| FI – Lansi Suomi | 10 | 0 | 0.075 | 1 | 0 | 0 |
| PT – Norte | 13 | 0 | 0.089 | 9 | 0 | 0.003 |
| GR – Attiki | 56 | 2 | 0.11 | 84 | 2 | 0.017 |
| IT –Emilia Romagna | 25 | 0 | 0.06 | 38 | 4 | 0.026 |

- Both networks display *small world* properties, even though the research network appears relatively more effective in information dissemination.
- The two networks overlap very little in terms of organizations, and even less in terms of links. The overall network (research and deployment projects jointly considered) is, however, relatively well connected.
- The types of organizations working as *hubs* in the two networks are relatively different:
  - In the research network, universities play a central role, while in the deployment network the more important hubs are private companies.

- Private companies are more locally connected in the deployment network than in the research network.
- In the deployment network, other organizations, such as city councils, play an important role, but they play a negligible role in the research network.
- "Other" organizations are the most locally connected.

As far as the examined regional networks are concerned:

- Each regional network has higher density than the density of the overall network: being co-localized makes it more likely to be connected.
- A large number of organizations does not automatically translate into a higher number of connections to external hubs: it is the presence of hubs in a region that increases the connectivity of the region to other external hubs.
- As a rule, the investigated regions are not hosts to either IST-RTD hubs or deployment hubs, with the exception of Attiki and Emilia Romagna.

## 4.  COMPLEMENTARITY BETWEEN RESEARCH AND DEPLOYMENT NETWORKS

### The Significant Presence of Gatekeepers

A key role in fostering complementarities between research and deployment networks is played by *gatekeepers*; that is, organizations that link the two networks together and, by doing so, allow others to access information and capabilities developed in other networks and contexts. As seen in Figure 10.4, the gatekeepers sit between the two networks: they are positioned in both networks. In our analysis, 277 organizations are identified as having this bridging position. Some of these 277 organizations are also hubs, a fact that has implications regarding their connectivity within the network.[15] We hypothesize that gatekeepers are in a unique position to speed up the process of innovation and technology diffusion, since they work as bridges between the two different networks.

Different types of organizations act as gatekeepers within the two networks. Figure 10.5 shows that higher education institutions and research organizations are more numerous than others, but they are definitely not the only important ones. Industrial organizations are also quite active as gatekeepers and, within this group, SMEs in particular play an active role, representing 17 per cent of these bridging organizations.

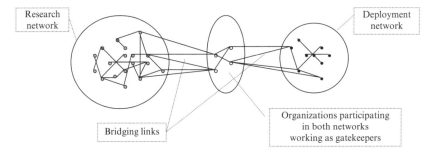

*Figure 10.4    Gatekeepers*

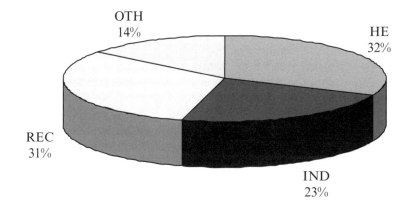

*Figure 10.5    Gatekeepers by organizational type*

The variety of different organizational types acting as gatekeepers means that different kinds of knowledge will be shared across the various networks. It became evident in the interviews that different types of organizations play different roles within the networks. Higher education and research institutes develop and diffuse advanced and frontier knowledge to the network, while businesses provide a major link to the market and provide information feedback in order to focus research on market relevance. Thus, a highly functional network would need gatekeepers from the different sectors in order to exchange and integrate different types of information and knowledge. This appears to be the case in the examined networks.

**The Bridging Role of Gatekeepers**

In our framework, *gatekeepers* are organizations that link the research with the diffusion network. By doing so, they allow others to access information and capabilities developed in other networks and contexts. It has already been shown in an earlier section that the linkage pattern between the two European networks (research, deployment) is quite significant (see Table 10.6). We can evaluate the key role of gatekeepers in that respect by considering the number of their links to the other organizations of the research and deployment networks. 20 264 out of a total of 61 686 (32.8%) links in the research network bridge gatekeepers with other organizations participating in that network; 2327 out of a total of 7422 (31.4%) links in the deployment network do the same there. In sum, more than one third of overall links bridge the two networks.

Gatekeeper organizations collaborate very frequently and actively in research networks, but they also work with private companies and public institutions that seek to deploy technologies. Their role is crucial since many organizations that are active players in the research networks are often not aware of deployment opportunities, as was evident from our interviews. Gatekeepers, on the contrary, are well aware of the deployment opportunities at the international, national and regional level. The opposite also happens frequently: poor links between research and deployment might arise in the case of organizations that are actively involved in deployment activities, but are not tied into the research network. The intermediary function of gatekeepers is therefore important and critical.

### The Complementarities Between the Two Networks

In order to grasp even more the complementarities between the two kinds of networks and the role of gatekeepers, we have juxtaposed the research network (FP6) with a network representing the links of the same organizations, this time involved in the deployment projects (Table 10.9), as exemplified in Figure 10.6.

Similarly, we have juxtaposed the deployment network and a network representing the links of the same organizations, this time involved in the research projects (Table 10.10).

A striking result is how little the research network is affected by the inclusion of the technology deployment linkages of its participants. All the structural properties barely change (see Table 10.9).

In contrast, the inclusion of the research links raises the degree of connectivity of the deployment network. The structural properties of the deployment network change significantly when the research links of its participating organizations are introduced (Table 10.10). The sizes of both the giant component and the giant bi-component increase significantly. Furthermore, this inclusion reduces the average distance between the participants. Therefore, an important effect of the IST research

*Table 10.9   Research network and deployment links: structural properties*

|  | IST research network | IST research plus deployment links |
|---|---|---|
| Number of nodes (organizations) | 2417 | |
| Number of edges (links) | 61 686 | 62 040 |
| Network density | 0.02 | 0.02 |
| Giant component | 2373 (98.18%) | 2375 (98.26%) |
| Giant bi-component | 2340 (96.81%) | 2353 (97.35%) |
| Average degree | 51.04 | 51.34 |
| Average distance* | 2.5 | 2.5 |
| Max distance* | 5 | 6 |
| Clustering coefficient* | 0.0377 | 0.0375 |

*Note:*   * These indexes refer to the giant component.

A simplified version of the IST research network

A simplified version of the IST research plus deployment links

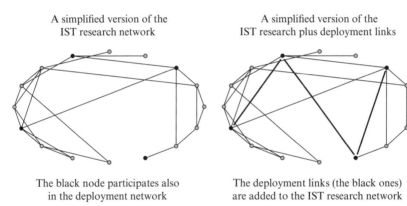

The black node participates also in the deployment network

The deployment links (the black ones) are added to the IST research network

*Figure 10.6   An example of how the IST research plus deployment links are built up*

network is the enlargement and widening of the number of organizations involved in sharing and exchanging knowledge and information and the speeding up of knowledge circulation among the deployment network organizations.

One also notices in Table 10.10 that the clustering coefficient decreases with the inclusion of the research links. This should not be interpreted as meaning the social capital of individual organizations drops. The lower clustering level also depends on the greater size of the component. More individuals can be reached, but only through one path. The decrease in the clustering coefficient depends mainly on arithmetical properties.

*Table 10.10    Deployment network and research links: structural properties*

|                                   | IST deployment network | IST deployment plus research links |
|-----------------------------------|------------------------|------------------------------------|
| Number of nodes (organizations)   |          1634          |                                    |
| Number of edges (links)           | 7422                   | 9948                               |
| Network density                   | 0.006                  | 0.007                              |
| Giant component                   | 1153 (70.56%)          | 1401 (85.74%)                      |
| Giant bi-component                | 733 (44.86)            | 1072 (65.6%)                       |
| Average degree                    | 9.08                   | 12.17                              |
| Average distance*                 | 5.08                   | 3.65                               |
| Max distance*                     | 11                     | 9                                  |
| Clustering coefficient*           | 0.1292                 | 0.0434                             |

*Note:*    * These indexes refer to the giant component.

*Table 10.11    Overlap between research and diffusion networks by region*

| Region | Overlap between research and diffusion network | | Overlap between IST networks and structural funds | |
|--------|------------------|-------|----------|------------|
|        | Organizations    | Links | Research | Deployment |
| UK – East Wales       | 0  | –  | –  | –  |
| FR – Rhône-Alpes      | 1  | 0  | 1  | 2  |
| DE – Bremen           | 3  | 0  | 1  | 2  |
| DK – N. Jutland       | 0  | –  | 0  | –  |
| FI – Lansi Suomi      | 0  | –  | 3  | 0  |
| PT – Norte            | 0  | –  | 6  | 3  |
| GR – Attiki           | 24 | 8  | 17 | 16 |
| IT – Emilia Romagna   | 7  | 0  | 5  | 8  |

For the regions examined in our analysis, the complementarity between the two networks is confirmed by the limited overlap between the research and deployment networks (Table 10.11).

The overlap between IST projects and structural funds is even smaller: there are no explicit links between the participation in IST networks and the use of structural funds. Structural policy instruments focus mainly on funding projects that improve the level of employment in a region, while programmes such as the FP6 prioritize different thematic topics. Given that the priority for regional funds is to help the transition to knowledge society and sustainable development,[16] however, one could argue for stronger linkages across networks to increase knowledge flows.

Thus, the empirical analysis of network data regarding the complementarity between IST research and deployment indicates that:

- There is relatively little overlap between IST research and deployment networks, which, however, may vary across regions.
- Several gatekeepers – organizations that participate in both networks – are universities or research centres (two-thirds of the total). However other organizations seem to play a relevant role, including SMEs.
- The population of gatekeepers includes a good number of network hubs: this significantly affects connectivity.
- The intense activity of gatekeepers – as observed through their linkages with other organizations – goes a long way in terms of balancing the relatively limited number of organizations participating in both activities. Put otherwise, gatekeepers effectively play their role of network bridge. For instance, one-third of the links of each network (research, deployment) correspond to connections between gatekeepers and other organizations.

## 5. THE VIEWPOINT OF PRACTITIONERS: NETWORKS AND DEPLOYMENT

A lot of linkages and relationships among actors that are quite relevant for innovation and diffusion escape from the aggregate quantitative examination. They can be identified only through in-depth case analysis. While the relatively limited set of interviews conducted in a selected set of regions means that our results can be taken as indicative rather than representative of the whole population of European organizations, some clear indications emerge from the field evaluation.

Networks were reported to play an important role in raising research diversity by allowing the involvement of more sectors, making research more relevant to problem-solving, and to increasing the research quality. In cases where there is potential for market application, the networks are also viewed as very important. As one gatekeeper organization told us:

> Yes, they [networks] do have a role [in deployment opportunities] since they allow us to integrate our competencies with foreign public institutions which can provide insights and experience . . . we apply the know-how developed within the research network to specific regional projects.

Although interviewees are nearly unanimous in saying that the IST-RTD networks play an important role in information exchange critical to product and process deployment, in some cases they report that IST projects are too much focused on research and do not provide support to deployment activities and market commercialisation.

In cases where projects had an explicit goal that included product development or deployment, specific new products or processes did result from IST research projects. More frequently, however, interviewees mentioned that many projects aim at improving the deployment of an existing product or process. A person from a gatekeeper organization said that their organization participated in IST projects because the networks offer the opportunity to cooperate with other institutions, such as universities, which aim at achieving different research goals from their own. This person also said that, while universities are the main source of research, they also play a role in deployment in cases where research allows the university to establish its own company.

A number of interviewees emphasized that the information that came through the networks also helped them to gain a better understanding of the markets that they are preparing products for. One interviewee in particular mentioned that the IST research network has helped to speed up diffusion of knowledge, and that this same network connected with a regional promotion agency aimed at diffusion in the region. However, interviewees stated that the physical location of the partners is less important than the existence of complementarity between capabilities among network participants.

In any case, a number of interviewees claimed that the IST projects encourage links among the institutions that interact across different types of programmes. The requirement to find partners from different sectors, for example, is seen as a point that strengthens regional links. Multinational firms participate in IST-RTD projects; as a result, some smaller institutions had access to these firms in a way they otherwise would not have had under national or regional projects. They may represent a unique opportunity for local organizations to broaden up their connectivity.

However, the interviewee from one of the gatekeeper organizations reported that the deployment of the products and processes developed within research networks is not always possible. Quite interestingly, this case refers to an IST network that had successfully accomplished the development of a product. The interviewee said that there had not been sufficient infrastructure for using the application and introducing it into the market. In this case, even the existence of an IST network could not advance the deployment. The problem appears to be one where the institution is not aware of other organizations that could help bring the product to market.

ICT diffusion activities are not always closely tied to regional strategies. In this respect, there seem to be some differences between the examined

Northern European regions, where there is little coordination with regional strategies, and the examined Southern European regions, where coordination activities take place more frequently. In general, large organizations are informed of and exploit regional links, while SMEs are often not aware of the existence of regional strategies for ICT deployment and do not have the resources and capabilities to use them efficiently. Creating a critical mass of resources and competencies therefore seems to be a necessary condition for exploiting regional policies aimed at connecting IST research and deployment. Very often interviewees cannot name a regional strategy to which they are linked. In many cases they did not have precise information about where they could go to get help with regional deployment and were not aware of direct links between national and regional networks in deploying ICT products developed within IST research projects. This is probably because organizations are aware of first tier linkages, but are less conscious of the *second and third tier* participants. In other words, while the global network (research and deployment) appears to be well connected when looking at the quantitative data, information about deployment projects and about potential indirect linkages with hubs and gatekeepers still remains scarce, especially for small organizations.

Most interviewees were not aware of explicit links between the participation in IST networks and the use of structural funds. In this respect, one interviewee said that the structural policy instruments focus mainly on funding projects and general concepts that improve the level of employment in a region, while programmes such as the FP6 prioritize different thematic topics. However, the priority for regional funds is to help the transition to knowledge society and sustainable development. Therefore, using structural funds to harness the research results of the IST networks for regional deployment should represent a major issue in the agenda of regional authorities. An interviewee from a hub told us: "Theoretically there certainly are [such explicit links]. However, at an operational level there are none. The institutions are invited to participate during the starting period, but during the execution period there is no participation at all."

Most of the interviewees report very little connection with regional networks in deploying products. As one interviewee told us: "The lack of significant regional economic agents to finance local deployment projects is a barrier. The resources to finance the higher educational institutions are also scarce at the local level, which has negative implications on working conditions." There are also cases where local connections appear to work, and where the local hub brought together a lot of local resources. For example, this is the case with the University of Cardiff, which actively coordinates a number of local and national activities in addition to EU projects. Although it does not show up as highly networked, this university clearly helps the local region by acting as a connecting point.

IST network participation is seen by several interviewees as less advantageous for the local region than for the European or international level. As one gatekeeper institution told us:

> The network had an advantage in identifying deployment opportunities at the European level. The advantage at the regional level was less significant. The network supported the partners to build thematic communities . . . this kind of community building occurred at a national or international level rather than at the regional level.

From these reports it follows that opportunities exist for improving the linkages between the research and deployment networks at the regional level. In order to promote the development of IST networks at the regional level there is the need, on the one hand, for national governments to play a catalytic role and provide significant value-added by initiating and supporting mechanisms for inter-regional cooperation and collaboration (this point is particularly important when regions have rather limited political power and a very limited budget). On the other hand, a clear understanding at the regional level of the concrete benefits resulting from the participation in the IST networks is required.

Bureaucracy and difficulty in coordinating across the network are mentioned a number of times as obstacles to the integration of the IST networks. Other obstacles include the transaction costs (travel, staff time) associated with involvement in IST-RTD networks. As one highly-connected hub institution says: "The main obstacle to participating in research, diffusion, and deployment networks is usually the cost associated with coordination. Bringing people together can be costly and time consuming." This also becomes an issue when looking for links between research and deployment networks. In this respect, regional agencies can play an important role as brokers and matching institutions, emphasizing the value of collaborations. Indeed, even if there may be high costs in entering the network, the benefits of deployment projects in general are quite high and usually greatly compensate for them.

## 6.  LESSONS LEARNED AND POLICY IMPLICATIONS

The present research has concentrated on the assessment of the effectiveness of network collaboration and of knowledge transfers between RTD, innovation and deployment activities related to IST at the EU and regional levels. It has done so by focusing on the intersection of research, innovation, and technology deployment networks at the EU, national, and regional levels. We have tried to point out the linkages and influences between the *research networks* built through FP6 funding in the thematic area "Applied IST research addressing major societal and economic challenges", on the one hand, and the *deployment networks* built through EU programmes (eTen, eContent) as well as at the regional level through structural funds or other member state and regional funds, on the other. The coalescence of these networks within nine selected regions of the European Community has received the bulk of our attention.

Regional networks are considerably strengthened by links into the IST-RTD network. The research network complements the deployment network by adding links that allow many organizations to be connected, and brings about effective knowledge exchange among organizations and fast diffusion of information within the network. Both research and deployment networks are highly connected. However, in the deployment network the number of organizations connected to others is proportionally smaller than in the research network and, even for those who are connected, the connection is weaker. If the research links are added to the deployment network, the structural properties of the deployment network are modified. In particular, the IST research network increases the number of the organizations of the deployment network that are involved in sharing and exchanging knowledge, and speeds up information transmission among its organizations. The overall network (the research and the deployment networks jointly considered) is well connected and the average distance between organizations is 3.

*Hub organizations* play a critical role in maintaining the ties of the smaller and more isolated members of the networks. They diffuse technological and market information, help define standards for emerging products, and provide demand (applications) for research results. It is the actual presence of hubs in a region (among the regions examined this is the case of Attiki and Rhône-Alpes for research and of Emilia Romagna for deployment) that increases the connectivity of the region to other external hubs. *Gatekeepers* have a uniquely important role of bridging research and deployment networks, thus helping both to disseminate knowledge of all kinds through various knowledge channels and to provide access to resources and opportunities. The intensity of the activity of individual gatekeepers – as observed through their linkages with other organizations – goes a long way in terms of balancing the relatively limited number of organizations participating in both activities. Thus gatekeepers effectively play their role of network bridge. From our quantitative evaluation analysis, we have found that one-third of the links of each network (research, deployment) correspond to connections between gatekeepers and other organizations.

Multinational firms participate in IST-RTD projects: as a result, some smaller institutions have access to these firms in a way that otherwise would not have been possible under national or regional projects. Multinational companies possess financial assets and human resources that are necessary in order to engage in large-scale projects that link research and deployment. SMEs are key players in deployment. They are deeply rooted in the territory and represent very efficient agents when it comes to deploying specific applications and building relationships with regional authorities.

In order to promote the development of IST networks at the regional level there is the need, on the one hand, for national governments to play a catalytic role and provide significant value-added by initiating and supporting mechanisms for inter-regional cooperation and collaboration (this point is particularly important when regions have rather limited political powers and a very limited budget). On the other hand, a clear understanding at the regional level of the concrete benefits resulting from the participation in the IST networks is required. Bureaucracy and difficulty in coordinating across the network appear to raise barriers to the integration of the IST networks. Other obstacles include the transaction costs (travel, staff time) associated with involvement in IST-RTD networks.

The stronger emphasis on innovation and the quest for balancing supply and demand side effects of technological advancement in Europe today imply that both research and deployment linkages become a core policy concern. On the basis of lessons learned from our analysis, the following policy recommendations are aimed at strengthening the links between research and deployment, including the linkages between European/ national and regional activities.

1. *Strengthen the links between research and deployment*
   While research across the ERA is highly networked, other parts of the system – namely those related to deployment – are less interconnected. Gatekeeper organizations in the networks play a critical role in that respect by providing interconnections across different networks. This implies that *regions should involve more of these types of organizations (gatekeepers and hubs) in order to bridge research and deployment at the regional level more effectively and to harness the results from FP6.*

   While somewhat overlapping, deployment activities, capabilities and skills are significantly different from those relating to research. Therefore, when programme objectives include dissemination and applications, they could be enriched with a regional deployment strategy as part of IST-RTD projects. *In its programmes the Commission should ensure that opportunities for regional organizations to engage and participate to deployment activities exist, so that connections between research and deployment programmes are strengthened at the regional level.*

Both research and deployment networks appear to be effective in information dissemination, the latter more so at the regional level (as expected). Nonetheless, having a large number of organizations in the network does not guarantee extensive connections to the outside world: the inclusion of hubs does. The investigated regions are not hosts to either IST research hubs or deployment hubs, with the exception of Attiki and Emilia Romagna. *Since the presence of hubs in a region raises disproportionately the connectivity of the region with others, the attraction of such organizations regionally certainly makes sense. Even more so given that many hubs also play the role of gatekeepers.*

In our interviews, many organizations are unaware of opportunities for support to deployment. *The provision of information about these opportunities could be the first step in the direction of more awareness. In order to promote ICT deployment there is the need for national governments to play a catalytic role and provide significant value-added by initiating and supporting mechanisms for inter-regional cooperation and collaboration.*

2. *Strengthen regional strategies for deployment of innovations*
   Regional strategies for economic development and ICT deployment are largely unknown to network participants. In many cases, participants are focusing on the global marketplace in their development process rather than on the regional level. This may be appropriate for frontier research, but it is not the most effective way to achieve innovation diffusion and deployment. *The development of regional policies for an ICT-based knowledge society is essential for regional knowledge hubs to establish links at the regional level.*

   Large multinational organizations play a central role in bridging research and deployment, as they possess financial, technical and human resources to enter research and deployment networks and to manage the complexity of collaborations. In this respect, *regions should support the presence of such large organizations that disseminate technological and market information, help define standards for emerging products, and provide demand (applications) for research results. Furthermore, they should strengthen links between multinational organizations and SMEs.*

In relation to this, knowledge about regional support systems (when they exist) is very patchy. In a number of cases, the interviewees did not know of regional structural programmes or opportunities for connections. *From a policy perspective, ensuring that this kind of information is available, possibly through a virtual clearing house, would be a step forward.*

3. *Simplify the exploitation of IST networks and project coordination*
The range of programmes and projects existing at the regional, national and European levels can be daunting and confusing to prospective participants, and may be a barrier to smaller enterprises. *The Commission together with regional agencies should provide clear information about the IST-RTD activities as well as other EU programmes. This would greatly help organizations at the regional level.*

The costs of joining IST networks, particularly for smaller institutions, can be a barrier to participation. In particular, bureaucracy and difficulty in coordination constitute important obstacles to the use of IST networks. This issue is already well known to the European Commission. Further efforts to ameliorate this problem should be considered.

## NOTES

1. J. Stefan Institute: *Data Mining and Decision Support for Business Competitiveness: A European Virtual Enterprise* (Cordis Project reference: IST-1999-11495); RAND Europe: *ERAnets: Evaluation of Networks of Collaboration between Participants in IST Research and their Evolution to Collaborations in the European Research Area (ERA)* (Tender OJ 2004/S 177-151255); CESPRI: *Evaluation of Progress Towards a European Research Area for Information Society Technologies* (contract number OJ 2004/S 177-151255).
2. Regional and research policies in the EU are seen as closely interlinked and, to a certain extent, interdependent. Increased regional cohesion and competitiveness are considered to be partly dependent on the existence of a suitable research infrastructure. See for example http://cordis.europa.eu/fp7/regional_en.html.
3. In analogy with previous works (see Note 1), we have considered all the participants in a project having similar roles; that is, we have not assigned any specific role to the prime contactor of the project.
4. This region is NUTS 3 level.
5. More formally, a component is a subpart of a network where there exists at least one *path* (i.e. an alternating sequence of node and edges) linking all its nodes. In other words, all the nodes belonging to a component have to be reachable at least in one way.
6. The giant bi-component is the largest one.
7. Of course, this is true if all the other network features are equals.
8. The clustering coefficient for a node is the proportion of links between the nodes within its neighbourhood divided by the number of links that could possibly exist between them. The clustering coefficient for the whole network is the average of the clustering coefficient for each node and captures the level of social capital, since it measures how many *direct* partners of a specific organization collaborate with each other.
9. Here *low average distance* means that the network has the same value as a random

network with the same size and density, *high clustering coefficient* means that the network has a value that is much greater than the value of the random network.

10. The giant bi-component is slightly smaller: 3150; that is 90 per cent of the size of the giant component.

11. This includes 11.5 per cent of the organizations participating in the research network, 16.9 per cent of the organizations participating in the deployment network, or 7.3 per cent of the total number of organizations (3774).

12. There are 3011 links among the 277 organizations participating in both networks and these links can depend on a partnership either in a research project or in a deployment project. Of these, 2526 out of 3011 (83.89%) links are related exclusively to research project participations, 354 (11.76%) only to deployment project participations and only 131 (4.35%) depend on participations in both programmes. This means that the overlap, in terms of links, is very poor.

13. The 2 per cent cut-off is obviously arbitrary but this arbitrariness in the cut-off value is hard to avoid in similar exercises. We considered different values (both higher and lower than 2 per cent) in order to check for robustness. The main results are not affected. Alternatively, hubs could have been defined on the basis of threshold values for centrality. This becomes impractical, however, because of the need to compare across different types of networks of different sizes.

14. Source: EUROSTAT, average for 1999–2004. We used the following indicators: GERD per capita, R&D personnel per inhabitant, human resources in science and technology, percentage of total employment in high-technology manufacturing, percentage of total employment in knowledge-intensive services.

15. Twenty-seven out of 48 (56.2%) of hubs in the research network and 22 out of 32 (68.7%) of hubs in the deployment network are also gatekeepers. It is worth noticing that 11 organizations are hubs in both networks: they could be classified as the strongest gatekeepers in our sample.

16. As Table 10.11 shows, only in Attiki is there a substantial overlap of organizations and links between research and diffusion networks, and between these networks and structural funds. However, one may recall that Attiki is a capital city region with a major concentration of national industry, quite different from the rest of the regions examined. Furthermore, Greeks are, in relative terms, the most frequent postgraduate students abroad and this helps them establish social networks that allow them to make connections within Europe. Finally, structural funds within Greece are strongly supported by government intervention.

# BIBLIOGRAPHY

Bathelt, H., A. Malberg and P. Maskell (2004) "Clusters and knowledge: local buzz, global pipelines and the process of knowledge creation", *Progress in Human Geography*, **28**, 31–56.

Breschi, S., L. Cassi and F. Malerba (2004) "A five-industry analysis of co-citation networks", Working Paper for the STI-NET project, European Commission, April.

Breschi, S., L. Cassi, F. Malerba and N. Vonortas (2007) "Networked research: European policy intervention for information and communication technologies", mimeo, Bocconi University, Milan.

Breschi, S. and L. Cusmano (2004) "Unveiling the texture of a European Research Area: emergence of oligarchic networks under EU Framework Programmes", *International Journal of Technology Management. Special Issue on Technology Alliances*, **27** (8), 747–72.

Burt, R.S. (1992) *Structural Holes. The Social Structure of Competition*, Cambridge, MA: Harvard University Press.

Caloghirou, Y., N. Constantellou and N.S. Vonortas (eds) (2005) *Knowledge Flows in European Industry: Mechanisms and Policy Implications*, London: Routledge.

Caloghirou, Y., N.S. Vonortas and S. Ioannides (2002) "Science and technology policies towards research joint ventures", *Science and Public Policy*, **29** (2), 82–94.

Caloghirou, Y., N.S. Vonortas and S. Ioannides (eds) (2004) *European Collaboration in Research and Development: Business Strategy and Public Policy*, Cheltenham, UK and Northampton, MA, USA: Edward Elgar.

Coleman, J.C. (1988) "Social capital in the creation of human capital", *American Journal of Sociology*, **94**, 95–120.

Cowan, R. and N. Jonard (2004) "Network structure and the diffusion of knowledge", *Journal of Economic Dynamics and Control*, **28** (8), 1557–75.

European Commission (2000), "Toward a European Research Area", COM 2000/6.

Gulati, R. (1999) "Network location and learning: the influence of network resources and firm capabilities on alliance formation", *Strategic Management Journal*, **20** (5), 397–420.

Hagedoorn, J., A.N. Link and N.S. Vonortas (2000) "Research partnerships", *Research Policy*, **29** (4–5), 567–86.

Jaffe, A.B. and M. Trajtenberg (eds) (2002) *Patents, Citations, and Innovations*, Cambridge, MA: MIT Press.

Peterson, J. and M. Sharp (1998), *Technology Policy in the European Union*, London: Macmillan.

Powell, W.W., K.W. Koput and L. Smith-Doerr (1996) "Interorganizational collaboration and the locus of innovation: networks of learning in biotechnology", *Administrative Science Quarterly*, **41**, 116–45.

Roediger-Schluga, T. and M.J. Barber (2006) "The structure of R&D collaboration networks in the European Framework Programmes", UNU-MERIT Working Papers, 36.

Storper, M. (1997) *The Regional World: Territorial Development in a Global Economy*, London: Guilford Press.

Vonortas, N.S. (1997) *Cooperation in Research and Development*, Boston, MA and Dordrecht, Netherlands: Kluwer Academic Publishers.

Watts, D. and S.H. Strogatz (1998) "Collective dynamics of 'small world' networks", *Nature*, **393**, 440–2.

# Index

Abernathy, William J. 126
additionality 23
  behavioural additionality 13–14,
    195–6, 199, 218–19
  input and output/ outcome
    additionality 14, 195, 199
Agrawal, A. 159
Ahuja, G. 57–8, 67
Albert, R. 64, 142
Almeida, P. 108, 158–60
Anderson, D. 71, 106
Argonne National Lab (USA) 185–6
Arora, A.A. 58, 158, 162
Arrow, K.J. 157
Attiki (Greece) 230, 236–8, 242, 247, 249
automobile industry 49, 53, 55, 62

Barabasi, L. 64, 142, 205
Barber, M.J. 228
Bathelt, H. 228
Bauer, L.L. 57, 59
Baum, J.A. 64, 67
Bayona, C. 57
Becker, W. 57–8
behaviour, corporate
  and networks, benefits of 3–4, 30,
    33–4, 40
behavioural additionality 13–14, 195–6,
    199, 218–19
benchmarking, of network indicators
    23
benefits, of networks
  control/ governance benefits 3–4, 30,
    33–4, 40
  informational benefits 30–33, 39–40
betweenness centrality 139–40, 203–4,
    215
  ego-betweenness 186–7
biotechnology industry
  interfirm technological alliances in,
    study 63, 66–7

M&A activity in 168–74
multi-applicant inventors/ mobility,
    study 11–12, 157–74
  network analysis 168–74
  study dataset and method 158,
    162–8
  role of networks in 5–6
Bocconi University (Italy) 128
Bonacich, P. 146
Borgatti, S.P. 181
Bourdieu, P. 29–30
Branstetter, L.G. 48, 66–7
Breschi, Stefano 6, 8, 48, 64, 66, 126,
    135, 143, 146, 159, 228
brokers, technology 10–11, 147–9,
    152–3, 217, 246
Burt, R.S. 29, 31–2, 36, 62–3, 67–8, 144

Calero, C. 96, 101
capital, types of 3–4, 18, 27–9
  social capital 29–30, 36, 39–41, 62–3,
    67
Carlsson, B. 126
centrality see betweenness centrality;
    degree centrality; power centrality
Centre National Recherche Scientifique
    (CNRS) (France) 184
chemical industry
  interfirm technological agreements
    in 49, 53, 55, 57–8, 64, 67
  network characteristics in 6
cliques 62–4, 71, 135, 144, 201–2
clustering 62, 64, 189
  clustering coefficient 144–6, 179,
    184, 232–3, 241–2
Cohen, W. 57–8
Coleman, J.S. 29–30, 33, 36, 62, 67, 144
collaboration 18 see also interfirm
    technological agreements; R&D
    networks
  cooperative capability 58–9

experience, role in 58–9
and locus of innovation, networks as
31–3, 39–40
and transaction costs, reducing
17–18
Colombo, M.G. 47, 57–8
commercial capital 27–8
communications industry 50, 62, 67,
113–14
communications networks, in
nanoscience research, study of
12–13, 178–90
information flows 178–9
lobal/ local networks 12–13, 180,
183–4, 189
study analysis 184–90
study dataset and method 179–82
companies, position/ role in research
networks
multinational companies 15, 83, 234,
248–9
SMEs (small and medium sized
enterprises) 14, 83, 195, 228,
243–6, 248–9
competition, and network activity
competing constellations 22
crowding, network 8–9, 105, 107–8,
110–13, 116–22
technical crowding coefficient 128,
146–51
location, in network 17, 32–3
networks as exclusionary/ protective
mechanism 5, 8, 17, 70, 105–6
complex technologies 15–16, 152, 227
computer industry
interfirm technological alliances in
49–50, 55, 62, 67–8
knowledge and partnership networks
compared, study 9–11, 127,
131–3, 136–7, 140–42, 149, 152
patent citation and alliance activity
in 113–14
connectivity
in IST-RTD programme networks
208–14, 218–20, 238
key nodes 9–10, 13, 139–40, 151,
184–6, 220, 238
in knowledge and partnership
networks 9, 135, 139, 141–4, 151
network connectors 203, 234

Contu, A. 33–4
cooperative capability 58–9
Coordinated Actions (CAs) 198
corporate/ organizational strategy
and networks *see also* interfirm
technological agreements
control/ governance benefits of
3–4, 30, 33–4, 40
and corporate evolution, impact
on 2, 6, 19–21, 45, 125–6
as corporate resource 17
influence on strategy 8–9, 39–41
participation in 4, 7–8
positioning in 4, 17, 30, 32–3,
39, 41, 127–8, 146–53,
217–18
publishing research, incentives
for 91
R&D incentives 84–7
and spin offs 12–13
strategic alliances, study of 8,
105–22
spin offs, impacts on network
activities 12–13, 189
COST network 200
Cowan, R. 62–4, 144
Criscuolo, P. 101
crowding, network 8–9
and competition, impact on
innovation 105, 107–8, 110–13,
116–22
reasons for 107–8
technical crowding coefficient 128,
146–51
Cusmano, L. 48, 64–6, 135, 143,
228
*CWTS Corporate Research Papers
(CRP)* database 92–3
Cyert, R.M. 38

data sources, problems with 47–8
De Nooy, W. 178
Debackere, C. 66
degree centrality 66, 139, 147, 184–6,
203–4, 211, 215
knowledge network thresholds 134,
136–8
degree distribution 142–3
Department of Energy (DOE) (US),
nanoscience lab networks *see*

*also* Nanoscale Science Research
Centers (NSRCs)
Jump Start Program 186, 188
research collaboration history
180–81
study of 12–13, 178–90
study analysis 184–90
study dataset and method 179–82
deployment networks
in IST-RTD programmes 14–15,
226, 228–50
and gatekeepers 238–40, 245,
247–50
regional networks 234–8, 244–7
and research networks, compared
15, 226, 228–50
Dietz, J. 57–8
diffusion networks *see* deployment
networks
discovery, scientific
as communication network 84–7,
177–8
self-organization of 2–3, 34–5,
177–8
Dosi, G. 2, 125
Duysters, G. 38, 64, 67–8

eContent 15, 229–30, 233–4, 247
Edquist, C. 2–3, 108, 125
ego-betweenness 186–7
Eisenhardt, K.M. 60
electronics industry
interfirm technological alliances in,
study 49, 53, 55
knowledge and partnership networks
compared, study 8–11, 127,
131–3, 137–8, 140–42, 150–52
knowledge search and strategic
alliance, study 8–9, 105–22
network crowding 105, 107–8,
110–13, 116–22
technical crowding coefficient 128,
146–51
embeddedness, of networks 31–3
Emilia Romagna (Italy) 230, 236–8,
242, 247, 249
entrepreneurs/ isolates 10–11, 147–9,
152–3, 211
and multi-applicant inventorship
163–5, 169–73

environmental factors, influence of 8,
17–20, 37–8, 40–41, 108, 195–6
EP-CESPRI database 128–9, 158, 165,
202, 214
eTen 15, 229–30, 233–4, 247
EUREKA network 200
Europe
European companies, knowledge
networks in 9–10, 148–9, 152
European Research Area (ERA)
197, 211–12, 227, 248–50
Lisbon Strategy 198
Plan i2010 198
policy implications, on networks
217–20, 246–50
research networks in, studies of
*see* IST-RTD programmes;
pharmaceutical industry
Sixth Research Framework
Programme (FP6) *see also* IST-
RTD programmes
background to 197
strategic objectives of 197–8
evolution, corporate
network impact on 2, 6, 19–21, 45,
125–6
and interfirm technological
agreements 4–5, 69–71
theories of 125–7
*ex ante/ ex post* motivations 62
experience, role in collaboration 58–9
exploitation, networks for 8, 19, 22,
37–8, 40–41, 106–7, 126–7
exploration, networks for 8, 19, 22,
37–8, 40–41, 126–7

Feldman, M.P. 157
Feldman, M.S. 37
first-mover advantage 5
followers, technology 10–11, 147–9,
152–3
France 184, 230, 236–8, 242, 247
Fritsch, M. 57, 59

Gambardella, A. 58, 126, 158, 162
Garcia-Point, C. 62
Garrone, P. 47, 57–8
gatekeepers
bridging role of 239–40, 247–50
in IST-RTD programme networks

14–15, 207–13, 216–17, 238–40, 245, 247–50
in knowledge and partnership networks 9, 140, 151
types of organizations acting as 238–9
geodesic distance 139
Geroski, P.A. 56, 157–8
Ghoshal, S. 29–30
'giant component' 205
bi-component/ giant bi-component networks 232–3, 240–42
Gibbons, M. 177
Gilsing, V.A. 28, 33–4, 37–8, 126–7
globalization, impact of 22, 83, 89, 228
Gomes-Casseres, B. 62, 69
Gort, M. 126
Granovetter, M.S. 29, 32
Griliches, Z. 157
Grodal, S. 45
Gulati, R. 27–8, 30, 33, 45, 58, 61, 70, 143–4

Hagedoorn, J. 28, 38, 45–6, 54, 57, 59, 66–8, 83, 96, 114
Henderson, R. 159
Hernan, R. 57–60
Hesse, M. 177
hubs
characteristics of 196, 217
connectivity, of 208–14, 218–20, 231–6, 238
role of
deployment hubs 236–8, 249–50
in IST-RTD programmes 14–15, 196–7, 204–20, 223–5, 231–8, 247, 249–50
in knowledge and partnership networks 9, 140, 151
human capital 4, 29
Hwang, Bob 187–8

ICT *see* information and communications technology (ICT)
industrial analysis
trends in 125–6
industry sectors *see also under* individual industry sectors
distinguishing elements of 126–7

innovation systems in, analyzing 2–3, 125–6
and networks, influence/ impact of 1–2, 4
information and communications technology (ICT) industry 13–15
Information Society Research and Technological Development programmes of Sixth Research Framework (EU) *see* IST-RTD
informational benefits of networks 30–33, 39–40
INNET database 201
input additionality 14, 195, 199
instruments industry
interfirm technological alliances in 49, 53, 55
knowledge and partnership networks compared, study 9–11, 127, 131–3, 138–42, 151–2
network characteristics in 6
Integrated Projects (IPs) 197–8, 200, 208–13, 218–20
interfirm technological agreements 71–2
cliques 62–4, 71
and corporate evolution, role in 4–5, 69–71
and corporate experience 58–9
and corporate size 57, 59–60, 70
defining 46–7
at dyadic level 56, 60–61, 69
and economic performance 65–8
at firm level 56–9, 69
frequency/ number, relevance of 66–7
hierarchies of 64–5
at industry level 56, 59–60
and innovative performance 65–8
modes of cooperation 51–2
motivations for 52–4, 61–2, 69
networks' impact on industry 61–5
newly established agreements 49–50
and R&D intensity 57–8
sectoral differences in 49–51, 53–5
study dataset 47–8
and technical capability 57–8, 68
and technological distance 60–61, 65, 67

trends in 48–56
trends over time 54, 56
inventorship
  academic
    relationship with industry 90–92,
      94, 158, 161–4, 170
  mobility of 11–12, 157–62
    applicant sequences 160–62
    and M&A activity 11–12, 157–8,
      163–74
  multi-applicant
    applicant sequences 160–62
    and individuals 163–5, 169–73
    knowledge spillovers 112–13,
      157–60, 162, 215
    and open science organizations
      163–5, 169–73
    and private technology
      organizations 163–5, 169–73
    study of, in biotechnology
      industry 11–12, 157–74
    taxonomy for 163–5
  isolates 10–11, 147–9, 152–3, 211
    and multi-applicant inventorship
      163–5, 169–73
IST-RTD programmes 13–15
  studies, of IST networks under
    affiliation networks 201–2
    background studies 200
    bi-component/ giant bi-
      component networks 232–3,
      240–42
    centrality in 202–3, 211, 215
    cliques 201–2
    deployment hubs 236–8, 249–50
    deployment and research
      networks, compared 14–15,
      226, 228–50
    field interviews 230–31, 243–6
    gatekeepers in 14–15, 207–13,
      216–17, 238–40, 245, 247–50
    global networks in 12–13, 180,
      183–4, 189, 201–4, 208–13,
      215–17
    hubs, connectivity of 208–14,
      218–20, 231–6, 238
    hubs, deployment 236–8, 249–50
    hubs, role in 14–15, 196–7,
      204–20, 223–5, 231–8, 247,
      249–50

Integrated Projects (IPs), role in
    197–8, 200, 208–13, 218–20
  IST-RTD only networks in 201–4,
    208–13, 215–17
  knowledge networks in 201–4,
    214–17
  knowledge spillovers 202
  network benefits/ problems
    218–20, 243–6
  Networks of Excellence (NoEs),
    role in 198, 200, 208–13,
    218–20
  partnership networks in 214, 226,
    228–50
  regional networks 234–8, 244–7
  'small world' networks 219–20
  Specific Targeted Research
    Projects (STRePs), role in
    198, 208–13
  study datasets and methods
    200–204, 214–15, 226,
    228–31
IST Thematic Priority of the Fifth
  Framework Programme 198

Jaffe, Adam B. 157, 159
Japan, knowledge networks in 9–10,
    148–50, 152–3
joint ventures 51–2
Jonard, N. 62–4, 144
Jump Start Program 186, 188

Klepper, S. 57, 69, 126
knowledge networks 13
  connectivity 9, 135, 139, 141–4, 151
  corporate roles in
    brokers 10–11, 147–9, 152–3, 217,
      246
    followers 10–11, 147–9, 152–3
    isolates 10–11, 147–9, 152–3, 211
    leaders 10–11, 147–9, 152–3
  degree centrality 134, 136–8
  in European companies 9–10, 148–9,
    152
  gatekeepers in 9, 140, 151
  hubs in 9, 140
  illustration of 129–30, 134, 136–8
  knowledge search and strategic
    alliance, in electronics industry
    8–9, 105–22

and multi-applicant inventorship/
    job mobility 11–12, 157–74
and partnership networks compared,
    sectoral study 9–10, 127–53 *see
    also under* individual industry
    sectors
    knowledge flow efficiency 143–6
    network analysis 128, 133–42,
        146–53
    positioning in 146–53
    robustness 9–10, 143, 145–6, 151
    study dataset and method 127–33
knowledge spillovers
    and cumulative innovation 106–13
    and multi-applicant inventorship
        157–60, 162, 215
    and network structure 34
    and prior experience 31, 106, 202
Kogut, B. 3, 28–31, 33–6, 63, 65, 71,
    158–60
Koput, K.W. 31–3
Kortum, S. 162

labor market, network implications for
    23, 34–5
laboratories, research networks *see*
    Department of Energy; Nanoscale
    Science Research Centers
Lawrence Berkley National Lab 185
leaders, technology 10–11, 147–9,
    152–3
Lerner, J. 162
Levinthal, D. 57
Link, A.N. 57, 59
Lisbon Strategy 198
Lissoni, F. 159, 166
lock-in/ lock-out 17, 21–2, 34, 40, 71,
    199, 220
locus of innovation, networks as 5, 20,
    23, 28, 196
    and inter-organizational
        collaboration 31–3, 39–40
Luhman, Nicolas 177
Lukas, R. 57, 59

M&A activity
    in biotechnology/ pharmaceutical
        industry 168–74
    and inventor mobility 11–12, 157–8,
        163–74

Madhavan, R. 71
Malerba, Franco 2, 6, 72, 126
March, J.G. 37–8
market failure rationale 157, 199
market relationships 23
    impact on R&D 84, 86
    oligopolistic markets, role in
        networks 59, 70
    role in networks 2
MERIT-CATI database 47–9, 51–2,
    114–15, 128–9
MERIT-CATI dataset 47–8, 114–15
Meyer, J.B. 33
Mitchell, W. 66–7
mobility, of inventors 11–12,
    157–74
    and knowledge spillover 157–60
Mohrman, S.A. 177, 183, 187
Mowery, D.C. 46, 61, 68, 81
Mueller, Denis C. 126
multi-applicant inventorship 11–12
    applicant sequences 160–62
    and individuals 163–5, 169–73
    and knowledge spillovers 112–13,
        157–60, 162, 215
    and open science organizations
        163–5, 169–73
    and private technology organizations
        163–5, 169–73
    study of 11–12, 157–74
        network analysis 168–74
        study dataset and method 158,
            162–8
        taxonomy for 163–5
multinational companies
    role in research networks 15, 83, 234,
        248–9
Murray, F. 161
Mytelka, L. 70

Nahapiet, J. 29–30
Nanoscale Science Research Centers
    (NSRCs) 12–13, 178–90
    lab networks, study of
        changes to networks after
            formation 12–13, 182–3,
            188–90
        global networks in 12–13, 180,
            183–4, 189
        information flows 178–9

network centrality 184–6
  study dataset and method 179–82
nanoscience research, communications
  networks study *see* Nanoscale
  Science Research Centers
National Institute of Advanced
  Industrial Science and Technology
  (AIST) (Japan) 184
Nelson, Richard R. 2–3, 38, 69, 106,
  125
network structure
  clustering 62, 64, 144–5, 179, 184,
    189, 232–3, 241–2
  degree distribution 142–3
  density 33–4, 37–8, 140, 238
  and division of labor 34–5
  embeddedness 31–3
  exploitation *vs.* exploration 8, 19, 22,
    37–8, 40–41, 106–7, 126–7
  influences on 15, 30–38
  knowledge flow efficiency 143–6
  niche overlap 146
  optimality 35–8, 40–41
  power centrality index 128, 146–51
  regional networks 234–8, 244–7
  scale-free 64–5, 142, 181, 200,
    216–17, 219
  self-organizational nature of 2–3,
    34–5, 177–8
  strong-tie 19–20, 22–3, 33–4, 37–9
  structural holes 20, 32–3, 36, 39,
    62–3, 67, 144
  weak-tie 19, 22–3, 37–9
networks *see also* interfirm
    technological agreements;
    knowledge networks; network
    structure; partnership networks;
    patent activity; 'small world'
    networks
  betweenness centrality 139–40,
    186–7, 203–4, 215
  control/ governance benefits of 3–4,
    30, 33–4, 40
  and corporate/ organizational
    strategy 4, 7–8
  and corporate evolution, impact on
    2, 16, 19–21, 45, 125–6
  corporate social networks
    context of 28–9
    importance of 27–41

crowding, and competition 8–9, 105,
    107–8, 110–13, 116–22, 128,
    146–51
degree centrality 66, 139, 147, 184–6,
    203–4, 211, 215
  knowledge network thresholds
    134, 136–8
embeddedness 31–3
emergence of 3–4
as exclusionary/ protective
    mechanism 5, 8, 17, 70, 105–6
for exploitation 8, 19, 22, 37–8,
    40–41, 106–7, 126–7
for exploration 8, 19, 22, 37–8,
    40–41, 126–7
globalization, impact of 22, 83, 89,
    228
industry/ sector differences, reasons
    for 15–21
influences on 15–21, 23, 30–38
  environmental factors 8, 17–20,
    37–8, 40–41, 108, 195–6
learning knowledge, role in
    establishing routines for 18–19
location in, and competition 17,
    32–3
lock-in/ lock-out 17, 21–2, 34, 40,
    71, 199, 220
as locus of innovation 5, 20, 23, 28,
    31–3, 39–40, 196
nanoscience labs, study of 178–90
  *see* IST-RTD Programmes
  information flows 178–9
network indicators
  and benchmarking 23
  as 'early warning systems' 21
as opportunities and constraints 17
path-dependency, impact of 5, 20–21
path length, between nodes 139,
    144–6, 180
public policy implications 21–3
reducing collaboration/ transaction
    costs 17–18
redundant contacts 63
regional, and IST-RTD programmes
    234–8, 244–6
scientific discovery, as
    communication network 177–8
social networks 27–41
and spin-offs, impacts on 12–13

value of, as corporate resource 17,
19–20, 27–41
Networks of Excellence (NoEs) 198,
200, 208–13, 218–20
Networks of Innovation in
Information Society:
Development and Deployment in
Europe (EU) 226
Newman, M.E.J. 171, 178
niche overlap 146
nodes *see also* gatekeepers; hubs
bi-component/ giant bi-component
232–3, 240–42
connectivity of 9–10, 13, 139–40,
151, 184–6, 220, 238
network connectors 203, 234
path length, between 139, 144–6,
180
Nohria, N. 62
Nooteboom, B. 28, 33–4, 37–8, 61–2,
126–7
Nowack, P. 59

Oak Ridge National Lab 185–6
Okamura, Koichiro 58–61
oligopolistic markets, role in networks
59, 70
Oliver, A.I. 28, 33
open science organizations, and multi-
applicant inventorship 163–5,
169–73
Orsenigo, L. 6, 126
output/ outcome additionality 14, 195,
199

Page, K.L. 33, 107
partnership networks 9–11, 14–15,
125–53
connectivity 9, 135, 139, 141–4,
151
gatekeepers in 9, 140
hubs in 9, 140, 151
illustration of 130, 135, 137–9
and knowledge networks compared,
sectoral study 127–53 *see also*
*under* individual industry
sectors
knowledge flow efficiency 143–6
network analysis 128, 133–42,
146–53

robustness 9–10, 143, 145–6, 151
study dataset and method 127–33
Patel, P. 81
patent activity, network impact on
network inventiveness 214–17
patent citation
and inventor mobility 159–62
in knowledge and partnership
networks, study 131–3,
150–51
self-citation 110–13, 117, 121–2
patent co-citation in electronics
sector, study of 8, 105–22
corporate age/ size, impact of
115–17, 121–2
and innovative performance
110–13
knowledge search strategies 8–9,
105–22
knowledge spillovers 112–13
network crowding 110–13, 116–22
self-citation 110–13, 117, 121–2
study dataset and method 113–17
and prior art/ experience 31, 106,
202
and technological capability 68
path-dependency 5, 20–21, 69, 106
Pavitt, K. 81
Pentland, B.T. 37
Peteraf, M.A. 27
Pfeffer, J. 59
pharmaceutical industry *see also*
biotechnology industry
co-authored research networks,
European study of 7–8, 92–101
corporate profiles 94–5
influences on partnership activity
98–9
publication output 94
research partnerships profiles 95–9
study dataset 92–5
study limitations 99–100
development of 87–8
interfirm technological alliances in
51–3, 55
inventor mobility in 171–4
knowledge and partnership networks
compared, study 9–11, 127,
131–5, 140–42, 147–8, 151–2
M&A activity in 168–74

networks in
  external influences on 8
  role in 5–6, 88–9
  R&D costs of 88–9
  R&D patterns in 88–9
Plan i2010 198
plastics industry
  knowledge and partnership networks
    compared, study 9–11, 127,
    131–3, 136, 140–42, 148
Podolny, J.M. 33, 68, 107, 109, 112,
  146–7
Powell, W.W. 31–3, 45, 58, 66, 70, 227
power centrality index 128, 146–51
public policy, network implications for
  21–3

R&D
  appropriability of 60
  corporate incentives for 84–7
  costs of 14, 85, 88–9
  intensity of, role in forming alliances
    57–8
  and market relationships 84, 86
  publishing research
    incentives for 91–3
    limitations on use of 99–100
    pharmaceutical industry co-
      authorship study 92–101
  relocation trends of 83
R&D networks *see also* interfirm
    technological agreements
  and corporate evolution, role in 2, 6,
    19–21, 45, 125–6
  and deployment networks, compared
    14–15, 226, 228–50
  deployment hubs 236–8, 249–50
  'discovery' research partnerships
    84–7, 177–8
  gatekeepers, role of 238–40, 247–50
  influences on 83–5
  and knowledge networks, compared
    13
  'open innovation' 83
  public sector involvement, trends in
    81–2
  regional networks 234–8, 244–7
  self-organizational character of 2–3,
    34–5, 177
regional networks 234–8, 244–7

relational capital 18, 27–8
relational embeddedness 32
research and development *see* R&D
Rhône-Alpes (France) 230, 236–8, 242,
  247
Roediger-Schluga, T. 228
Roijakkers, N. 96
Rosenberg, Nathan 3
Rosenkopf, L. 71, 108, 159–60
Rowan, B. 33
Rowley, T. 28, 32–3, 37

Sakakibara, M 48, 57–60, 66–7
Sampson, R. 65, 67
scale-free networks 64–5, 142, 181, 200,
  216–17, 219
Schakenraad, J. 57, 66–8, 114
Schoonhoven, C.B. 60
Schumpeterian patterns of innnovation
  70–71
scientific discovery
  as communication network 84–7,
    177–8
  self-organization of 2–3, 34–5,
    177–8
scientific instruments *see* instruments
    industry
SDC Platinum Joint Ventures and
    Strategic Alliances dataset 47–53
sectors, industrial *see* industry sectors
self-organization, as network
    characteristic 2–3, 34–5, 177–8
semiconductor industry 58, 60, 66–8,
    113–14
Shan, W. 29–30, 35–6, 63, 66
Siebert, R. 57, 66
Simon, H.A. 38
Singh, J.H. 159
Singh, K. 66–7
Sixth Research Framework Programme
    (FP6) (EU)
  background to 197
  research networks under, studies of
    *see* IST-RTD programmes
  strategic objectives of 197–8
size, corporate
  bi-component/ giant bi-component
    nodes 232–3, 240–42
  interfirm technological alliances, role
    in forming 57, 59–60, 70

and patent activity, impact on
    115–17, 121–2
and regional networks 238
'small world' networks 10
    clustering 62, 64, 144–5
    and IST-RTD programmes 219–20
    in knowledge and partnership
        networks, compared 152
    regional networks 237
    and scale-free networks 219–20
    short-cuts in 63–4
SMEs (small and medium sized
    enterprises) 14, 83, 195, 228,
    243–6, 248–9
Smith-Doerr, L. 31–3
social capital 3–4, 27–8
    closure concept 36, 62–3, 67
    defining 29–30
    as network resource 39–41
Song, J. 159
Specific Support Actions (SSAs) 198
Specific Targeted Research Projects
    (STRePs) 198, 208–13
spin offs, impacts on network activities
    12–13, 189
Stolpe, M. 160
Storper, M. 228
Strogatz, S.H. 63, 145
structural embeddedness 31–3
structural holes 20, 32–3, 36, 39, 62–3,
    67, 144
Stuart, T.E. 58, 60–61, 66, 68, 107, 121
Swan, G.M.P. 166

technical capital 27–8
Teece, D.J. 81

Tether, B. 57, 59
Teubal, M. 3
Tilton, J. E. 126
Trajtenberg, M. 159–60, 167
Tsai, W. 29–30
Tushman, M.L. 71, 106

United States *see also* Department
    of Energy; Nanoscale Science
    Research Centers
    US companies, knowledge networks
        in 9–11, 149–50, 152–3
University of California-Berkley
    185
University of Cardiff 245–6
University of Maastricht 128
Utterback, James A. 126

Verspagen, B. 64, 144–5
Von Bertalanffy, L. 177
Vonortas, Nicholas 28, 48, 57–61,
    143–4

Wacquant, L. 29–30
Wagner, Caroline S. 177, 183,
    187
Wales 230, 242, 245–6
Walker, G. 29–30, 35–6, 63
Watts, D.J. 63, 145
*Web of Science (WoS)* 92–3, 179
Whitley, R. 177–8
Willinger, W. 142
Wilmott, H. 33–4
Winter, S.G. 38, 69, 106

Zander, U. 33–4